Library of
Davidson College

# Apathy in America, 1960-1984:

*Causes and Consequences of Citizen Political Indifference*

Stephen Earl Bennett

Transnational Publishers, Inc.
Dobbs Ferry, New York

**Library of Congress Cataloging-in-Publication Data**

Bennett, Stephen Earl, 1941-
  Apathy in America, 1960-1984.

    Bibliography: p.
    Includes index.
    1. Political participation—United States.
  2. United States—Politics and government—1945-
  —Public opinion. 3. Public opinion—United States.
  I. Title.
  JK1764.B46 1986      323'.042'0973      85-24711
  ISBN 0-941320-39-1

© Copyright 1986 by Transnational Publishers, Inc.

All rights reserved. No part of this publication may be reproduced in any form or by any electronic or mechanical means including information storage and retrieval systems without permission in writing from the publisher.

Manufactured in the United States of America

This book is for my mother, Lucille Josephine Bennett (nee Riddle), and my father, Clifford Earl Bennett. They taught me it was my responsibility and in my interest to pay attention to public affairs, . . . although I don't think they've always approved of the direction mine has taken from time to time.

# Table of Contents

Preface .................................................................................... ix

Chapter 1: Introduction ............................................................. 1
   Plan of the Book ................................................................. 9

Chapter 2: Apathy in Political Theory and Political Behavior    11
   Introduction ........................................................................ 11
   Citizen Political Interest in the American Past ............... 13
   Political Apathy and Social Scientists ......................... 24
   Apathy in Theories of Democracy ............................. 28

Chapter 3: The Conceptualization and Measurement of
        Apathy .................................................................... 31
   Introduction ........................................................................ 31
   Conceptions of Political Apathy in the Literature .......... 31
   Apathy Reconsidered .......................................................... 37
   Measurement of Political Apathy ............................... 39
   Conclusion ......................................................................... 58

Chapter 4: The Demographic and Political Correlates of Interest in Public Affairs ......................................... 61
   Introduction ........................................................................ 61
   Change Over Time: The Entire Citizenry ..................... 61
   → Apathy Among Selected Subgroups ........................... 67
   Political Factors and Apathy ...................................... 78
   → Conclusion: The Influence of Political Forces on Political
      Interest ................................................................. 88

Chapter 5: The Causes of Political Apathy: A Multivariate
        Investigation ............................................... 93
    Introduction ....................................................... 93
    Untangling the Effects of Age, Education, and Gender .... 96
    The Impact of Partisanship, External Political Efficacy,
    Education and Age ............................................. 113
    The Results of OLS Regression Analysis ...................... 118
    Conclusion ....................................................... 122
    Appendix ......................................................... 123

Chapter 6: The Consequences of Apathy ......................... 125
    Introduction ..................................................... 125
    Exposure to Political Information and Knowledge About
    Public Affairs .................................................... 131
    Political Interest and Political Activity ........................ 140
    Apathy, Basic Political Orientations, and Political Activity 152
    Conclusion ....................................................... 160

Chapter 7: Summary and Conclusions ........................... 163
    The Future Study of Political Apathy: What Is to Be
    Done? ............................................................. 172

References ............................................................ 179
    Index ............................................................. 195

# List of Tables

| | | |
|---|---|---|
| 3.1: | Interest in Election Campaigns, 1960-1984 | 46 |
| 3.2: | Interest in Public Affairs, 1960-1984 | 48 |
| 3.3: | Reliability of the Political Apathy Index, 1960-1984 | 53 |
| 3.4: | Forms of Political Participation by the Political Apathy Index | 57 |
| 4.1: | Political Apathy in America, 1960-1984 | 63 |
| 4.2: | Political Apathy by Social Factors, 1960-1984 | 73 |
| 4.3: | Political Apathy by Political Factors, 1960-1984 | 80 |
| 5.1: | Political Apathy by Birth Cohort by Gender, 1960, 1968, 1976, 1984 | 98 |
| 5.2: | Political Interest by Gender, Controlling for Education and Age | 107 |
| 5.3: | Political Interest by Gender, Controlling for Employment Status and Age | 110 |
| 5.4: | Political Interest by Partisanship, Controlling for Education and Age | 114 |
| 5.5: | Political Interest by External Political Efficacy, Controlling for Education and Age | 117 |
| 6.1: | Zero-Order and First-Order Partial (Education Controlled) Correlations between the Political Apathy Index and Forms of Political Participation | 130 |
| 6.2: | Mass Media Usage by Political Apathy Index, 1960-1984 | 133 |
| 6.3: | Political Information Index by Political Apathy Index, 1960-1984 | 137 |
| 6.4: | Reported Turnout by Political Apathy Index, 1960-1984 | 142 |
| 6.5: | Validated Turnout by Political Apathy Index, 1964-1984 | 144 |

6.6: Campaign Activism by Political Apathy Index, 1960-1984 ............ 146
6.7: Nonelectoral Political Participation by Political Apathy Index, 976 ............ 150
6.8: Validated Vote by Political Apathy Index and External Political Efficacy, 1964-1984 ............ 155
6.9: Validated Vote by Political Apathy Index and Trust in Government Index, 1964-1984 ............ 157
6.10: Validated Vote by Political Apathy Index and Political Alienation Index, 1976 ............ 159

# Preface

I wonder how many authors should admit that, "this is not the book I set out to write." Certainly such is the case here. When, a few years ago, after almost a decade of laboring in the increasingly muddied fields of mass belief systems research, I decided to take up the study of another facet of American political behavior, I initially wanted to do a more general analysis of changes in ordinary citizens' basic political orientations since the halcyon days of the late 1950s and early 1960s.

Two factors dissuaded me from that effort. The first was the appearance of several studies with a similar thrust: Paul Abramson's *Political Attitudes in America* (1983), David Hill and Norman Luttbeg's *Trends in American Electoral Behavior* (1983), and especially Seymour Martin Lipset and William Schneider's *The Confidence Gap* (1983). Not only did these books plow some of the same ground I had wanted to till, they had probably borne a richer harvest than the work I had in mind.

The second factor was more personal. At about the same time I was doing background work for the original work, a young lady who was in her late teens uttered two wonderful lines. First, she admitted she had no idea of what Skylab was. It was about to fall out of the sky. Later, she asked: "Who's Ted Kennedy, anyway?" At the time the senior senator from Massachusetts was a possible contender for his party's nomination to the highest elective office in the land.

The young lady in question was then a very bright, outgoing college undergraduate who was doing well in her classes. (She has since graduated and gone on to a professional career.) Her remarks started me to thinking about why some people pay more, and some less, and a few, none at all, attention to government and public affairs.

From that beginning, the present effort has evolved. I wonder if she remembers how she indirectly caused me finally to write a book.

It is said that scholarship is a lonely enterprise, and work on this book has been no exception. Nonetheless, I find that in the process I have acquired a substantial number of debts, acknowledgement of which cannot begin to repay. To the following, then, my heartfelt thanks. Roger Stuebing, of the University of Cincinnati's Institute for Policy Research. He gave much counsel on statistical analysis techniques which I have haltingly tried to follow. Professor Seymour Martin Lipset of Stanford University. He critiqued an article which became the basis of this work. At the time I did not accept all his suggestions, but later I came to see he was probably right. Samuel Long, editor of *Micropolitics*, who published that paper, and encouraged me to expand it. Professor Abraham H. Miller, my colleague in the Political Science Department at the University of Cincinnati. He stepped in at a critical moment with very good advice. Ms. Heike Fenton, publisher of Transnational Publishers, Inc. She encouraged me to set a deadline which, lo and behold, I beat, . . . barely. Ms. Donna Scheeler, assistant editor at Transnational, who gave encouragement.

Finally, I come to the one person without whom I literally could not have done this book: my wife, Professor Linda L. M. Bennett of Wittenberg University's Political Science Department. "She who must be obeyed!" She is at once my best friend, confidant, coauthor, and . . . well, . . . you know. Without her sometimes gentle, *sometimes not so gentle*, prodding, I could not have done it. Thanks, "Emma."

Xenia, Ohio<br>
September 20, 1985

# CHAPTER 1

# INTRODUCTION

Have Americans become less interested in public affairs than formerly? Have they become, in a word, more "apathetic"? Certainly they are less likely to vote in national elections. Since reaching a postwar peak of 62.8% of the eligible electorate in 1960, turnout in presidential elections fell to 52.6% in 1980. Between 1962 and 1982, voting in off-year congressional elections declined from 45.4% to 38.7%.[1] Despite expectations of a sizable increase of voter participation in 1984, turnout only inched up to 53.3%, still nearly ten percentage points below 1960's mark. The decline in turnout has occurred despite efforts to make the voting process easier for all citizens and more accessible to groups (primarily southern blacks) formerly denied the franchise, and despite changes in society (chiefly increased levels of education and the entry of more women into the work force) that ought to have led to higher rates of voting (Brody, 1978; Reiter, 1979; Cassel and Hill, 1981; Cavanagh, 1981; Shaffer, 1981; Abramson and Aldrich, 1982).[2]

Small wonder, therefore, that many students of American politics have been worried about rising apathy (Gans, 1978; Hadley, 1978). In the view of some, "the continuing and sharp decline in the level of voting and citizen involvement cannot help but adversely affect the health of the American body politic" (Gans, 1978: 55).

Some scholars disagree that apathy has increased (Abramowitz,

---

1. Actually, turnout in the 1978 congressional elections had been even lower (35.2%) than it was in 1982. Indeed, the latter year was the first time since 1962 that voting in a national election was higher than in the preceding contest of the same type.
2. For complete citations, *see* the reference section at the end of the book.

1980; W. Miller, 1980). They point out that participation in other forms of political activity has either remained constant or increased since the early 1960s. For example, the University of Michigan's Survey Research Center/Center for Political Studies' National Election Studies show that participation in campaign activities has remained steady since 1960 (Miller, Miller, and Schneider, 1980). Between 1964 and 1976, the percentage of adults reporting having written to a public official rose from 16.9 to 27.7 (see also Abramowitz, 1980: 199). In the same period, the percentage of people saying they had written to a newspaper or magazine editor expressing a political opinion rose from 3.3 to 7.7. Finally, during the mid- and late-1960s, more people engaged in various forms of political protest (Skolnick, 1969; Barnes, Kaase, et al., 1979; Abramowitz, 1980).[3] Participation in activities outside the electoral arena has probably increased because "[m]ost Americans no longer regarded voting as the only effective means of influencing government officials" (Abramowitz, 1980: 199; see also Converse, 1972: 326-330). In any event, according to Warren Miller (1980: 24), "declining turnout cannot be attributed to an aggregation of decreased individual commitments to democracy because none of the general indicators of interest in politics show [sic] a parallel decline."

Those who contend that the decline in voting does represent a cause for concern about apathy counter with two points. First, voting is democracy's most fundamental act, for most modern theories of democracy recognize the irreplacable significance of the ballot box for the potential control of elites by ordinary citizens (Pomper, with Lederman, 1980: 21-25). Second, voting is the only form of political participation undertaken by more than half the adult populace. Other forms of political activity are engaged in by a minority, often by only a tiny fraction of the citizenry (Bennett and Bennett, 1986). Even though the demographic profile of voters differs systematically from that of nonvoters, the difference is far less than that between the few who undertake more demanding forms of political activity and the passive majority (Verba and Nie, 1972). Thus, as the ratio of those casting ballots in presidential elections has fallen from just over three-in-five in 1960 to a little over one-in-two in the 1980s, worry about the implications for democratic politics in America seems justified.

   3. While engagement in protests of varying political purpose and orientation fell decidedly during the 1970s, there has been a slight resurgence of such activities in the last two years.

*Introduction*

Concern about the consequences for representative government becomes especially poignant because the diminution in voting has not occurred equally throughout society, but has been concentrated in precisely those social orders that had already been at a disadvantage in the electoral arena by virtue of lower rates of participation (Reiter, 1979; W. Miller, 1980; Cavanagh, 1981). As Gans (1978: 55) puts it, "To the extent that American political participation dwindles and the business of politics becomes increasingly the province of organized interest groups, the ability of the political system to produce public policy in the interest of society as a whole declines correspondingly."[4] If one result of declining turnout means a political process less and less likely to produce government of, by, and especially for "the people," it is easy to understand why students of American politics worry about any signs of increasing political apathy.

But, do declining rates of voting in elections necessarily signify increased political apathy? For those who equate apathy with lack of political participation, particularly voting in elections, the question is tautological. But, if apathy's meaning is kept closer to its Greek etymon, *apatheis* ("without feeling"), the answer becomes less apparent. Just as people may vote who say they are not interested in public affairs, so may others who are politically interested abstain from voting.

This is a study of psychological involvement in public affairs at the grassroots level in America between 1960 and 1984. The work is addressed to five primary concerns. First, a review of social science research on apathy shows that the concept has been given a variety of meanings. Quite often it is treated as the equivalent of nonparticipation. When it is conceived as a political disposition it is very often so interwoven with other personality maladies, social pathologies, and basic political dispositions that it is hard to see the significance of the term *in and of itself*. Hence, one purpose of the work is to argue for a clearer, leaner, and straightforward conceptualization of the concept (see Chapter 3).

---

4. Gans' statement is predicated upon the assumption that people who are politically passive have different views than those who are active. Evidently, such does not seem to be the case, at least insofar as voting is concerned (De Nardo, 1980; Shaffer, 1982; however, see Perry, 1973). On the other hand, when it comes to consideration of political activists, *i.e.*, those who take part in more demanding political activities, Gans is on safer ground (see Nexon, 1971; Shaffer, 1980).

3

A second goal is to demonstrate the utility of an operationalization of the concept first put forward, but never used, by Almond and Verba (1963: 88-89) in their classic study, *The Civic Culture*. Specifically, I propose (in Chapter 3) to employ both a measure of interest in election campaigns and an indicant of general political interest. While many studies have utilized the former, all too often as an index of political interest *per se*, only a few have drawn upon the latter (see, *e.g.*, Jennings and Niemi, 1974, 1981; W. Miller, 1980; Bennett, 1984b). Fortunately, both items have been repeatedly included on large-scale nationwide public opinion surveys over the last quarter of a century, although there are some technical problems associated with their use (see Chapters 3 and 4). Happily, none is fatal to the project.

Some might question whether an item asking a respondent to give a subjective assessment of his interest in campaigns or politics generally can be taken at face value. The problem is probably especially relevant to the item on general political interest. As Jennings and Niemi (1981: 28) have noted, the general interest question "is nothing more than a subjective self-appraisal offered by an individual. It has few concrete referents." Therefore, it might not be surprising to find that answers to such items lack meaning, or honesty for that matter.

Fortunately, as Jennings and Niemi (1981: 28) report, despite its relative lack of concrete reference, the general interest item "elicits a strong degree of continuity over time," which is one of the more strenuous tests of a survey item's reliability (see also Chapter 3). Four decades ago, Lazarsfeld, Berelson, and Gaudet (1968: 41) explained why a question about self-interest in politics would be trustworthy:

> It is not surprising that people's self-rating on interest stands up well on a series of tests of consistency and validity. For being interested is a clearly recognizable experience, as anyone knows who has ever been unable to put down a detective story or been bored to tears at a cocktail party. Given any two activities, we can frequently tell at once which is the more interesting for us.

While one can always wish for better measures of key concepts, those available for secondary analysis of survey data over an extended period of American history are adequate to the present task.

The third main purpose of the book is to trace the American people's psychological involvement in politics between 1960 and

*Introduction*

1984. No excuse need be offered for the time frame. I have already mentioned that 1960 witnessed the highest level of turnout in a national election in our time. 1984 marked the first time since that voting did not sag in a presidential election. The two years, therefore, make as good a beginning and an end to a study of political apathy as one could wish. Of course, honesty requires the admission that 1960 just happens to be the first time both components of our measure of political apathy were included on the same nationwide survey questionnaire.

The two and one-half decades between 1960 and 1984 also happen to be a period of momentous changes in American society and politics (Morris, 1984). The events, issues, and personalities of the era are among the most important to have dotted the pages of American history since the 1860s. Beginning with John F. Kennedy's "New Frontier," the next twenty-five years saw Lyndon Johnson's "Great Society," Richard Nixon's promise to "bring us together again," Jimmy Carter's promise to build "a government as good as its people," and ended with Ronald Reagan's attempt to achieve a "Second American Revolution." A score of major American personalities arose, some flourished, and many disappeared: JFK, Dr. Martin Luther King, LBJ, Barry Goldwater, Eugene McCarthy, Bobby Kennedy, George Wallace, Nixon, Spiro Agnew, George McGovern, Henry Kissinger, Jerry Ford, Carter, and Reagan. All added color, and some substance, to the politics of the time. The issues and movements which characterized the period were some of the most important of the twentieth century: the civil rights revolution, poverty, Vietnam, urban riots, campus unrest, law and order, consumerism, environmentalism, feminism, energy conservation, stagflation, Iran, terrorism, abortion, and on and on. The list could go on. One underlying development of the time was the steady growth of the federal government's power over the lives of its citizens, a movement which has been only arrested, hardly reversed, under Reagan. Clearly there were sufficient reasons for the ordinary citizen to pay attention to public affairs.

The fourth goal of the work is to determine the major factors responsible for political interest or apathy. While in many ways based on limited evidence of varying quality, previous research has established several factors that appear related to political involvement. Several propositions taken from earlier studies are tested with nationwide survey data between 1960 and 1984 (see Chapter 4). Some are confirmed, many require modification, and some are rejected. Moreover, unlike most previous research, which has utilized primarily bivariate methods of analysis, the data utilized here permit in-depth analyses of several important factors alleged to affect political interest, often with two or three background factors statistically controlled (see Chapter 5). Finally, while the effort strains some of the technical assumptions undergirding the technique, a brief effort is made to determine the relative impact on political interest of key independent variables in a multivariate context (Chapter 5).

The last purpose is, in some ways the most important. Political scientists are interested in political apathy mainly because of its impact on the citizen and especially upon the polity itself. Political philosophers from Aristotle to John Stuart Mill have contended that political involvement and participation can have beneficial results to the individual citizen. In the twentieth century, a number of "citizenship" theorists have revised and extended this view (Thompson, 1970). While Aristotle, Mill, and most of the "citizenship" thinkers specifically mention participation as the source of self-improvement, it is also worthwhile to determine whether and in what ways the interested citizen differs from his apathetic neighbor. Although it is not always possible to determine whether interest *per se* is responsible, it is important to learn that the psychologically involved person is both qualitatively and quantitatively a different political actor than the indifferent individual.

Perhaps even more important is the determination of apathy's consequence for the political system. Throughout American history, political thinkers, moralists, educators, and statesman have insisted that the ordinary person has a duty and a self-interest to maintain an active interest in the public affairs. Extolment of the virtues of the interested citizen was especially prevalent during the first two or three decades of the twentieth century. After a review of textbooks on citizenship in the 1920s, Walter Lippmann (1925: 24) wryly concluded that the good citizen "is apparently expected to yield an unlimited quantity of public spirit, interest, curiosity, and effort." Lippmann felt that such expectations were unrealistic and unreasonable, since not even *he* could meet the standard. Worse, Lippmann believed the requirement that the ordinary individual be continually interested in every conceivable public problem was bound to cause confusion and disillusionment. As Lippmann put it (1925: 25),

*Introduction*

> Unless . . . [the citizen] can discover some rational ground for fixing his attention where it will do the most good, and in a way that suits his inherently amateurish equipment, he will be as bewildered as a puppy trying to lick three bones at once.

Contemporary educators may have downplayed the requirement for sustained and active political interest in citizenship education in favor of "values clarification" and the student's personal "growth" as a moral being (Shaver, 1981). However, critics of current practices have recently called for a rebirth of civic consciousness as a goal of the educational process (Janowitz, 1983).

As might be expected, there are a variety of views about what apathy means for the democratic political system (see Chapter 2). Is it harmful, as most democratic theorists, especially the advocates of the so-called "participatory democracy," have contended (Pateman, 1970; Benello and Roussopoulis, eds., 1971; Kramer, 1972; Parry, ed., 1972; and Pennock and Chapman, eds., 1975)? Or does it have beneficial effects, as the so-called "empirical" (a.k.a. "elitist") democratic theorists have argued (see Schumpeter, 1975; Berelson, 1952; Berelson, Lazarsfeld, and McPhee, 1954; Dahl, 1961)? These arguments are reprised in Chapter 2.

The answer, of course, depends upon several factors. A very important one is one's view about democratic government in general, and especially the role(s) one thinks ordinary citizens ought to play. It also depends even more on the other basic political orientations found to be related to political interest/apathy. Is the apathetic citizen indifferent because he is basically satisfied with the way things are going, so much so that political involvement would be a waste of his time and effort? Does he think politicians are his "public servants," who are much like him and his kind, and therefore will produce policy outputs much as he would if he himself were running things? Or is he indifferent to public affairs because he is convinced that democratic politics is fraudulent, that the system is controlled by alien and perverse forces, and beyond the control of decent, ordinary people like himself? Does he believe politicians can't be trusted, they are fools, or naives, or worse: the tools of well-organized, well-heeled, narrow special interests bent on achieving their own ends at the expense of the public good? Or is it possible that lack of interest in public affairs is simply another symptom of the political orientation characterized many years ago by Almond and

Verba (1963) as "parochial?" This is the individual who sees no relevance for himself or his family of what goes on in the public realm. Since what government does is irrelevant to his personal existence, it is small wonder the "parochial" pays little or no heed to public affairs. Or is the apathetic individual so weighed down by personal concerns, such as health difficulties, family problems, or financial reverses, that he has little or no time or psychic energy left to "give a damn" what happens in such a remote environment?

Clearly it makes a difference, for the individual, and more so, for the political system, which comes closest to the data. It also makes a significant difference whether any of the combinations of apathy with other basic political orientations affects people's participation in the political fray (see Chapter 6).

Part of the difficulty in any attempt to approach political interest from an empirical perspective is the relative paucity of comparable measures of major concepts, and the problem is especially serious if the concern is with comparison over time. In the ideal world, one would have data gathered expressly for the purpose at hand.

Alas, such is not the case. Rather, one must rely upon information gathered over nearly a quarter of a century, for quite different purposes (see Chapter 3). Someone who wishes to do secondary analysis of survey data is often under severe constraints (Glenn, 1972). Not only must the secondary analyst be dependent upon whether other researchers have chosen to plumb a given political disposition or behavior, he is also constrained by how such has been done.

There was a time when secondary analysts of survey data approached the analysis of over-time phenomena in rather cavalier fashion (see, *e.g.*, Bennett, 1973, Nie, with Andersen, 1974; Nie, Verba and Petrocik, 1979). It now turns out that such strategy was ill-chosen (Schuman and Presser, 1981). So sensitized has a portion of the discipline become, some methodological monists have declared that, unless a variable be measured in precisely identical wording and at exactly the same point during an interview, over-time comparisons are inherently suspect (see Chapter 3).

Happily, at least in the present instance, such does not appear to be the case. There are differences in question wording (between 1960 and thereafter), the wording of the most politically involved option on the general interest item was altered after 1964, and there were varying placements of both items on the questionnaires from time to

*Introduction*

time. Such alterations require sensitivity in handling over-time comparisons, but the evidence seems to be that each item is sufficiently robust to be usable over nearly a quarter of a century.

Before closing, a brief note is needed about what this study is *not*. First, it is not a study in normative political theory. I have my own views about the questions raised throughout, and no doubt they not only influence the discussion but even the manner in which questions are raised, or ignored. However, I have tried to hew to the data in hand, and let the results of data analyses drive the discussions. I am sure I shall hear about the odd place here and there where I have failed to do so. Second, this is not a study in the psychodynamics of citizen political interest. While such can be very useful, the data are not in hand for a study concerned primarily about citizen political interest over a quarter of a century. Perhaps they shall be in the future (see Chapter 7). Nor is it a formal analysis of the causal dynamics of interest. While some might argue the data exist for such an endeavor, I am not convinced either that they do, or that the theoretical framework to sustain such an analysis yet exists. It is my hope that a study such as this will help lay such a foundation.

Finally, this is not an analysis of "the attentive public" or of the role this specialized "public" plays in the policy processes of American democracy. As originally conceived by Gabriel Almond (1960), and as it has been used by scholars such as V. O. Key, Jr. (1961) and Donald Devine (1970), the attentive public has been used as a key concept in the study of linkage mechanisms between the American people and their rulers. There is no question that the operationalization of political interest developed here (Chapter 3) can be utilized in work on this vitally important topic. It is similar to the indicant relied on by Devine (1970), although he includes media usage variables that are separate behavioral consequences of political interest (Chapter 6). While there is no doubt as to the importance of the "attentive public's" role in any analysis of contemporary democracy, that task must await another day.

The Plan of the Book

In the main the organization of the work is conventional. Chapter

2 presents a brief analysis of the role of citizen political interest in democratic theories, both normative and empirical. Along the way, it also presents a partial assessment of levels of grassroots attention to public affairs throughout the American past prior to the development of scientific public opinion surveys. The chapter also reviews some of the attempts by social scientists to analyze political apathy from an empirical perspective.

Chapter 3 contains a much more in-depth analysis of the conceptualization and measurement of political interest in social science research. The chapter argues for a narrowing of conceptualization of apathy, and proposes an operational definition of the concept that can be used over the entire period from 1960 to 1984. Some of the technical problems with the indicant's components are reviewed, and the measure is shown to be both reliable and valid.

Chapter 4 opens with an analysis of grassroots political interest over the years from JFK to Ronald Reagan. The more important sections contain bivariate determinations of the demographic and political factors associated with attention to politics and government.

The fifth chapter continues some of the thrust begun in Chapter 4. Utilizing different methods of multivariate data analysis, Chapter 5 assesses the relative impact on political interest of several demographic and political variables that have been considered key determinants.

In some ways, Chapter 6 is even more important, for it focuses on the consequences of apathy for the citizen and for the American political system. The interested citizen is shown to behave differently than his apathetic neighbor, and apathy is shown to be, if not a serious problem for the democratic process, at least a worrisome thing.

The book closes with a brief summary of the findings and an exploration of work that needs to be done on apathy in the future.

With this overview of the work in mind, it is time to turn to the analysis of citizen political interest in contemporary democratic politics. First, however, let us briefly return to ancient Athens.

# CHAPTER 2

# APATHY IN POLITICAL THEORY AND POLITICAL BEHAVIOR

## Introduction

In his rendition of Pericles' famous "funeral oration," Thucydides (1972: 147) has the Athenian statesman say this about grassroots psychological involvement in the politics of his city:

> Here each individual is interested not only in his own affairs but in the affairs of the state as well: even those who are mostly occupied with their own business are extremely well-informed on general politics — this is a peculiarity of ours: we do not say that a man who takes no interest in politics is a man who minds his own business; we say that he has no business here at all.

It is a nice historical question whether Pericles' description of the highly involved Athenians was accurate or merely a fifth-century B.C. example of "Fourth of July" hyperbole. While historians have long debated the issue, the conclusion of W. G. Forrest (1969: 143) seems balanced and fair: "The Athenians were probably more alive politically than any people has been since but it would still be strange if the normal pattern of political interest did not roughly repeat itself there." As M. I Finley recently noted (1983: 72-73), if the objections against participation by ordinary citizens raised by contemporary aristocrats have any "evidentiary value," they argue in favor of widespread popular involvement.

In any event, Pericles' point about widespread grassroots political interest has been a central theme of popular government over the centuries. Many philosophers have staked the future of democratic politics upon the responsibility and the capability of the typical citizen to maintain an active interest in the public affairs. Three decades ago, Bernard Berelson (1952) catalogued the "requirements" he claimed traditional philosophers had made of ordinary citizens in democracies (see also Berelson, Lazarsfeld, and McPhee, 1954: chap. 14). One of these Berelson (1952: 316) called *"the factor of interest and participation:"*

> Political democracy requires a fairly strong and fairly continuous level of interest from a minority, and from a larger body of the citizenry a moderate-to-mild and discontinuous interest but with stable readiness to respond in critical political situations. Political disinterest or apathy is not permitted, or at least not approved.

An illustration of the requirement is found near the beginning of Rousseau's *The Social Contract* (1968: 49): "Born as I was the citizen of a free state and a member of its sovereign body, the very right to vote imposes on me the duty to instruct myself in public affairs, however little influence my voice may have in them." Of course, Rousseau was one of the most radical theorists of the eighteenth century, and has been called "the theorist *par excellence* of [political] participation . . ." (Pateman, 1970: 22; see also Miller, 1985; Shklar, 1985). It is not surprising, therefore, that someone with his orientation would expect widespread citizen attention to the public affairs.

It is startling, however, to discover that the conservative British statesman, Edmund Burke (1959: 119), could write to his Bristol constituents that, "In a free country every man thinks he has a concern in all public matters; that he has a right to form and a right to deliver an opinion upon them. They sift, examine, and discuss them. They are curious, eager, attentive, and jealous. . . ."

Indeed, most proponents of democratic government assumed that an essential ingredient to its successful operation was a vigorous and watchful citizenry. In his seminal work on *Modern Democracies* (1921, I: 47-49), Viscount James Bryce opens his description of "an Ideal Democracy" thusly: "In it the average citizen will give close and constant attention to public affairs, recognizing that this is his interest as well as his duty."

Of the multitude of reasons given for paying attention to politics, two stand out. First, it is a matter of civic duty, of fulfilling one's "public spiritedness" (Bryce, 1913: 2). Also, by following politics one could become a better informed, wiser, and possibly a more rational citizen participant. Therefore, one could better protect one's self-interests, which has been the second main justification for attending to the political process. Those who did not keep a weather eye on politics ran the risk of being victimized by political elites. As Thomas Jefferson warned in 1787, "If once . . . [the people] become inattentive to the public affairs, you, I, and Congress, and the Assemblies, judges and governors, shall all become wolves" (1977: 415).

Of course, it is one thing to hold up the ideal of the attentive, involved citizen. Practice is often quite another matter. How well have ordinary Americans lived up to the expectation by democratic theorists that they will pay heed to what goes on in politics and government?

## Citizen Political Interest in the American Past

Immediately the topic of past grassroots political behavior is raised we confront one fundamental problem: absence of hard information upon which to base judgments about the relative incidence of a political disposition among ordinary people in the American past (Benson, 1967-1968; Kann, 1968). The problem is complicated when the focus is on a widespread cultural desideratum, such as the expectation of citizen political interest, where there is a tendency, in the absence of hard evidence to the contrary, to assume the equivalence of hope and habit.

The most obvious source of the problem is the unavailability prior to the late 1930s of nationwide scientific public opinion polls. Until a historical survey reaches that late date, then, all that one can use is impressionistic evidence picked up from a variety of sources: comments by political practitioners and politicians that have come down to the present in one form or another, observations by a succession of (mostly) foreign travellers who have written about the American scene, documents (mostly letters) produced by ordinary citizens, and the reconstruction of the past by contemporary American historians.

Admittedly, none of these is entirely satisfactory, and even when — as in the 1830s with de Tocqueville, the 1880s with Bryce, or the 1920s with the Lynds — one is given a tantalizing tidbit of evidence to consider, it must be recognized how partial and inadequate such is. Still, even in the face of the very great odds against the enterprise, a brief historical survey of grassroots political interest is warranted in order to set contemporary data in proper chronological relief.

Someone who has studied the electoral process and voting behavior in early American history is Robert J. Dinkin. He has written two monographs (1977, 1982) on voting during the colonial period and during the revolution and confederal era. If Dinkin is correct, the expectation that the colonist had a duty to keep abreast of politics and government was a part of the American political culture even before the breach with the mother country (1977: 188). However, Dinkin also presents evidence that there must have been many who were inattentive, for there were "[m]any writers" who commented on "the 'criminal indifference' to who was elected, and the profound feeling of general apathy toward the electoral process." Nor were apathetic colonists necessarily apologetic. As Dinkin notes, "it was not uncommon" to hear, as a justification for political indifference, expressions such as: " 'What can one man do against a Torrent? It is not our Business, let those who are upon the Watch look out.' " Dinkin wryly notes that such sentiments are hauntingly familiar in our own time.

Given the conditions of colonial society and politics — the primitive means of transportation and communication, fairly severe limitations on the franchise, and the control of politics in many of the colonies by a relatively narrow elite — it is perhaps not surprising to find significant numbers of the people indifferent to the public affairs. However, one would certainly expect greater citizen political involvement during the revolutionary war and in the first decade or so of national independence. In all likelihood, such was the case. Yet there also must have been many who still remained indifferent to politics, for Dinkin (1982: 137) writes there were "[s]everal contemporaries [who] complained of voter apathy and of the people's 'fatal omission of their duty.' " Lack of political interest during the revolution and immediate post-war period also must have contributed to substantial political ignorance among the electorate, for it was alleged that many people cast ballots innocent of anything save " 'who was in last. . . .' "

As noted above, in eighteenth century America, the belief was widely held that the citizen had a duty to maintain an interest in government and politics. That duty, evidently, was not only to protect one's self-interest, but also to posterity. In an oft-quoted letter to his wife Abigail, written in 1780, John Adams declared that,

> I must study politics and war that my sons may have liberty to study mathematics and philosophy. My sons ought to study mathematics and philosophy, geography, natural history, naval architecture, navigation, commerce, and agriculture, in order to give their children a right to study painting, poetry, music, architecture, statuary, tapestry, and porcelain.

In short, the purpose of the revolutionary generation's attention to public affairs was less because of some intrinsic value thereto, than because, if successful, the fruits of their concern would leave their offspring free to attend to more personally rewarding subjects.

Once the revolution was fought, the problems associated with the Articles of Confederation withstood, and the new Constitution in place,[1] what became of citizen political interest in the first decades of the American Republic? If political scientist James Young's study of *The Washington Community* during the first three decades of the nineteenth century (1966) is any indication, the public was characterized more by apathy than interest, at least where national affairs were concerned. Young points out that the attempt to launch the new capital city — begun during the administration of George Washington in the early 1790s — nearly foundered on a sea of citizen apathy (1966: 17-23). As Young notes, to some degree the problems encountered in securing widespread popular backing in creation of the new seat for the national government were due to the location of the city in a pestilential swamp and to poor communication facilities and inept management of the enterprise (1966: 26-27). But there was a more fundamental reason: public indifference to the national government itself.

Why was that? According to Young, the primary source of widespread citizen indifference to national politics during the Jeffersonian

---

1. Certainly it would be reasonable to have expected an unusually high grassroots involvement during the war itself, while the Constitution was being framed at Philadelphia during that hot, muggy summer of 1787, and during the period when its ratification was under debate.

era and thereafter was the limited role of the federal government in American politics. Government was simply too limited an affair to be of much significance to ordinary people's personal lives. As Young puts it (1966: 30-32):

> What government business there was was not, most of it, of a sort to attract any widespread, sustained citizen interest. . . . Almost all of the things that republican governments do which affect the everyday lives and fortunes of their citizens, and therefore engage their interest, were in Jeffersonian times *not* done by the national government. . . . An institution whose involvement in the internal life of the nation was limited largely to the collection and delivery of letters could hardly have expected to be much in the citizens' consciousness. . . .

This widespread citizen apathy toward the national government also must have influenced the tenor and tempo of politics during the first three decades of the nineteenth century. According to Young (1966: 34), "The comparatively low 'temperature' of national politics and its relative decorum before the Jacksonian era may have testified not so much to the skill of a ruling Republican oligarchy as to a generalized or residual indifference among citizens toward national government itself."

Perhaps. But if Alexis de Tocqueville's comments on the importance of attention to public affairs among the Americans during the early 1830s are correct, things changed, and quickly, with "Old Hickory" in the White House. Based on his travels about the country during the Jacksonian Era, the young French aristocrat concluded that (1966: 243),

> It is hard to explain the place filled by the political concerns in the life of an American. To take a hand in the government of society and to talk about it is his most important business and, so to say, the only pleasure he knows. That is obvious even in the most trivial habits of his life; even the women often go to public meetings and forget household cares while they listen to political speeches.

Moreover, "if an American should be reduced to occupying himself with his own affairs, at that moment half his existence would be snatched from him; he would feel it as a vast void in his life and would become incredibly unhappy." If Tocqueville's characterization of the intense politicization of the people during the 1830s is correct, Pericles would have felt right at home in Andy Jackson's America.

It is not hard to account for the intense interest shown by ordinary people in the politics of the time. While the election of Andrew Jackson in 1828 did not immediately herald "the rise of the common man," it did "provide the ordinary citizen — who had been 'rising' for decades — with an elaborate party machine through which he could more effectively control the operation of government and shape public policy" (Remini, 1963: 203). The successes of Jackson's party — "the Democracy" — were brought about by a new type of politician who created a "new style" of electioneering, one which engaged the emotions of the ordinary people much more fervently than hitherto (Hofstadter, 1970: chap. 6). According to Richard McCormick (1973: 350),

> Politics in this era took on a dramatic function. It enabled voters throughout the nation to experience the thrill of participating in what amounted to a great democratic festival that seemed to perceptive foreign observers to be remarkably akin to the religious festivals of Catholic Europe.

McCormick also makes another important point. Since there were so few alternative forms of popular entertainment, people viewed the political process as a dramatic spectacle. Small wonder, then, that Tocqueville and other European travellers found such high levels of political interest in the 1830s (see, *e.g.*, Grund, 1959).

The extensive grassroots interest and participation in elections and politics generally that had begun with the election of 1828 continued throughout the next three decades. Certainly turnout in national elections surged ahead, although at an uneven pace, throughout the 1830s and 1840s (Chambers and Davis, 1978). Nor was the intense politicization of the citizenry simply confined to election time. According to Chambers and Davis (1978: 196), "Once voters were politically socialized to a pattern of political involvement, at least at the polls, they were likely to continue their concern for and excitement over political issues, parties, and campaigns."

Between 1848 and 1861, a series of political events, issues, and personalities marched across the American scene, all joined by the growing sectional crisis which would eventually produce what one historian dubbed *The Disruption of American Democracy* (Nichols, 1967; see also Potter, 1976). While historians have long debated the "causes" of the civil war, for present purposes Nichols focuses on the "hyperemotionalism" of the people by 1860 (1967: chap. 27). Not only did the people of that era fail to comprehend the cultural differences underlying sectional rivalries (Nichols, 1967: 503-504),

> This lack of understanding was accompanied by a deep-seated enjoyment of political activity by Americans which proved dangerous. They gave themselves so many opportunities to gratify their desire for this sport. There were so many elections and such constant agitation. . . . A great disruptive fact was the baneful influence of elections almost continuously in progress, of campaigns never over, and of political uproar endlessly arousing emotions.

The endless campaigning, fought out by virtually independent party organizations in each of the states, gave demagogues of every political stripe in all regions multiple opportunities to whip public interest into such an emotional fervor that compromise became impossible, and the Union was torn asunder (Nichols, 1967: 504-507).

Nichols' contention that an excess of public spirit and popular involvement in public affairs played a determinative role on the onset of civil war may be correct. However, according to Converse (1964: 251), letters written by ordinary Ohioans during the 1850s and 1860s reveal a growing awareness of and interest in the crisis on the eve of secession and war, but "later than is customarily assumed."

Whatever its causes, the sectional crisis of the 1850s and the Civil War ushered in a new era of grassroots political participation that was characterized by exceptionally high rates of turnout (Burnham, 1965; Kleppner, 1979, 1982b). While there is general agreement that voting in national elections was quite high (however, see Shortridge, 1981b), scholars are at loggerheads over the factors responsible. According to some, "The second half of the nineteenth century was an era of strong partisanship, high levels of political enthusiasm and involvement, and a more fully mobilized electorate than this country had ever before, or ever since, witnessed" (Kleppner, 1982b: 28; see also Burnham, 1965: 22). Other researchers demur, contending that a variety of technical factors associated with electoral administration in the thirty years after 1865 accounted for what only seem to be atypically high levels of voter participation (Rusk, 1970; Converse, 1972). Given the low levels of formal schooling and large portions of the electorate living in rural isolation, these scholars argue it is highly unlikely that the late nineteenth-century electorate was especially politically aware or interested (Converse, 1972: 271-276). Converse also warns that evidence from contemporary third-world countries reveals "how risky it is to draw simple equations between turnout levels and public involvement or alienation from the affairs of state" (1972: 287).

Not surprisingly, the question of how politically engaged and sophisticated the late nineteenth century electorate was has generated a lively intellectual debate (in addition to the citations above, see Burnham, 1971, 1974; Converse, 1974; Rusk, 1971, 1974; Kleppner and Baker, 1980; Shortridge, 1980, 1981a; Claggett, 1981). For the most part, this scholarly controversy is beyond the present volume's scope.

Suffice it to say that both quantitative and qualitative historical evidence support the proposition that, between 1865 and 1896, Americans maintained a fairly high level of interest in public affairs. First, as Kleppner has shown (1970, 1979, 1982b), the type of partisan divisions of the era which, especially in the northeast and upper midwest, were rooted in ethnoreligious identifications, produced a "quasi-confessionalism" in virtually all strata of society (see also, Jensen, 1971). Partly because they were closely linked with such basic social identifications as ethnoreligious group membership, the partisan struggles of the period were especially intense (Kleppner, 1982b: 46). Consequently, as Kleppner notes (1982b: 47),

> In that earlier society, politics occupied a greater share of the individual's life-space [than today]. Political matters were not complex, intangible, and remote, but simple, concrete, and directly related to the concerns of daily life. Because ethnoreligious and political communications reinforced each other, it placed no severe cognitive burden on most citizens to perceive the relationship.

In short, not only was the citizen of the late nineteenth century under a fairly strong goad to follow what was happening in political life, the psychological "costs" associated with political involvement were less than today.

Jensen (1971: 2-4) points to another factor behind the relatively greater citizen political involvement of the late nineteenth century: "Perhaps people who lacked electronic amusement and commercialized sports sought entertainment from the political arena." As he notes, there was a sufficiency of "spellbinders, oddballs, cranks, and demagogues" to more than meet the demand. Partly because they wanted entertainment, partly because political attachments were imbued with an intensity akin to religious affiliation (Jensen, 1971: 3), people not only voted at higher rates, but also were much more likely to take part in more demanding activities than is true today.

> The electorate followed political developments, recognized politicians, and understood the issues. They sat through hours of speeches without a break, not only to display their support of favorite candidates but also to soak up the details and the minute points of the tariff, the money question, educational policies, prohibition laws, and the myriad of minor issues that erupted from time to time.

Not only did they read "a good many pamphlets," the people also avidly consumed the strongly partisan newspapers of the time (Jensen, 1971: 4-6). While Jensen's account deals with the Midwest, it is unlikely that things were much different in other regions.

Even though it appears that political interest and concern were fairly high during the last third of the nineteenth century, there were observers who worried about signs of public apathy. One such was James Bryce (1891, II: chap. 84), who wrote of what he called "the fatalism of the multitude." By this he meant the tendency for even well-educated Americans to believe that the majority must be right and ought to prevail, and therefore "to acquiesce in the dominant opinion, to submit thought as well as action to the encompassing power of numbers" (1891, II: 331). While it is difficult to know how prevalent this tendency was in the 1880s, Bryce believed that, "there are in the United States signs of such a fatalistic temper" (1891, II: 333), and that it was rooted in certain cultural beliefs and practices: among them were "the unbounded freedom of discussion" and "the intense faith which the Americans have in the soundness of their institutions, and in the future of their country." Both work to "dispose . . . a man to acquiescence and submission" (II: 334).

Although it is likely that Bryce's concerns about political fatalism were in a minority among observers of the American scene in the

1880s, within a couple of decades or so many had become worried about apathy. Several factors account for this. First, beginning in 1896, turnout in national elections began to decline. This turn-down in turnout would continue unabated throughout the 1920s (Kleppner, 1982b). While some have blamed the admission of women into the electorate in 1920 for most of the turnout decline, Kleppner (1982a) has shown that it began much earlier and affected men's voting participation as well.

There is a good deal of controversy about why voting fell after 1896. Some, such as Burnham (1965, 1971, 1974) believe that the causes are primarily the result of the domination of the post-1896 party system by politico-economic elites determined to insulate themselves from the vagaries of a completely democratic electoral process. As Burnham puts it (1965: 26), "Confronted with a narrowed scope of effective democratic options, an increasingly large proportion of the eligible adult population either left, failed to enter or — as was the case with Southern Negroes after the completion of the 1890-1904 disenfranchisement movement in the old Confederacy — was systematically excluded from the American voting universe." Other scholars point to changes in the administration of the electoral process, most notably the institution of voter registration and residency requirements — in order to clean up fraudulent voting practices in urban areas — as the primary factors in the decline of voting (Converse, 1972, 1974; Rusk, 1974). Still other researchers believe that the partisan realignment after 1896, which replaced a generally competitive party system rooted in ethnoreligious group memberships with a largely uncompetitive system based primarily on regional cleavages (Kleppner, 1982b; see also Burnham, 1981). The resulting "politics as usual" could not attract the interests nor integrate large segments of the population, particularly younger persons, into the active citizenry (Kleppner and Baker, 1980; Kleppner, 1982b).

Had the decline in voting been the only factor of grassroots political behavior between 1896 and 1930, it would be difficult to characterize the period as one of growing citizen indifference to politics. However, there are other indications of widespread disengagement from public affairs by ordinary Americans. Fortunately, some have been documented by classics in social science research. Two are particularly relevant to present purposes: Merriam and Gosnell's *Non-Voting* (1924) and the Lynds' *Middletown* (1929).

The former deals with abstention from Chicago's mayorality election of 1923, and is based on in-person interviews with 6,000 nonvoters in that contest. As such, the monograph was based on the first sample survey recorded in the annals of American political science (Bennett and Bennett, 1986). While several factors accounted for the decision not to vote, the most important one was what Merriam and Gosnell (1924: 159) call "general [political] indifference." Depending upon how it is conceived, somewhere between one-quarter and two-fifths of the nonvoters did not take part in selection of the city's mayor because they were politically apathetic (Merriam and Gosnell, 1924: 158). While most prevalent among older women of foreign stock, no section of Chicago's society was completely free of political indifference at the time (Merriam and Gosnell, 1924: chap. 7).

The final chapter of the book deals with "methods for controlling non-voting." Although they had some ideas for dealing with the problem (1924: 235-238), Merriam and Gosnell admit that (235), "It is in the area designated as 'general indifference,' 'inertia,' or 'disbelief' [in women's suffrage] that the most serious difficulties are encountered in the effort to obtain a 100 per cent vote."

Another classic social science work that permits some insights into political apathy during the 1920s is Robert and Helen Lynd's analysis of "Middletown" (actually, Muncie, Indiana). In their chapter on the "machinery of government" (24), the Lynds distinguish the prevailing apathy toward politics and elections of the 1920s from the much greater citizen politicization of the 1880s and 1890s. Not only were "Middletowners" less likely to vote in local and national elections than had the previous generation, they were also less prone to be politically engaged in other ways. For example, they were less likely to go hear political stump speeches, and less likely even to care who won. Moreover, local newspapers devoted much less space to coverage of the electoral process.

The Lynds attribute the greater apathy of contemporary (*i.e.*, 1920s) residents to two factors: (1) "new inventions [especially radio] offering a variety of alternative interests are pressing upon politics as upon lodges, unions, and churches;" and (2) "in the minds of many citizens, politics is identified with fraud" (1929: 416, 420). There were two main consequences of citizen indifference: (1) fewer of the "best citizens" sought public office (1929: 421), and (2) ordinary citizens, unless their personal interests were directly engaged, did not concern themselves with what happens in politics but felt much more critical of anything that happened (422-424). Finally, as apathy more and more pervaded "Middletown," politics and government was increasingly left to the influence of what a later generation of political observers would call "special interests" (Lynd and Lynd, 1929: 425-427).

Granted, both the monograph by Merriam and Gosnell and the Lynds' book dealt with local affairs. However, there was also ample commentary during the 1920s on a pervasive public indifference to national politics as well (see, e.g., Munro, 1928; Wilson, 1930). A particularly interesting example was Walter Lippmann's essay on "The Causes of Political Indifference To-day" (1927). According to Lippmann, there were three primary factors behind the political apathy of the 1920s. First, unlike the case when Theodore Roosevelt or Woodrow Wilson were on the scene, "There are no parties, there are no leaders, there are no issues" (1927: 18). Second, there had been a deliberate effort by President Calvin Coolidge to dampen down "popular interest in popular government," mainly in order not "to distract business" (1927: 21). The third reason is more basic: so ample were opportunities to make money during the 1920s that "it was a waste of time to think about politics" (1927: 23). Given both the economic boom of the decade and the more enlightened policies of corporate leadership, the major causes for "political agitation" had been removed. With economic conflict, which is always the prime mover in politics, alleviated by prosperity, the issues that remained — prohibition, nativism, xenophobia, and fundamentalism — were orthogonal to the traditional issues that had historically divided the major political parties. Since both the Republicans and Democrats were internally divided over the "new" issues, they had become essentially irrelevant to large segments of the public, and the result was political indifference. Worse, there was no leadership prepared to bring either party to grips with the current "realities of American life" (1927: 34).

While Lippmann's conclusions were basically pessimistic, the one major factor he did not reckon with was a quick return of economic conflict as a primary source of political discord, and interest. Within a few years of the appearance of his essay, such and more had happened. The onset of the Great Depression, the emergence of a new generation of political leaders attuned to contemporary issues, and the rise of Nazism, Fascism, Communism, and Japanese expansionism had, by the end of the 1930s, combined to effect a resurgence of citizen political interest and electoral participation (Kleppner, 1982b: chap. 5). However, at least in terms of citizen turnout, the 1930s saw only an incomplete remobilization of the electorate.

Fortunately, the 1930s also witnessed the emergence of both nationwide scientific surveys of public opinion. Unhappily, another decade would pass before there was serious concern by quantitatively oriented social scientists in the problem of political apathy. It is to those early attempts by scholars to deal with citizen indifference that we now turn.

## Political Apathy and Social Scientists

With the advent of nationwide public opinion polling in the 1930s, political scientists had for the first time the chance to plumb systematically how interested people were in public affairs, and to determine which segments of the population were politically engaged and which were apathetic. It is surprising, therefore, that students of American politics were relatively slow to take advantage of the opportunity. In large measure, of course, this was because the dominant research paradigms in the discipline at the time eschewed quantitative studies (Somit and Tanenhaus, 1967: chap. 9). Other than the famed "Chicago school," of which *Non-Voting* was a prime example, most political scientists' work was little different from that of historians, philosophers, and legal scholars. As a result, most of the early work on apathy was done by either sociology or social psychology scholars.

Many of the early social scientists who studied the phenomenon tended to equate apathy with nonvoting (Connelly with Field, 1944; Knupfer, 1947; see Chapter 3). One important exception was the study of grassroots voting behavior during the 1940 election by Lazarsfeld, Berelson, and Gaudet (1968: chap. 5). At that, however, the approach taken by the authors of *The People's Choice* toward conceptualization and measurement of their respondents' interest was narrowly focused; they plumbed only interest in the election campaign (1968: 40-41). Nonetheless, self-reported campaign in-

*Apathy in Political Theory and Political Behavior*

terest gave Lazarsfeld and his colleagues very useful purchase on other forms of political involvement and participation. People who were highly interested were more likely to have opinions on a wider range of issues, were more likely to expose themselves to communications about the Roosevelt-Wilkie campaign, and were more likely to take part in campaign activities (1968: 41-42). In their efforts to pin down who was more likely to be politically interested Lazarsfeld, Berelson, and Gaudet (1968: 45) discovered that, "the person most interested in the election is more to be found in urban areas among men on higher levels of education, with better socio-economic status, and among older age groups." As will be seen in Chapter 4, their finding is, with few alterations, still relevant today.

While Lazarsfield and his associates conceptualized political interest in fairly simplistic terms, social scientists gradually came to view apathy as "a fairly complex psychological orientation" (Riesman and Glazer, 1950: 531). Riesman and Glazer conceive of apathy as a product of two distinct but closely related dimensions: "affect" and "competence" (1950: 536-547). "Affect" refers to the individual's investment of genuine but "appropriate" feelings of involvement and concern with the political arena. The adjective "appropriate" serves to warn against including the excessive feelings of those with psychopathological orientations "who look for opportunities of releasing indignation onto politics" (1950: 539). "Competence" means the mastery of political terminology and skills that are suitable to the individual's station in life.

By combining the components of affect and competence, Riesman and Glazer claim to be able to identify three different variants of apathetic orientations toward politics in the twentieth century[2] (1950: 537): (1) the "indifferents," who are low on both dimensions; (2) the "indignants," who are high in affect but low in competence; and (3) the "inside-dopesters," who are affectless but high in competence (see also Riesman, with Glazer and Denney, 1961: 180-187). Unfortunately, despite the theoretically rich discussion they provide, Riesman and Glazer are forced to concede that their efforts to provide empirical indicators of key concepts were not particularly successful (1950: 544-547).

2. Riesman and Glazer believe that, although absolute levels of apathy did not change much from the nineteenth to the twentieth centuries, the bases and manifestations in each were considerably different (1950: 506-530).

*25*

More recently, as political scientists have focused on apathy, one approach has been to concentrate on the links between political indifference and alienation. For example, Gilmour and Lamb (1975: 111) create a typology of the different ways people can respond to American politics by superimposing an indicator of "extreme political alienation" upon an indicant of apathy. Despite some technical questions about the underlying measures (see 1975: 160-165), Gilmour and Lamb's scheme has the advantage of having been constructed from at least reasonably direct empirical measurements of key concepts.[3]

Gilmour and Lamb differentiate four separate variants of apathetic orientations to American politics in 1972. The largest bloc of apathetics is labelled the "Indifferents;" this grouping made up 46 percent of all apathetics. These were people who, because they were disillusioned with contemporary American politics, did not participate. The second largest group of apathetics — 39 percent of the total — were the "Withdrawn." These were persons who were extremely "alienated" from politics, and did not take part in what they believed was a hopelessly spoiled political system. Making up 11 percent of all apathetics, the "Disgruntled" were people who were either severely disillusioned or even outright "alienated" from American politics. In some ways, this variant of apathy is the most interesting of all, for, although politically indifferent, they tended to engage in political participation, usually to spew their bile. When given the chance these people vote, usually against incumbents. They are the "agin," or "crank" voters. (This points to a fact worth remembering: some persons low in interest may still vote, either out of a sense of duty or, more likely, to "get even.") Finally, there was a small group of apathetics that Gilmour and Lamb call the "Contenteds." Making up only four percent of all apathetics, they were both disinterested and inactive because they were basically satisfied with things as they were. (This grouping reminds one of Arthur Hadley's [1978: 68] "positive apathetics," who did not vote in the 1976 election "because at present their lives are too full for the act of voting to seem important.")

Gilmour and Lamb's approach to the analysis of apathy can be criticized on conceptual grounds (see Chapter 3). However, it is

---

3. Gilmour and Lamb utilize the Center for Political Studies' 1972 national election study as their data base.

important because it points indirectly to some of the factors social scientists have alleged to be responsible for political indifference. One of the more interesting efforts to identify the major factors that influence apathy is by Morris Rosenberg (1954-1955). Based on an admittedly non-random sample of 70 individuals in the early 1950s, he identifies three main factors that contribute to political indifference and inactivity. Some people are apathetic because they view political involvement as threatening. Politics, after all, often involves conflict, and many view such as potentially detrimental to business interests, friendships, and even, on occasion, family relationships. Other individuals fear that political involvement could result in serious blows to already fragile egos. (In this connection, one is reminded of Abraham Lincoln's famous dictum that it is better to remain quiet and be thought a fool than to speak out, thereby removing any possible doubts about it.)

Another factor responsible for apathy is the perception that political activity is ultimately futile. Man may not be a completely rational political actor, but people do like to think there would be at least the possibility of a successful payoff to their involvement. When the likely results of engagement are seen as dismal at best, it is small wonder that people lose interest. According to Rosenberg, the belief that political activity would be futile has two components. Some individuals focus on their own incompetence as political actors; politics is a complicated business, involving the actions of many far more powerful actors than a single individual. Hence, it would be foolish to expect much to happen as a result of one's measly endeavors. The second component focuses on the relative political impotence of the ordinary citizen. Many people subscribe to the traditional American belief about the domination of our political system by powerful, well-organized forces (A. Miller, 1974a; Citrin, 1974; Gilmour and Lamb, 1975; Sniderman, 1981; Abramson, 1983; Lipset and Schneider, 1983a). They are thus likely to disparage the clout of the "little man." The "system" is also seen as unresponsive to grassroots attempts at influence. Since they feel powerless, they withdraw from political attention and involvement. (It should be noted that Rosenberg's two components of the sense of political futility are similar to the two dimensions scholars have found in the Survey Research Center's concept of political efficacy [Balch, 1974; Abramson, 1983]).

Rosenberg labels the third factor "absence of spurs to action." By this he means that many people find the subject matter of government and politics to be dull and boring, that there are seldom direct, palpable satisfactions to be gained from political involvement, and that people are much more likely to be concerned with direct, immediate, and concrete personal needs. Moreover, some people are indifferent simply because they have never been asked to take a personal hand in public affairs.

Rosenberg also points out that other factors also affect one's psychological involvement in public affairs. Those who are basically satisfied with how things are going may be under no goad to pay heed to politics. Others are indifferent because they see no basic differences between the major political parties. Still others lack any firm convictions about politics. Finally, others may be subjected to social pressures against political involvement.

Rosenberg's work reminds us that a variety of factors shape the individual's usual level of political interest or indifference. However, he was unable to determine how much interest/apathy there was at the grassroots level in the early 1950s. Someone who could was Bernard Berelson (1952), and it is to his work we return.

## Apathy in Theories of Democracy

According to Berelson (1954: 316), public opinion surveys of the time indicated that, "Less than one-third of the electorate is 'really interested' in politics, and that group is by no means a cross-section of the total electorate." The discovery that citizens remained basically uninterested in politics led Berelson and other scholars (Parsons, 1959; Lipset, 1981; Dahl, 1961; Almond and Verba, 1963; Milbrath, 1965) to attempt reformulations of democratic philosophy to bring theory more into line with practice. In the new version, rather than being detrimental to democracy as older notions had held (Bryce, 1913), a sizable bloc of apathetic persons became an advantage, for it provided a "cushion" for elites against the actions of highly interested, intense partisans. Apathy gave political decision-makers leeway to bargain and compromise. Berelson believed that if everyone were intensely interested, the political system ran a serious risk of political immobilism (see also Berelson, Lazarsfeld, and McPhee, 1954: chap. 14; Dahl, 1961; Almond and Verba, 1963). He con-

*Apathy in Political Theory and Political Behavior*

cluded that democracy might be better suited if most people maintained a lukewarm interest in political life, and elites had to secure their approval or acquiescence. Later (Berelson, Lazarsfeld, and McPhee, 1954: 315), he added: "Some people are and should be highly interested in politics, but not everyone is or needs to be" (see Chapter 3).

Attempts to create an "empirical theory" of democracy elicited criticism by scholars who believed the reformulated versions had denuded traditional democratic theory of its radical thrust (Duncan and Lukes, 1963; Davis, 1964; Walker, 1966; Bachrach, 1967; Pateman, 1970; Thompson, 1970). To its critics the reconstituted version of democratic theory was more "elitist" than "democratic." According to Thompson (1970: 25), "Elitist democratic theory reinforces the potent historical forces toward centralized, bureaucratic power that make citizens feel remote from politics and that discourage citizenship."

Critics of empirical democratic theory especially rejected its notions about citizen apathy. In Jack Walker's view (1966: 289),

> The most unsatisfactory element in the theory is its concept of the passive, apolitical common man who pays allegiance to his governors and to the sideshow of politics while remaining primarily concerned with his private life, evenings of television with his family, or the demands of his job.

In the main, however, even Berelson's critics had to agree that most citizens were politically indifferent. The bones of contention centered on whether apathy dampened the fires of political cleavage and provided room for elites to maneuver in the quest for political solutions, as Berelson (1952) and Almond and Verba (1963) contended, or insulated them from grassroots political influence, as critics of the "elitist" theory of democracy believed.

Another element in the "debate" about apathy was the diversity of conceptualizations of the concept. There were many, often-conflicting, ways of defining what apathy meant. In addition, the "debate" over apathy took place in the absence of satisfactory operationalizations of the term. Because they conceived it and measured it differently, scholars very often talked "past," rather than "at," one another. Until this conceptual and operational disarray is resolved, it is unlikely that the "debate" can be resolved. Chapter 3 seeks to address each of these problems.

# CHAPTER 3

# THE CONCEPTUALIZATION AND MEASUREMENT OF APATHY

## Introduction

This chapter has two parts. The first is a reconsideration of the concept of political apathy as it has been presented in the literature on political behavior. Previous analyses have either misconceived the concept or added several conceptual dimensions that tend to obfuscate, rather than clarify, its meaning. Some are drawn from social psychological research on attitudes and personality traits. Some come from studies of other basic political orientations such as political efficacy and cynicism. These extraneous attributes are not integral to apathy, and must be stripped from conceptual treatments of the concept.

The second part of the chapter reviews previous measurements of political interest, and develops an operational definition of the concept, based on the Survey Research Center/Center for Political Studies' data that are available for over-time research. At this point, the technical aspects of the new measure are explored.

## Conceptions of Political Apathy in the Literature

Given the volume of research on political participation, it is not surprising that a number of scholars have studied interest in politics (Milbrath and Goel, 1977: 35-42, 46-49). However, a sizable portion of this work deals with interest or involvement in specific election campaigns (Lazarsfeld, Berelson, and Gaudet, 1968: 40-45; Berelson, Lazarsfeld, and McPhee, 1954: 24-28; Campbell, Gurin, and Miller, 1954: 33-35; and Campbell, Converse, Miller, and Stokes, 1960: 101-103). While the two are related, interest in a particular campaign is a narrower construct than is the notion of political apathy.

Another tendency has been for many students of political behavior to equate apathy with the absence of participation (Rosenberg, 1954-1955; Kornhauser, 1959: 46-47; Lane, 1965: 108, 116-118; DiPalma, 1970: 2; Verba and Nie, 1972: 28, 33; Milbrath and Goel, 1977: 11; and Hadley, 1978: 39-40, 68-74). This is unfortunate, as there are several good reasons for making a conceptual distinction between apathy and nonparticipation.

For one thing, people may not take part in politics for a variety of reasons, some having nothing to do with apathy. Riesman and Glazer (1950: 535) point out that it is possible to be genuinely interested in politics but to remain passive because no appropriate mode of activity is presently at hand. Also, people may be interested in politics but abstain from acts such as voting because they believe politicians to be insincere, corrupt, or even incompetent (Johnson, 1980: 122-123). Also, some persons — such as southern blacks prior to passage of the 1965 Voting Rights Act — may dearly wish to take part in politics, by voting, for example, but avoid doing so because they fear harassment, intimidation, or even outright violence (Salamon and Van Evera, 1973; but see also Kernell, 1973). Finally, a more tendentious point is made by those who regard nonparticipation, especially by the most disadvantaged segments of society, as "a justifiable reaction to a politics that is meaningless in its electoral content and disappointing in its policy results" (Parenti, 1977: 208).

On a different note, Riesman and Glazer (1950: 518-520) contend that, increasingly in this century, as the nature of politics and the relation of citizens to the political process have changed, some people have engaged in various forms of participation for what are "apolitical," possibly even "apathetic," reasons. This happens when politics is not used for its own sake, but instead to conform to group pressures, or as a form of personal reaction, or even for the displacement of individual psychopathology. According to some, projection of psychopathological tendencies has been an especially compelling motivation for engagement in politics during the twentieth century

(Lasswell, 1960, 1962; Neumann, 1957: chap. 11; Hofstadter, 1965). It should be noted in passing that most of the studies in which psychopathological dispositions figure heavily as goads to political participation have focused on engagement in right-wing social protest (see, for example, Adorno, et al., 1950; the essays in Bell, ed., 1963; and Lipset and Raab, 1977), although some have also looked at various forms of leftist extremism (Almond, 1954; Liebert, 1971).

For these reasons, and because apathy originally meant "without feeling," it seems more appropriate for the concept to signify a particular type of political disposition rather than a pattern of (in)action. Among those who have used apathy to mean a particular political orientation, most seem to have had in mind some notion of "indifference," or similar terms such as "disinterest," "withdrawal," "passivity," or "lack of motivation" (Bryce, 1913: 2-3; Lippmann, 1927: 18-34; Riesman and Glazer, 1950: 531-547; Berelson, 1952: 316; Dean, 1960: 187; Lipset, 1981: 226; Riesman, Glazer, and Denney, 1961: 165-171; Campbell, 1962: 9; McClosky, 1968: 252; Pranger, 1968: 27-28, 51; and Gilmour and Lamb, 1975: 21, 91-111). As Gilmour and Lamb (1975: 96) put it, apathy is "simply a matter of [lack of] political interest."

However, in most previous analyses of apathy, the concept has seldom been so narrowly conceived. Rather, the term has usually bee made to carry a heavy load of normative and/or empirical freight. It was typical for earlier generations of political observers to castigate the disinterested for their "failure" to abide by the norms of "good citizenship" (Bryce, 1913; Connelly, with Field, 1944). The indifferent citizen was informed, nay, lectured, about his "slackness," "indolence," or "laziness," which was believed to be harmful to democracy.

Especially during the early decades of the twentieth century, a legion of what Roelofs (1957: 3) would later call the "professional preachers of good citizenship" travelled about the country, appearing at Chatauqua meetings, lecturing before learned foundations, and writing pamphlets, monographs, and textbooks, reminding the ordinary citizenry of the responsibility to maintain an active interest in the public affairs. To some degree, these sentiments were a carry over of sentiments expressed even before independence from Great Britain was achieved (Dinkin, 1977: 188; see also Dinkin, 1982: 137). It was also common among politicians of the progressive era to threaten the political indifferent with loss of their political liberties (Roosevelt, 1958: 73).

Occasionally, someone tried to justify, if not excuse, grass-roots disinterest (Lippmann, 1925: 16-39, 1927: 18-34; Dewey, 1927: 134-135). Far more common, however, was the expression of disdain, and even outright hostility toward those who, in the pursuit of private business or pleasure, neglected their civic responsibilities (see esp. Bryce, 1913).

Even though later generations of social scientists would jettison much of the hyperbole and excess normative baggage, they would continue to conceptualize apathy in multifaceted terms. One approach has been to link apathy with basic personality traits, so that discussion of the concept became almost an exegesis on political psychopathology (Knupfer, 1947; Riesman and Glazer, 1950: 536-546; Lipset, 1981: 103-104, 115-116; Campbell, 1962: 10-13). The apathetic citizen, especially if from the lower social orders, was found to suffer from enervating personality maladies (such as low self-esteem), and to manifest a variety of sociopathic attitudes (including xenophobia, racial and ethnic bigotry, and authoritarianism).

Another multifaceted approach has been to conceptualize apathy in conjunction with such basic political orientations as trust, cynicism, and alienation (Dean, 1960; Campbell, 1962; Gilmour and Lamb, 1975). A particularly interesting study is Campbell's "The Passive Citizen." Although quick to recognize that some people are apathetic simply out of detachment, he also claims that there are many whose orientation to politics is one "of suspicion, distrust, hostility, and cynicism" (1962: 14). As Campbell puts it, "It would appear that some part of political apathy is more than simple passivity. With some individuals an active rejection of political matters is involved" (1962: 14).

Another perspective on the multiple meanings that have been attached to apathy comes from the scholars who have focused on the consequences of indifference for the future of democracy. Reacting to the breakdown of democratic regimes, especially the case of Weimar Germany, several analysts have worried about the implications for democracy should substantial proportions of the previously apathetic become suddenly mobilized. Based on findings from early studies of participation, special attention was drawn to the tendency for the chronically apathetic to come disproportionately from the same population elements, namely those that were least socialized into the norms of democratic politics. It was felt that such previously disinterested groups could, especially if a severe economic or social crisis were to arise, comprise a potentially mobilizable public on behalf of an anti-democratic demagogue or mass movement (Kornhauser, 1959: 46-47; Lipset, 1981: 226-227). The sudden emergence into the political arena of the chronically apathetic, who would bring their sociopathic attitudes along, would constitute a grave threat to the democratic order.

There has been a consistent worry among students of political participation that the sudden irruption of the previously apathetic —whether defined attitudinally in terms of indifference or behaviorally with regard to abstention from voting — into the political arena would drastically alter the political process. An obvious question has been what the entry of chronic nonvoters into the electoral process would portend. Some analysts fret over the potential for realignment of the political agenda and/or the balance of power among contending political parties. As E. E. Schattschneider (1960: 103) put it a quarter-century ago, "Anyone who finds out how to involve the forty million [nonvoters] in American politics will run the country for a generation." Other students of political behavior are concerned about the potential for transformation of the political system itself. According to Arthur Hadley (1978: 17, 126),

> The [apathetic] nonvoters tamp our political system with an explosive mass, waiting for some trigger to change the course of history. . . . As there is a critical mass of nuclear material necessary to trigger an atomic explosion, so there appears to be a critical percentage of nonvoters necessary to produce rapid social change. Historically that percentage has been close to the 50 percent we now approach. They sit out there, . . . disconnected from the process of democracy, but able at any moment to dominate our future. . . . To start them back now as voters is important. Not because our country will necessarily be governed better if they return, but because their growing presence menaces any government.

Whether one's concern is as profound as the impact of the previously apathetic on the character of the regime or as mundane as their consequence for the alignment of political forces, evidence from studies of nonvoters indicates the problem may have been overblown. Not only are nonvoters essentially indistinguishable from voters in their ideological proclivities and policy opinions (Wolfinger and Rosenstone, 1980; Shaffer, 1982), it is unlikely that the sudden entry of the previously passive into the voting booth would alter the balance of power between the major political parties (De Nardo, 1980; however, see also Perry, 1973).

While studies of the likely consequences of the addition of chronic nonvoters into the political process are important, they do not indicate what might happen should the indifferent suddenly become mobilized. That query is addressed in Chapter 6.

Some scholars view political apathy from a different angle. They are not especially troubled by the presence of substantial numbers of disinterested citizens. According to this view, rather than being detrimental to democracy, a sizable bloc of apathetic persons becomes an advantage, for it provides a "cushion" for elites against the actions of highly interested, intense partisans. Apathy thus gives political decision-makers leeway to bargain and compromise. As Bernard Berelson (1952: 317) puts it, "If everyone in the community were highly interested, the possibilities of compromise and of gradual solution of political problems might well be lessened to the point of danger" (see also Berelson, Lazarsfeld, and McPhee, 1954; Dahl, 1961; Almond and Verba, 1963). Berelson concludes that, "Perhaps what . . . [democracy] really requires is a body of moderately and discontinuously interested citizens within and across social classes, whose approval of or at least acquiescence in political policies must be secured." In a similar vein, Almond and Verba (1963: 478-479) contend that to maintain the delicate balance between governmental power and responsiveness, "the democratic citizen is called on to pursue contradictory goals; he must be active, yet passive; involved, yet not too involved; influential, yet deferential." (Needless to say, the argument that apathy is beneficial to democracy has not gone unchallenged [see, *e.g.*, Duncan and Lukes, 1963; Davis, 1964; Walker, 1966; Pateman, 1970; Thompson, 1970]).

Regarding either the contention that apathy constitutes a potential threat or that it is a blessing to democracy, one sees a superimposition onto political indifference of extra conceptual dimensions. On the one hand, there is the blending of disinterest with sociopathic dispositions such as bigotry, authoritarianism, and anti-civil libertarianism. On the other hand, there is an admixture of political ignorance and acquiescence to elite policy decisions. In either case, political indifference has lost its pristine conceptual status and, in the end, becomes important only in terms of its real or imagined consequences for the functioning of democratic politics.

This partial review of research on apathy reveals that some conceptual reworking of the concept is in order. It is necessary to prune the concept, to strip away the extra baggage that has been added over the years.

## Apathy Reconsidered

The concept of political apathy refers to the varying degrees to which people are or are not interested in and attentive to politics and public affairs. It is similar to Almond and Verba's (1963: 88) idea of "civic cognition" and to Verba and his associates' (Verba, Nie, and Kim, 1978: 47-48, 70-73) notion of "general psychological involvement in politics and public affairs."

To describe levels of political interest across a large population, imagine a continuum of awareness, interest, and attention. At the one end is the individual who is so engrossed with his own psychological needs, or the affairs of his family, his work, or even his entertainment and recreational activities, that he has little or no psychic energy left for interest in public affairs. When such an individual declares that he "hardly thinks about politics at all," or does not "follow public affairs much at all," he can be classified as politically disinterested, or apathetic. At the opposite end of the continuum is the person who says he follows public affairs "very closely," or thinks about politics "most of the time."[1] This person can be considered to be psychologically involved in governmental affairs.

The concept of political apathy serves a dual utility in the study of political behavior. First, it is an important indicator of an individual's potential for political activity. Political behavior research has

---

1. I have deliberately shortened the continuum somewhat to exclude the political activists, who constitute the shock-troops of political campaigns, causes, organizations, and movements. Their activities provide American politics with much of its driving verve. Much good research has been done on them recently (Rosenau, 1974; Kirkpatrick, 1976; Broder, 1980; Lamb, 1982); there is little I can add to this literature.

repeatedly found that those who are highly interested in politics are considerably more likely to be active than those who are not (Milbrath and Goel, 1977: 46-47).

However, it would be mistaken too readily to accept the proposition that high levels of psychological involvement necessarily result in participation. As Dahl (1961: 280) has pointed out, it is considerably easier to be "merely" interested, which demands only "passive participation," than it is to be actually active Interest "costs" but little in terms of psychic and physical energy and time; activity demands much more of each. Moreover, Dahl argues, "mere" political interest can even be a form of "escape" (see also Riesman and Glazer, 1950: 510-518). Without leaving a favorite easy chair or missing a TV soap opera, "interest" allows the expression of a range of emotions, from admiration to abhorrence. Or the person can daydream about the easy achievement of miraculous solutions to today's vexing problems, while denigrating the "measly" accomplishments of those who actually grapple with them in the mundane world of reality. "Interest" also permits Riesman's "inside dopster" (Riesman, with Glazer and Denney, 1961: 180-186) to use any information gleaned thereby to impress his peers with his "savvy," without having to sully himself through actual participation in the political fray. Finally, on a more prosaic level, the expression of "interest" in public affairs may offer partial absolution of the guilt that accompanies real or imagined failure to live up to culturally ingrained expectations of a high level of political participation (Lane, 1973: 286).

Nevertheless, the concept of political apathy remains useful as a device for estimating the degree to which citizens are psychologically "engaged" in the political process. As Almond and Verba (1963: 88) put it, "We may assume that if people follow political and governmental affairs, they are in some sense involved in the process by which decisions are made." They are aware, of course, that this may be a minimal involvement. Yet, someone with even a minuscule level of political interest has at least a dim and hazy awareness that he is a member of a polity and that the governmental process does, however, marginally, affect his daily life. In this sense, he is, however slightly, more involved than the individual Almond and Verba (1963: 17-18) call a "parochial." The latter is virtually without any awareness of the commonwealth, and does not see government as encroaching in any significant way upon his existence (1963: 79-83).

Of course, as noted above, it is possible to be aware that governmental decisions affect one's life, but to be politically disinterested nonetheless.[2] But those who do admit to even a minimal degree of political interest have made some small investment of psychological involvement in the political system. *Citizens who claim interest in public affairs may not yet have crossed the border into the realm of political participation, but they have made a substantial down payment on the keys to the kingdom.*

Considered as either an indicator for potential for participation or an estimate of psychological engagement in the governmental process — the two are, of course, related — the concept of political apathy is clearly a very important one for grassroots political behavior. However, before empirical assessments can be made, a workable operationalization of the concept is needed.

## Measurement of Political Apathy

Several approaches have been followed to measure political interest. They range from a simple measure of interest in election campaigns (Berelson, Lazarsfeld, and McPhee, 1954: 24-28) to the complex "Index of Psychological Involvement in Politics" developed by Verba and Nie (1972: 367-369). The latter consists of an admixture of general interest in politics, engagement in political discussions, and media utilization for political purposes, combined via an elaborate algorithm into a composite index. Intermediate between these extremes stand the SRC's measures of "Political Involvement" (Campbell, Converse, Miller, and Stokes, 1960: 102-107).

In their efforts to account for voting turnout, Campbell and his associates created two separate indicants of psychological involvement. The simpler, and perhaps better known, is a simple combination of interest in the election campaign with concern about which

---

2. The Five Nation Study and the Comparative State Election Project included the same question on perceptions of the central government's impact on the individual's daily life (Almond and Verba, 1963: 529; Black, Kovenock, and Reynolds, 1974: 182). Each study also had a measure of general political interest (Almond and Verba, 1963: 527; Black, Kovenock and Reynolds, 1974: 180). Despite the fact that the interest questions were worded differently, it is instructive that, in each survey, people who saw the national government as having a great effect on their lives were more than twice as likely to be highly interested than were those who did not think their lives were affected by government.

political party won the election (Inter-University Consortium for Political Research, 1974: 172). The more elaborate version is a linear combination of measures of "intensity of partisan preference," campaign interest, concern about the election's outcome, with the SRC's original four-item version of the Political Efficacy Scale and its four-item Sense of Citizen Duty Scale (Campbell, Converse, Miller, and Stokes, 1960: 107; Robinson, Rusk, and Head, 1968: 456-458).

The pitfalls entailed in utilizing only a measure of campaign interest to tap the more general phenomenon of political involvement are too apparent to require comment. Also, much as one might admire the statistical prowess involved in Verba and Nie's indicant, it suffers from the introduction of forms of political activity — engagement in conversations, use of mass media — in what is alleged to be only an indicator of psychological involvement.

On the other hand, each of the SRC's indicators of political involvement has much to recommend it, especially in comparison to the other operationalizations considered hitherto. The components of the simpler version — campaign interest and concern about which party won the election — are sufficiently related to form a unidimensional index, and each has been shown to predict turnout fairly well (Campbell, Converse, Miller, and Stokes, 1960: 103-104). Turning to the more complex version, principal components factor analyses of the 1952 and 1956 SRC National Election Studies show that at least four of the elements load on a component that accounts for half the variance of the separate measures (Campbell, Converse, Miller, and Stokes, 1960: 102), and the composite index created by the five elements robustly predicted reported turnout in 1956 (Campbell, Converse, Miller, and Stokes, 1960: 107).

However, problems crop up with each version of the SRC's political involvement measure. Concerning first the more complex indicant, since the early 1970s the original four item version of the Political Efficacy Scale has come increasingly under fire for a variety of technical problems (Converse, 1972: 326-330; Asher, 1974; Balch, 1974; McPherson, Welch, and Clark, 1977; Craig, 1979; Craig and Maggiotto, 1982; Abramson, 1983: chap. 8). More recently, some concern has surfaced about possible problems with the Sense of Citizen Duty Scale (Brody, 1978: 305; W. Miller, 1980: 18), at least insofar as it relates to turnout in national elections.

Nor is the two-item version of the SRC's indicator of involvement free of difficulty. While some scholars have pointed to the decline since the 1960s in concern with which a political party wins the election as a causal factor in the turndown in turnout (Ferejohn and Fiorina, 1979), Rollenhagen (1984) has shown that lessened concern with party victory at the polls is a consequence of the diminution in attachment to the major parties, which began about 1966.

This discovery forces attention to the fact that the item about concern with the election's outcome centers on partisan fortunes. Hence, the variable depends, in large part, upon intensity of partisanship. All other things being equal, strong partisans will care more about which party is victorious than do lukewarm adherents, or especially independents. An item that adds the contamination of partisanship into what is supposed to be a measure of political interest is best left out.

Inspiration for the measure of political interest used in this volume comes from Almond and Verba's (1963: 88-89) indicator of what they call "civic cognition." They propose (p. 91) combining a measure of general political interest with a campaign interest variable to form an index of psychological involvement in politics. As Almond and Verba (1963: 88) put it, "Following governmental and political affairs and paying attention to politics are limited civic commitments indeed, and yet there would be no civic culture without them."

Despite their suggestion to combine general with campaign interest, Almond and Verba treat the two separately. Following their idea, the "Political Apathy Index" used here is a linear combination of interest in election campaigns with an indicant of more general interest in public affairs.

The data used for this study come from a variety of sources. The bulk comes from most of the University of Michigan's Survey Research Center/Center for Political Studies' National Election Studies from 1960 to 1984. Occasionally, they will be supplemented by the American data from the Five Nation Study, the University of North Carolina's Institute for Social Science Research's 1968 Comparative State Election Project, the University of Chicago's National Opinion Research Center's Amalgam survey of December, 1973; the CPS special surveys in 1980 (P1-P4, C1); NORC's General Social Surveys of 1982 and 1984; and the CPS's Continuous Monitoring Survey of 1984. All the information was made available by the Inter-University

Consortium for Political and Social Research to the University of Cincinnati's Behavioral Sciences Laboratory.[3]

As is often the case with secondary analysis of sample surveys, especially when the aim is to trace a phenomenon over an extended period, problems with the comparability of measures crop up. For example, the wording of the item on campaign interest in the Five Nation Study differs from that used by the SRC/CPS since 1952. In the former case, the item reads so:

> What about the campaigning that goes on at the time of a national election — do you pay much attention to what goes on, just a little, or none at all?

The SRC/CPS version is more elaborate:

> Some people don't pay much attention to political campaigns. How about you? Would you say you have been very much interested, somewhat interested, or not much interested in following the campaigns so far this year?

Students of the methodology of public opinion research have repeatedly shown that even minor fluctuations in the wording and/or format of a question can produce profoundly different response patterns (Schuman and Presser, 1981). Some researchers have contended that, where even minuscule changes are made in the wording and/or format of a survey item, trend analysis becomes virtually meaningless (Sullivan, Piereson, and Marcus, 1978; Sullivan, Piereson, Marcus, and Feldman, 1979).

There is no gainsaying the fact that any attempt to compare distributions of response to questions that differ in question wording and format must be done with great care, sensitivity to the nuances of wording, and concern with the vagaries of format. For example, consider again the wordings of the Five Nation Study question on campaign interest and that of the SRC item. In the former, the survey respondent is asked to recall whether he pays "much attention to what goes on" in the campaigning "at the time of a national election," or "just a little," or "none at all." For the SRC version, the respondent must declare whether he was "very much," "somewhat," or "not much" interested "in following the political campaigns this year."

---

3. Naturally, I alone am responsible for all analyses and interpretations.

The two questions, therefore, differ on three dimensions. First, there is the element of specificity; the SRC version denotes attention to the campaign just completed, while the Five Nation item pinpoints no specific election. Second, the timing of the two questions is very important. The SRC survey was done immediately before the election, while the American data from the Almond and Verba study were gathered in March, 1960, during the primary season of the presidential election, but well before the general campaign had begun. It is likely, therefore, that the Almond and Verba item calls for more recall of attention during past election campaigns, with all the vagaries such responses entail in the survey context (Gutek, 1978; Adamany and Shelley, 1980). Finally, the options offered by the Five Nation item — "much," "just a little," or "none at all" — are at once less precise and more discriminating than those presented by the SRC version — "very much," "somewhat," or "not much". The Michigan question is probably better able to detect persons very interested in the campaign, but less able to distinguish between the moderately interested and the apathetic. What, after all, does the survey respondent mean if he replies "not much" rather than "somewhat"? On the other hand, if someone, in response to the Five Nation question, says "none at all," his is probably a more pristine exemplar of campaign apathy than his neighbor who says "just a little." In short, with so many differences built into the two versions of campaign interest, one would be amply justified to conclude that any attempt to compare respective distributions is an exercise in futility.

But, is it? Consider for a moment the following information. In March, 1960, 43.3% of adult Americans claimed to pay "much" attention to national campaigns, 44.4% said it paid "only a little" heed, 11.3% replied "none at all," and one percent said either something else or did not know how much attention it gave (N = 970). In the six weeks immediately before election day, the SRC's 1960 National Election Study reports campaign interest thusly: "very much" = 37.6%, "somewhat" = 37.3%, and "not much" = 25.1% (N = 1919).

Immediately one notes the Five Nation Study data reflect a lower level of campaign apathy, by 14 percentage points (11% vs. 25%). On second thought, however, if the Almond and Verba item uses "none at all" as its most disinterested option, compared with the SRC's "not much" alternative, is it at all surprising to find a smaller percentage falling into the most "apathetic" category in the Five Nation study?

Indeed, when distributions on the other options of the two campaign interest questions are compared, one is as struck by the similarities in response patterns as by any divergences. Differences of about six percentage points may be statistically "significant," but substantively they pale into unimportance. In either instance, the substantive interpretation is the same: In 1960, roughly two-in-five adult Americans were "highly interested" in the campaign while almost the same proportion was "moderately" attentive. When the substantial differences in the two versions of campaign interest are taken into account, and due allowances are made for the very divergent wordings of the least interested option, it seems safe to conclude that both can be utilized in a study such as this.

Happily, of course, since most of the data for the book come from SRC/CPS national election studies, the wording of the campaign interest item will be invariate. Unfortunately, however, over the years the placement of the item on SRC/CPS questionnaires does vary, and for some methodologists, variation in questionnaire location — both in terms of the order and context of the item — produces such widely divergent reports on campaign interest as to invalidate an extended trend analysis such as this (Bishop, Oldendick, and Tuchfarber, 1982, 1984).

The particular bone of contention centers on the fact that, in 1978, the CPS changed its questionnaire so that the campaign interest item was the first one in the interview, rather than appearing later on, and after a series of questions about the campaign (Bishop, Oldendick, and Tuchfarber, 1982: 179). According to Bishop and his colleagues, a series of question wording experiments done on a local population show that the change made by the CPS in 1978 artifactually diminished reported campaign interest, and thus accounts for most, if not all, the lower rate of attention to the campaign that year compared with previous years, such as 1976 (Bishop, Oldendick, and Tuchfarber, 1982: 185). Subsequent research indicates that the questionnaire context within which campaign interest is elicited also affects levels of reported attention (Bishop, Oldendick, and Tuchfarber, 1984). If the contention by Bishop and his co-authors is correct, trend analysis of the SRC/CPS's campaign interest question must be suspect.

Of course it is necessary to consider technical factors such as the

*The Conceptualization and Measurement of Apathy*

questionnaire order and the contextual framework within which almost any survey item is posed. However, at least in terms of campaign interest, the situation is not as bleak as Bishop and his associates construe. First, the results of their experiment are not dramatically different from treatment to treatment (Bishop, Oldendick, and Tuchfarber, 1982: 183). Second, subsequent surveys show results inconsistent with their contention. In particular, CPS surveys in 1980, 1982, and 1984, which kept the order and context of the question on campaign interest as it had been in 1978, show higher levels of attention (see Table 3.1). The differences between reported campaign interest in 1978 and during the early months of 1980 are especially noteworthy. (Unfortunately, the CPS altered the placement of the campaign interest question on its 1984 Continuous Monitoring Study.) while the data in the table do not totally overturn Bishop's contention, they do suggest that question order may be less important than the time during the campaign when the survey is taken (note especially the data from the 1984 NES). In any event, there is sufficient variation in the data in Table 3.1 independent of question order and context to warrant inclusion of the campaign interest item in an indicator of political apathy.

At first blush, there are even more problems with the question on general political interest. Prior to 1960, no measure of general interest in public affairs was included on SRC questionnaires. In that year, the SRC included two, one on the pre-election wave (V115), the other on the post-election wave (V225). Unfortunately, the two are worded differently. The item asked before the election reads:

> Generally speaking, how interested are you in politics — a great deal, somewhat, or not at all?

After the election, the question was as follows:

> We'd also like to know how much attention you pay to what's going on in politics generally. I mean, from day to day, when there isn't any big election campaign going on. Would you say you follow politics very closely, fairly closely, or not much at all?

As a further complication, neither of the SRC versions is the same as the general political interest item on the Five Nation Study. It was worded thusly:

45

## Table 3.1:
## Interest in Election Campaigns, 1960-1984

|  | Very Much | Somewhat | Not Much | (N =) |
|---|---|---|---|---|
| 1960 (V98) | 37.6% | 37.3% | 25.1% | (1919) |
| 1962 (V39) | 36.1 | 37.8 | 26.1 | (1294) |
| 1964 (V157) | 38.2 | 36.6 | 25.1 | (1564) |
| 1966 (V87) | 30.1 | 40.4 | 29.5 | (1272) |
| 1968 (V130) | 38.9 | 40.3 | 20.8 | (1546) |
| 1970 (V201) | 33.6 | 42.6 | 23.8 | (1506) |
| 1972 (V163) | 31.5 | 41.1 | 27.4 | (2699) |
| 1974 (NA) |  |  |  |  |
| 1976 (V3031) | 36.5 | 42.3 | 21.2 | (2856) |
| 1978 (V43) | 21.6 | 44.6 | 33.8 | (2299) |
| 1980, Jan. (V42) | 34.1 | 45.8 | 20.1 | (1003) |
| 1980, Apr. (V9) | 34.6 | 43.3 | 22.0 | ( 962) |
| 1980, Je./Jl. (V9) | 34.7 | 43.3 | 19.1 | ( 842) |
| 1980, Sep./Nov. (V11) | 29.7 | 44.2 | 26.1 | (1567) |
| 1980, Nov./Dec. (V5) | 45.0 | 42.5 | 12.4 | ( 764) |
| 1982 (V23) | 25.9 | 44.2 | 29.8 | (1415) |
| 1984, Jan. (V147) | 50.5 | 37.8 | 11.7 | ( 196) |
| 1984, Feb. (V147) | 47.0 | 40.2 | 12.8 | ( 321) |
| 1984, Mar. (V147) | 48.5 | 39.5 | 12.0 | ( 332) |
| 1984, Apr. (V147) | 46.2 | 37.5 | 16.3 | ( 325) |
| 1984, May. (V147) | 44.4 | 37.8 | 17.9 | ( 347) |
| 1984, Je. (V147) | 51.2 | 34.8 | 13.9 | ( 201) |
| 1984, Sep./Nov. (V75) | 28.3 | 46.8 | 24.8 | (2251) |
| 1984, Nov./Dec. (V722) | 35.0 | 45.0 | 19.9 | (1978) |

Source: University of Michigan's Survey Research Center/Center for Political Studies' National Election Studies, Special Surveys in Jan. (P1), Apr. (C1), Je./Jl. (P2), and Nov./Dec. (P4), 1980, and Continuous Monitoring Surveys between Jan. and Je., 1984.

Do you follow the accounts of political and governmental affairs — would you say you follow them regularly, from time to time, or never?

In short, between March and December of 1960, three different questions on general interest in public affairs were asked by two different survey organizations. Not surprisingly, the distributions on the three questions are different (see Table 3.2). The variation between the two SRC versions is especially dramatic; the post-election item shows a much more apathetic adult population than had the question posed prior to election day. (Note also that, in 1962, the only time the SRC asked the post-election version after 1960, indifference to public affairs was even higher.)

Someone who wishes to begin a study of political apathy in 1960 faces a quandary; especially in the case of the two SRC versions of general interest: which is the more accurate indicant? (The problem grows because, as will be discussed momentarily, none of the three versions described above has been asked since 1962.) The strategy adopted here is straightforward. First, due to the substantial differences in question wording, the American data from the Five Nation Study will be used sparingly, primarily as a means of underwriting points made by Almond and Verba in *The Civic Culture* (1963). Second, rather than use either the pre- or the post-election version of the SRC's 1960 National Election Study in isolation, the two were combined linearly into an index of general interest in public affairs.[4] Given the association between the two (r = .486), there is no problem with the construction of a unidimensional index. Once combined, the two versions produce the following index of general interest: 36.3% of the SRC's respondents to both pre- and post-election interviews were classified as "very interested," 28.5% were "slightly interested," and 35.2% were "politically indifferent" (N = 1789). With the new index created, it can be combined with the measure of campaign interest to create the "Political Apathy Index" that will be described below.

First, however, some additional problems with the measure of general interest in public affairs must be resolved. As indicated in

---

4. Responses to V115 and V225 were simply added together and recoded to form a composite "general interest" variable. Cases with missing data on either were excluded from further analysis.

## Table 3.2:
## Interest in Public Affairs, 1960-1984

|  | A Great Deal | Somewhat | Not at All | (N=) |
|---|---|---|---|---|
| 1960 (V115) | 32.2% | 56.0% | 11.8% | (1915) |

|  | Very Closely | Fairly Closely | Not Much at All | (N=) |
|---|---|---|---|---|
| 1960 (V225) | 20.8% | 41.7% | 37.5% | (1826) |
| 1962 (V40) | 15.9 | 42.5 | 41.6 | (1293) |

|  | All/Most of the Time | Some of the Time | Only Now and Then | Hardly at All | (N=) |
|---|---|---|---|---|---|
| 1964 (V324)[a] | 30.3% | 41.6% | 16.9% | 11.2% | (1477) |
| 1966 (V64) | 34.8 | 30.3 | 17.7 | 17.7 | (1287) |
| 1968 (V30) | 33.0 | 30.7 | 18.7 | 17.6 | (1345) |
| 1968CSEP[a] | 31.0 | 45.5 | 15.3 | 8.2 | (7604) |
| 1970 NA | | | | | |
| 1972 (V476) | 36.6 | 36.2 | 15.9 | 11.4 | (2186) |
| 1973 NORC (V20) | 49.5 | 30.6 | 12.3 | 7.6 | (1484) |
| 1974 (V2027) | 38.8 | 36.0 | 14.0 | 11.1 | (2497) |
| 1976 (V3599) | 38.2 | 31.4 | 18.4 | 12.0 | (2380) |
| 1978 (V310) | 23.3 | 34.0 | 25.2 | 17.5 | (2266) |
| 1980, Jan. (V103) | 43.4 | 36.4 | 13.9 | 6.4 | (1001) |
| 1980, Apr. (V82) | 45.0 | 35.8 | 12.1 | 7.0 | ( 957) |
| 1980, Je./Jl. (V73) | 38.4 | 40.4 | 14.3 | 6.9 | ( 830) |
| 1980, Nov./Dec. (V973) | 26.4 | 34.9 | 23.4 | 15.3 | (1400) |
| 1980, Nov./Dec. (V1319) | 39.5 | 38.5 | 14.6 | 7.4 | ( 754) |
| 1982, NORC GSS (V532) | 35.8 | 35.5 | 18.4 | 10.2 | (1494) |
| 1982, (V286) | 28.6 | 35.5 | 21.2 | 14.8 | (1410) |
| 1984, Jan. (V146) | 45.9 | 32.7 | 15.3 | 6.1 | ( 196) |
| 1984, Feb. (V146) | 45.0 | 30.1 | 17.7 | 7.1 | ( 322) |
| 1984, Mar. (V146) | 41.1 | 29.9 | 18.9 | 10.2 | ( 334) |
| 1984, Apr. (V146) | 45.8 | 30.2 | 16.6 | 7.4 | ( 325) |
| 1984, May (V146) | 39.6 | 33.5 | 16.5 | 10.4 | ( 346) |
| 1984, Je. (V146) | 42.3 | 39.3 | 11.9 | 6.5 | ( 201) |
| 1984, Nov./Dec. (V988) | 26.4 | 36.3 | 23.1 | 14.1 | (1926) |

[a]These surveys used "all of the time" as the most interested option.

Sources: Unless otherwise indicated, the University of Michigan's SRC/CPS's National Election Studies. The University of North Carolina's Institute for Research in Social Science's Comparative State Election Project, 1968. The University of Chicago's National Opinion Research Center's Amalgam survey, December, 1973, and General Social Survey, Spring. 1982. The CPS's Special Surveys of Jan. (P1), Apr. (C1), Je./Jl. (P2), and Nov./Dec. (P4), 1980. And the CPS's Continuous Monitoring Survey of Jan. - Je., 1984.

## The Conceptualization and Measurement of Apathy

the foregoing paragraph, neither of the 1960 versions of general interest has appeared on a SRC/CPS national election study since 1962. Instead, beginning with 1964, the SRC modified the general interest item to read so:

> Some people seem to think about what's going on in government all the time, whether there's an election going on or not. Others aren't that interested. Would you say you follow what's going on in government all the time, some of the time, only now and then, or hardly at all?

Two years later, on the SRC's 1966 National Election Study, the item had changed again. Now it read:

> Some people seem to follow what's going on in government and public affairs most of the time, whether there's an election going on or not. Others aren't that interested. Would you say you follow what's going on in government and public affairs most of the time, some of the time, only now and then, or hardly at all?

This revised version has been included on all SRC/CPS national election studies since except 1970, when there was no general interest item on the questionnaire.

The differences between the 1964 and later versions and either of the 1960 items are so obvious they require no comment. Comparisons between general interest in 1960 and subsequently must be made tenuously. In fact, were it not for the presence on the 1960 survey of two different questions on general interest, it would be very difficult to compare this with subsequent years. What was the effect of the alterations made between 1964 and 1966? Most serious, of course, is the modification of the "most interested" option from "all" to "most" of the time. No doubt the new wording had some effect on reported levels of interest; it is one thing to say you think about what's going on in government "all the time," another to say you follow what's happening "most of the time." But how much? In the absence of experimental data, the best guess stems from comparison of the 1964 SRC version with the revised question in 1966 and 1968, and with the 1968 Comparative State Election Project's data. In the CSEP survey, the general interest item followed the SRC's 1964 version verbatim. (The data are contained in Table 3.2.) Although a crude comparison, it is clear that alteration of the most involved option increased levels of reported interest in politics, hardly a surprising conclusion. But, although the evidence must be dealt with gingerly, the amount of change is small — between two to four percent — not enough to invalidate an over-time comparison such as this.

Perhaps not, but according to Bishop and his collaborators (Bishop, Oldendick, and Tuchfarber, 1982), changes in the context within which the general interest item was asked — again in 1978 — do precisely that. They conclude that experimental data show the contextual shifts in the CPS's questionnaires between 1976 and 1978 "created an artificial drop in reported interest in government and public affairs" (1982: 192). Hence, efforts to trace changes in this measure over time have been "irrevocably contaminated" (1982: 193). Unfortunately for Bishop's contention, the CPS repeated its 1978 questionnaire in 1982, only to produce an increase in levels of reported general attention to public affairs (see Table 3.2). Moreover, the item was identically situated on the Continuous Monitoring Surveys in 1984, with results just as variable as Bishop and his colleagues report (see Table 3.2). Moreover, looking at the entire array of data in Table 3.2 suggests the conclusion that, the 1973 NORC Amalgam Study excepted, it is the similarity of the pattern in general political interest over the 20 year span that is most striking. With very few exceptions, the data show repeatedly that, as tapped by the Michigan item, *somewhere from a third to a fifth of adult Americans has been "very attentive" to public affairs, somewhere between roughly a tenth and a sixth has been fairly "apathetic," and the rest in between*. Again, a more balanced conclusion appears to be that changing the context within which the general interest query is posed may alter the marginals, but the substantive implications of the data remain basically intact. In brief, treated sensitively, the general interest item can also be employed in the study of political apathy over time.

In the creation of the Political Apathy Index, the campaign interest and the general involvement variables were weighted equally. They were combined so that someone who was interested on both could be classified as "very involved." Those who were least interested on both were categorized as "very apathetic." An individual in the middle category(ies) on both was considered to be "neutral." Persons with other combinations of responses were placed into the remaining categories.[5] Persons who said they "did not know" in response to either item were placed in the "apathetic" category. Finally, those with missing data on either were excluded from all analyses.[6]

Virtually any measure of abstract social science concepts is problematic to some degree, and the Political Apathy Index is no exception. Two potential problems stem from inclusion of the campaign interest item. First, someone who wishes to write about general political interest must recognize that inclusion of this variable in a composite index could lead to bloated estimates of grassroots psychological involvement. Students of American politics have argued that there is a cyclical quality to ordinary people's political interest, "relatively high during campaigns and low at other times" (Lane, 1965: 141; see also Bryce, 1891, II: 324). Save for very brief periods of intense interest in the midst of national emergency or travail (assassinations, scandals, international crises, *etc.*), Americans are seldom more politically aroused than during national election campaigns. The CPS surveys between January and December, 1980 indicate that psychological involvement was high in January, just two months after the seizure of the U. S. Hostages in Teheran, peaked in April, at the time of the aborted rescue mission, and fell off substantially afterward. Nor is interest at a uniform level during the course of a campaign (Berelson, Lazarsfeld, and McPhee, 1954: 24-28). The CPS surveys during 1980 and its 1984 Continuous Monitoring Study show a good deal of variation in campaign interest over the course of a national campaign (Table 3.1).

Of course, it could be argued that the Political Apathy Index systematically over-estimates interest, for all the data come from election years. If information from non-election years were available, would it show lower levels of general political interest? A tentative answer comes from Verba and Nie's "Participation in America" study — the data were gathered by NORC in March, 1967 — and from the NORC Amalgam Survey of December, 1973. The distribution on Verba and

---

5. Other than recoding "don't know" replies to the most "apathetic" category, the SRC/CPS's original codes on each variable were left intact. Once the Apathy Index was created, the result was recoded to produce five categories: very involved, slightly involved, neutral, slightly apathetic, and very apathetic.

6. This is the strategy followed on all variables throughout this volume. The price, of course, is diminution of cases available for certain analyses, and the possibility that distortions could creep into the results if certain types of individuals become under-represented in the study. However, provided checks are made to detect this possibility, it is preferable to conduct the investigation only on cases with "actual" rather than "manufactured" data.

Nie's general interest variable is similar to those of the SRC in 1966 and 1968. According to Verba and Nie (1972: 368), 34.9% of adult Americans were "interested" in politics and national affairs, 38.3% showed "some interest," and 26.8% had "no interest." The data from the 1973 NORC Amalgam Survey are even more interesting, for this study used the 1966 version of the SRC's question. As can be seen from Table 3.2, the 1973 data manifest one of the highest rates of general political interest found for the nearly twenty-five year period under consideration. December, 1973 was an unusual time, for the public's attention was drawn to both the ongoing domestic scandal of Watergate and the shortages of gasoline brought on by the Arab oil embargo. It would be helpful if more data were available from non-election years. Still the two NORC surveys offer evidence that the present effort is not without merit.

The inclusion of the campaign interest variable raises a second problem. Generally, people tend to be somewhat less interested in off-year elections than in presidential contests (see Table 3.1). The Political Apathy Index will reflect this for 1962, 1966, 1978, and 1982, the only off-year elections in which both variables were on the questionnaire. Therefore, in making comparisons over time, it may be necessary to distinguish trends in presidential election years from those in off-years.

Granted, one can point to aspects of the Apathy Index which are troublesome. However, it presents no difficulties of a technical nature. As the data in Table 3.3 clearly show, it is an unidimensional measure. For each data point over the 24 years covered in the table, Cronbach's coefficient alpha — which is known to be a "conservative" estimate of unidimensionality (Carmines and Zeller, 1979: 45) — is well above the minimum value that measurement theorists feel is necessary for construction of unidimensional indicators (Nunnally, 1967: 210). Alpha's value remains high whether the data come from SRC/CPS national election studies, its special surveys (such as the Continuous Monitoring Study), the Five Nation Study, or the CSEP survey. Moreover, the estimate of the Index's unidimensionality is not substantially affected by either the type of election year in which the data are gathered, or the relative placement of the component items on the questionnaires.

How stable are the scores on the Index over time? If the 1972-1976 CPS New Panel Study are any indication, there is a remarkable

## Table 3.3:
## Reliability of the Political Apathy Index, 1960-1984

| Year | Pearson's r | Alpha | Standardized Item Apha | (N=) |
|---|---|---|---|---|
| 1960 (Civ. Cult.) | .440 | .518 | .611 | ( 954) |
| 1960 (SRC) | .609 | .755 | .757 | (1781) |
| 1962 (SRC) | .613 | .759 | .760 | (1292) |
| 1964 (SRC) | .445 | .567 | .616 | (1443) |
| 1966 (SRC) | .595 | .712 | .746 | (1270) |
| 1968 (SRC) | .510 | .654 | .675 | (1327) |
| 1968 (CSEP) | .432 | .597 | .603 | (7569) |
| 1970 (SRC) | NA | NA | NA | NA |
| 1972 (CPS) | .448 | .582 | .619 | (2182) |
| 1974 (CPS) | NA | NA | NA | NA |
| 1976 (CPS) | .517 | .652 | .681 | (2375) |
| 1978 (CPS) | .519 | .655 | .684 | (2263) |
| 1980 (Jan./P1) | .448 | .608 | .656 | ( 997) |
| 1980 (Apr./C1) | .558 | .664 | .716 | ( 954) |
| 1980 (Je.-Jl./P2) | .556 | .666 | .714 | ( 829) |
| 1980 (Sep.-Dec./C3PO) | .457 | .607 | .637 | (1353) |
| 1982 (CPS) | .500 | .636 | .666 | (1408) |
| 1984 (Jan.-Je.) | .458 | .595 | .628 | (1721) |
| 1984 (Sep.-Dec.) | .521 | .655 | .685 | (1921) |

Sources: University of Michigan's Survey Research Center/Center for Political Studies National Election Studies, 1960-1984; 1960 (Civ. Cult.): American data from the Five Nation Study; 1968 (CSEP): University of North Carolina's Institute for Social Science Research's Comparative State Election Project.

degree of constancy in people's psychological involvement in politics. Following the procedures of Converse and Markus (1979), the continuity coefficient for the interval bounded by 1972 and 1976 is $r = .561$. Of the 1184 cases with valid data on the Index in both years, 41.5 percent had the exact same score in 1972 and 1976. The CPS's P1-P4 panel data, from January to November/December, 1980, indicate that over a much shorter span the continuity coefficient is higher, $r = .629$ ($N = 748$). But, the increase is much less than might have been anticipated. From January to year's end, just over 48 percent of the cases had exactly the same index score.

Although comparisons based on just these data must be tentative, psychological involvement in politics is slightly more stable than are other basic political orientations such as internal and external political efficacy (Abramson, 1983: chap. 10), sense of citizen duty (Bennett, 1983), and perceptions of governmental attentiveness (Bennett, 1984a). It is substantially more so than trust in government (Abramson, 1983: chap. 13). While information over a longer period is needed, apathy does not appear to be particularly sensitive to factors idiosyncratic to particular campaigns. Hence, the data on the stability of scores on the Apathy Index support the belief of Campbell, Converse, Miller, and Stokes (1960: 102) that, "the individual develops a characteristic degree of interest and involvement in political affairs, which varies widely among individuals but which exhibits a good deal of stability for the same person through successive election campaigns." Additional support for the contention that the individual's level of political interest is basically stable over time comes from Jennings and Niemi's (1981: 28-29) reinterviews of the high school senior class of 1965 and its parents after an eight-year interval, although they tap only the general interest variable.

Although not a perfect measure, the Political Apathy Index is both unidimensional and fairly stable over time. In short, it meets two of the criteria required for a reliable indicant. But, does it really tap the individual's characteristic level of psychological involvement in public affairs? Is it, in other words, valid?

There are three major types of validity: content, construct, and criterion (Nunnally, 1967: chap. 3; Zeller and Carmines, 1980: chap. 4). Each can be approached in several ways, none of which is definitive. Indeed, unlike the case with estimates to reliability, the case for the validity of an indicant is never completely established. Here, the concern will be primarily with criterion validity. Of course, one could easily argue that the Political Apathy Index satisfies the criterion of content validity, but that is a notoriously slippery enterprise. Rather, the question centers on the extent to which the measure correlates with variables that would logically be expected if it taps psychological involvement in public affairs.

Obviously, there is a wide variety of factors that could be expected from someone who is highly interested in public affairs, ranging from something as simple as reading one's favorite columnist in the morning paper to much more taxing activities such as running for public office. Hence, in interests of economy of time and space, attention will be addressed to just a few. Two considerations guided the choice, one theoretical, the other, practical. First, there had to be some theoretical reason to believe that scores on the Apathy Index should be correlated with the factor in question (Lane, 1965: 143-146; Milbrath and Goel, 1977: 46-47). At a minimum, it ought to lead people to vote (Campbell, Converse, Miller, and Stokes, 1960: 102). Beyond "the simple act of voting" (Lane, 1965), one might expect the politically interested to utilize more mass media for political purposes, to be better informed, and to engage in political activities more demanding than voting (Lane, 1965; Milbrath and Goel, 1977). In the ideal world, this includes a wide variety of activities. In the real one we all inhabit, it means those regularly tapped by the SRC/CPS, which is the second, more practical criterion for selection of factors.

Utilization of both criteria leads to selection of four variables: turnout, a three item measure of campaign activism,[7] a four-item indicant of use of the mass media for political purposes,[8] and a two-item "Political Information" Index.[9] In the case of turnout, two different measures will be reported: (1) the respondent's report of

---

7. The three items are: attempting to influence others' vote, attendance at campaign meetings or rallies, and working for a candidate or party. On each, persons who said they had not performed the act were coded "0", while those who had, were coded "1". The Index is a simple summation.

8. Actually, the respondents were asked if they had relied on any of four media — television, newspapers, radio, and magazines — for news about the campaign. On each variable, a reply of no received a code of "0", while a yes was coded "1". Then the four were summed.

9. First, people were asked if they knew which political party had held the larger number of seats in the House of Representatives before the most recent election. Then, they were queried about which party had won the more house seats in the election. Don't know and incorrect responses were coded "0", while the correct answer was coded "1". Then the two were summed. Other, more extensive tests of "knowledge" were available occasionally, but not over the entire span of time.

whether or not he went to the polls, and (2) where available, verified vote as established by the SRC/CPS Voter Validation Studies of 1964, 1976, 1978, 1980, and 1984. There are sufficiently different results between self-reported turnout and validated vote to warrant treating them separately (Clausen, 1968-1969; Traugott and Katosh, 1979; Katosh and Traugott, 1981; Sigelman, 1982; Hill and Hurley, 1984). While there are some excellent candidates for inclusion in a validation check of the Index here and there in SRC/CPS surveys, none is available over the entire span of time covered in this book.

Table 3.4 presents the Pearsonian correlations[10] for the relations between the Political Apathy Index and the several modes of political involvement and participation. Detailed descriptions of some of these data awaits Chapter 6; here, the import of the data is their confirmation that the Index "predicts" the four types of political involvement and participation as would be expected if it taps interest in public affairs. In the main, it does so handsomely. The Pearsonian coefficients range from .224 (for validated vote in 1964) to .566 (for the Mass Media Usage Index in 1982). The average coefficient for the 40 observations in the table is just under .400, with the lowest values observed for validated vote — about which, more in Chapter 6 — and the highest for the media usage index. The value of the average coefficient, therefore, is sufficiently robust to be reassuring that the Index taps some component of political interest without being so high as to indicate it is epiphenomenal, another way of talking about participation generally. The fact that, on average the relations between the Apathy Index and the two modes of involvement — media usage and political information — are higher than for the two "behavioral" variables — vote and campaign participation is not surprising. One would expect more "slippage" between a measure of psychological interest and measures of political activity than between the former and other components of political involvement.

Another comforting datum in Table 3.4 is the limited range of variation over time in the relations between the Index and the five variables. Greatest variation occurs with the two measures of turnout,

---

10. Of course, Pearson's r requires interval measurement, and most, if not all, these variables are ordinal. I have nonetheless relied on this statistic for two reasons: (1) the violation of the requirement of interval measurement, at least for these variables, is only a technicality (see Labovitz, 1967, 1970); and (2) the product moment correlation coefficient is sufficiently robust to be unaffected by associations with different shapes (*i.e.*, variations in the number of categories on each variable).

## Table 3.4:
## Forms of Political Participation by the Political Apathy Index[a]

|  | Reported Vote | Validated Vote | Campaign Activism | Media Usage | Political Information |
|---|---|---|---|---|---|
| 1960 | .353 (1780) | NA | .454 (1769) | .465 (1761) | .407 (1770) |
| 1962 | .355 (1290) | NA | NA | NA | NA |
| 1964 | .265 (1443) | .224 (1169) | .463 (1436) | .463 (1436) | .414 (1434) |
| 1966 | .413 (1267) | NA | NA | NA | .436 (1262) |
| 1968 | .321 (1325) | NA | .493 (1309) | .493 (1309) | .385 (1322) |
| 1972 | .359 (2181) | NA | .472 (1103) | .472 (1103) | .424 (1106) |
| 1976 | .347 (2375) | .262 (2301) | .557 (2351) | .557 (2351) | .443 (2365) |
| 1978 | .387 (2259) | .353 (2192) | .546 (2189) | .546 (2189) | .424 (2248) |
| 1980 | .391 (1352) | .318 (1215) | .496 (1341) | .496 (1341) | .352 (1350) |
| 1982 | .456 (1398) | NA | .566 (1378) | .566 (1378) | .414 (1397) |
| 1984 | .343 (1921) | .331 (1916) | .476 (1914) | .476 (1914) | .372 (1916) |

[a]Entries are Pearsonian Product Moment Correlation Coefficients.

Source: University of Michigan's SRC/CPS National Election Studies.

something that would be expected, given the changes in rates of turnout in national elections after 1960 (Brody, 1978; Reiter, 1979; Cassel and Hill, 1981; Cavanagh, 1981; Shaffer, 1981; Abramson and Aldrich, 1982). It is not surprising that the associations between the Index and turnout tend to be somewhat higher in off-years than in presidential elections, when the "core" electorate (Campbell, 1960, 1964) is joined by "peripheral" voters. Least variation over time occurs with the Political Information Scale, followed closely by the media usage index and the Campaign Activism Index. Given that most of these data have been collected over almost a quarter of a century — a period marked by sometimes fundamental and rapid change in American politics — the data in the table offer substantial confirmation that the Political Apathy Index continually taps the individual's characteristic level of interest in public affairs.

All in all, there are two ways of looking at these data. Given what is already known about the effect of interest on political involvement and participation, nothing in the table is surprising. And that is precisely what one would expect if the Apathy Index is a valid indicant of political interest.

## Conclusion

This chapter sought to achieve two major purposes. First, it was necessary to review previous conceptualizations of the concept of political apathy, and to show why earlier notions needed revision. Once done, it became clear why the definition of political apathy favored here — the individual's typical degree of interest in and concern with government and public affairs — is an advance over older notions.

The second goal was to propose and test a new operationalization of the concept. Because it is a new indicant, extended consideration was addressed to the component items and to the Index itself. Given the limitations of secondary analysis of survey data, the Political Apathy Index is a workable indicator and an improvement over other operationalizations of political interest.

The Index is not perfect, by any means. Some methodological purists would rule out any study such as this, contending that altered questionnaire context and differences in question wording create artifactual barriers. Fortunately it can be shown that the CPS's revised placement of the interest questions in 1978 and thereafter comprises a smaller hurdle than some have contended. The changes in question wording are, however, a bigger barrier to overcome. Variations in the wording of the general political interest variable — especially between 1960 and 1964 — make some over time comparisons more complicated. Fortunately, the availability of two different general interest items in 1960 allows for confidence that the Index for that year is at least an adequate baseline from which to begin the study. It is to the American public's psychological involvement in public affairs over the past two and one-half decades that attention can now be addressed.

# CHAPTER 4

# THE DEMOGRAPHIC AND POLITICAL CORRELATES OF INTEREST IN PUBLIC AFFAIRS

## Introduction

This chapter has two parts. The first details the American public's psychological involvement in politics from 1960 to 1984. This period witnessed a substantial downturn of turnout in national elections, and it is important to compare that development with people's interest in public affairs. The second and more important section looks at trends in political apathy among important subgroups of the population. Drawing on earlier research, initial probes are made to understand the social and psychological factors that affect the ordinary individual's attention to political affairs. These preliminary findings are given more extensive analysis in the next chapter.

## Change Over Time: The Entire Citizenry

There was once a time, not so long ago, when Almond and Verba (1963: 440-441) could characterize Americans' basic political orientations as "allegiant" and "participant." Compared to citizens of four other western democracies, Americans held very favorable opinions about their governmental system and had activist conceptions of their political roles. A nationwide survey taken in the twilight of the Eisenhower Era (March, 1960) showed that adult Americans were very interested in public affairs and were emotionally involved in election campaigns (1963: 88-89). The Americans were more psychologically involved in public affairs than the Mexicans, Italians, and Britons, but less so than the West Germans.

Interestingly, although they propose combination of the general and campaign interest indicants into a composite index of the "civic cognition," Almond and Verba do not do so themselves. Combining their measures of general and campaign interest (see Chapter 3) into an index of political apathy, 7% of the Americans were "very apathetic," 15% were "slightly apathetic," 29% were "neutral," 30% were "slightly involved," and 19% were "very involved" (N = 954). In short, there was an excess of 27 percent "involved" over "apathetic" dispositions in early 1960. Almond and Verba were evidently correct when they declared that, in America, "the role of the participant is highly developed and widespread" (1963: 440). According to Abramowitz (1980: 180), "the portrait of American political attitudes contained in *The Civic Culture* does appear to be accurate for the time period in which the research was conducted: the late 1950s and early 1960s."

↳ Using Almond and Verba's data as a benchmark, what has happened since? Two studies which have looked at political interest over approximately the same period come to different conclusions. Nie and his associates (1979: 272-277) contend that political interest rose substantially between 1956 and 1960, remained high throughout the 1960s, and fell in 1972. However, Warren Miller (1980: 13) believes that interest was relatively low in 1960, rose thereafter, and remained high throughout the 1960s and 1970s. Part of the reason for the differences is undoubtedly because Nie, Verba, and Petrocik relied just on the campaign interest item while Miller used only the general interest variable.[1]

What would a composite measure, such as the Political Apathy Index, show? Table 4.1 depicts levels of psychological involvement in politics among the adult population between 1960 and 1984. Several aspects of these data merit attention.

Immediately, of course, one's attention is drawn to the data from 1960 and 1962, for these are the two years in which the wording of the general interest question deviates most from that from 1964 on-

---

1. Interestingly, Warren Miller (1980: 13) uses only V225 (which is the more "apathetic" of the two general political interest variables) to talk about interest in 1960. Had he used either V115, or both general interest items, he would have had to modify his claim that interest was especially lukewarm in 1960.

## Table 4.1:
## Political Apathy in America, 1960-1984

|   | Very Apathetic | Slightly Apathetic | Neutral | Slightly Involved | Very Involved | PDI | (N=) |
|---|---|---|---|---|---|---|---|
| 1960 | 17.4% | 18.1% | 22.8% | 14.9% | 27.6% | 7.0 | (1781) |
| 1962 | 21.7% | 20.4% | 24.1% | 19.7% | 14.1% | -8.3 | (1292) |
| 1964 | 7.5% | 16.8% | 29.7% | 27.1% | 19.0% | 21.8 | (1443) |
| 1966 | 13.4% | 16.2% | 29.8% | 20.1% | 20.6% | 11.1 | (1270) |
| 1968 | 9.0% | 15.5% | 29.2% | 24.5% | 21.9% | 21.9 | (1327) |
| 1970 | NA | NA | NA | NA | NA | NA | NA |
| 1972 | 7.5% | 16.3% | 31.6% | 24.2% | 22.2% | 20.7 | (2182) |
| 1974 | NA | NA | NA | NA | NA | NA | NA |
| 1976 | 7.2% | 14.2% | 30.8% | 22.8% | 25.0% | 26.4 | (2375) |
| 1978 | 13.2% | 21.9% | 34.6% | 18.5% | 11.8% | -4.8 | (2263) |
| 1980 | 8.9% | 17.9% | 36.5% | 20.3% | 16.4% | 9.9 | (1353) |
| 1982 | 10.9 | 19.0% | 34.1% | 21.0% | 15.0% | 6.1 | (1408) |
| 1984 | 9.1% | 16.3% | 37.2% | 21.4% | 16.0% | 12.0 | (1921) |

PDI = Very Involved + Slightly Involved − Slightly Apathetic − Very Apathetic

Source: University of Michigan's Survey Research Center/Center for Policical Studies' National Election Studies.

ward (see Chapter 3). No doubt the inclusion of the second of the SRC's earlier versions of the general interest item, which seems to accentuate "apathetic" responses (see Table 3.2), results in exaggerated estimates of indifference among the public. Thus, in any comparisons between these two and subsequent years, this "artifactual" problem must be kept in mind.

Nevertheless, despite the problem, 1960 and 1962 are included for three reasons. First, they allow us to plumb general psychological involvement in public affairs over the entire span between 1960 — when voting turnout peaked in the postwar era — and 1984 — when, for the first time in nearly a quarter-century, turnout in a presidential election inched upward. Second, even if comparisons between 1960 and 1962 and subsequent data points must be somewhat tenuous, it is still possible to look at the underlying social-psychological dynamics of interest in each year. Should it be found that, even when the operationalization of apathy contains a different general interest item, the same demographic and political factors are involved, more confidence redounds to the results of later years.[2] Third, even with the differences allotted to question-wording changes, the substantive conclusions reached about these data are not all that different from those arrived at looking just at 1964 and thereafter. Hence, it is possible to trace over-all levels of interest between 1960 and 1984.

At first blush, it appears that the type of election year during which the data are gathered has some effect on observed levels of apathy. As measured here, interest was lowest in the congressional election years. To some degree, of course, this is due to the inclusion of the campaign interest item in the index (see Chapter 3).

However, one should guard against making too much of the differences. First, with the exceptions of 1962 and 1978—about which, more below—the "typical" citizen fell somewhere from "neutral" to "slightly involved" in off-years as well as in presidential ones. Second, again 1962 and 1978 excepted, there was an excess of "involved" over "apathetic" citizens in congressional election years, albeit smaller than in most of the presidential years. Indeed, the diminution of psychological involvement in politics between presidential and congressional election years is a good deal less than the fall-off in voting turnout, which has averaged almost 18 percent since 1960. Finally, the PDI values show that aggregate levels of apathy

---

2. Scanning ahead to Tables 4.2 and 4.3, one sees precisely this result.

in 1960 and 1980 were about the same as they had been in 1966, and only a little different from those in 1982. It is possible, in short, to find at least two instances of over-all interest during presidential years which were virtually indistinguishable from two congressional years. (While it is possible to slough off 1960 as strictly a question of artifact, 1980 is not so easily dismissed on a technicality.) In any event, the generally small variations between presidential and off-year elections are a testament to the validity of the Political Apathy Index as a measure of a general orientation to public affairs.

Indeed, the impression these data give is one of generaly stability of the mass public's psychological involvement in politics during the period. Even considering the methodological problems posed by the 1960 and 1962 data, the constancy in levels of interest over most of the period is the most impressive datum in the table. Between 1964 and 1972, other than a slight increase in apathy in 1966, there was no change at all. Of course, it is likely that individual-level data would show a good deal more volatility. Nevertheless, the data from 1964 to 1972 provide an initial warning against the argument that the decrease in voting which occurred during these years necessarily signified a more apathetic populace.

A particularly interesting finding is that political interest rose slightly in 1976. Care should be taken not to impute too much to the increase. In absolute terms, the public was not much more politically engaged than formerly. However, the low turnout in 1976 had led a number of analysts to argue that apathy was rising, and some believed that this portended serious consequences for the political process (Gans, 1978: 55; Hadley, 1978: 17, 126). Nonvoting did increase between 1972 and 1976. But, apathy, when conceived as citizen indifference, did not. This compels the realization that the relation of psychological involvement in public affairs to turnout may be more complicated than is usually believed. I shall return to this point in Chapter 6.

After more than a decade of generally stable levels of psychological involvement in politics, apathy rose substantially in 1978. Political interest was lower than at any time since 1962. Moreover, other than 1962, 1978 is the only time that the percentage of the citizenry that was "apathetic" exceeded that which was "involved."

Some would account for the heightened level of political indifference in 1978 in terms of methodological artifact (Bishop, Oldendick, and Tuchfarber, 1982), and assuredly there is an element of truth in that view (Chapter 3). However, there is also evidence that Americans were unusually disengaged that year. First, turnout in the congressional elections sagged to 35.2%, lower than in any off-year election in a quarter of a century (Hinckley, 1981: 20). More important, the low level of psychological involvement for 1978 shown in Table 4.1 is corroborated by evidence from the Gallup Organization's finding that the electorate was especially disinterested in that year (*Public Opinion*, 1983: 24). In short, while some of the decline of interest in 1978 can be put down to methodological artifact, a goodly portion is not epiphenomenal.

After the nadir of 1978, involvement in politics rebounded in the 1980s. Considering that 1980 and 1984 were presidential years, an increase should occasion no surprise. However, citizen political interest in the early 1980s did not regain pre-1978 levels. Indeed, the 1980 CPS National Election Study data reveal the lowest level of grass-roots political interest during any presidential year save 1960. This occurred despite the fact that there was much about the 1980 election and its aftermath that should have stimulated a fairly high level of citizen interest (Abramson, Aldrich, and Rohde, 1983). Moreover, even though interest in 1982 was considerably higher than in 1978, it remained at a lower rate than in 1966. Thus, 1982 marked the third time in succession that levels of political involvement were well below the norm established between 1964 and 1976.

While political interest rose slightly in 1984, it was lower (PDI = 12.0) than in any other presidential election year save 1960 and 1980. This slight increase in psychological involvement in politics was accompanied by a small enhancement in turnout in 1984, the first time voting had risen since 1960. However, the increase was less than had been anticipated, given the massive voter registration drives conducted by both political parties and key interest groups.

Lest one conclude that political interest in the early 1980s has fallen permanently below what it had been as recently as 1976, consider the data from the CPS's special surveys of 1980 and from early 1984. In 1980, the January, April, and early summer surveys had an average of 30.4% excess of involvement over apathy. The Continuous Monitoring data from January through June, 1984, show a 42.4% excess of interest over disinterest (N = 1691). That is the highest level of political interest in any SRC/CPS survey.[3]

---

3. However, the CSEP data from 1968 show an even more politically engaged electorate (PDI = 68.0 [N = 7569]). That is the highest PDI value for any of the surveys used in this volume.

To summarize, the data in Table 4.1 show approximately five "periods" of the American public's interest in public affairs: (1) a relatively modest political involvement in the early 1960s, which may be exaggerated by the general interest question(s) available in 1960 and 1962; (2) a remarkably stable and relatively high attention to politics between 1964 and 1972; (3) a slight increase of interest in 1976; followed by (4) a surge of apathy in 1978; which was, in turn, (5) superseded by a restoration of interest in the 1980s, albeit on a slightly lower level than during the 1964-1976 era.

While the above paragraph captures the flavor of the data in Table 4.1, there is a more powerful message to be read: the generally uniform pattern to the data over the 24 years. Over the entire span of time, only a few Americans — generally less than one-fifth, and usually less than one-in-seven — are very apathetic, from 15 to 20 percent is very interested, and the rest somewhere in between. Although the data are not shown, the average scores on the Political Apathy Index repeatedly place the "typical" citizen between the "neutral" and "slightly involved" categories. (The only exceptions are, of course, 1962 and 1978, when the "average" citizen fell between "slightly apathetic" and "neutral".) All in all, then, perhaps the best conclusion to be derived from these data is that, for almost a quarter of a century, and almost regardless of changes in political seasons and/or questionnaire construction, the typical American has maintained a lukewarm involvement in public affairs. Indeed, in light of the great changes that characterized American political life between the election of John F. Kennedy and the re-election of Ronald Reagan, this constancy in over-all levels of citizen political interest is truly remarkable.

Assessment of the public's over-all levels of political interest is an important exercise, but it only scratches the surface of the topic. To understand more fully what has happened to Americans' psychological involvement in public affairs, it is necessary to plumb apathy separately for important demographic and political subgroups. Such is the topic of the next two sections.

## Apathy Among Selected Subgroups

At the outset a brief note is in order concerning the thrust of this section. The purpose is *not* assignment of relative predictive weights to independent variables. That will be dealt with in Chapter 5. Here the aim is to trace how political interest among important population subgroups changed from 1960 to 1984. This is a more modest goal, to be sure, but it is indispensable to the analysis of political involvement over time.

Given the importance attached to political interest in both normative and empirical writings on democracy, it is not surprising that a substantial literature exists on the factors associated with psychological involvement in public affairs (Almond and Verba, 1963: 88-95; Lane, 1965: 135-141; Milbrath and Goel, 1977: 46-48; Bennett, 1984b: 516-533). While there are differences, the consensus on the social, psychological, and political factors alleged to affect one's level of political interest is significant, especially given the variety in measurement of the concept and methods of data analysis in past research. The treatment of the factors said to influence attention to political affairs follows the observation by Berelson, Lazarsfeld, and McPhee (1954: 25) that interest is a function of both social and political factors.

Among the former, it is generally conceded that persons with higher socio-economic status backgrounds are more likely to be politically interested than those among the lower social orders. Why are those with higher socio-economic status more inclined to be politically interested? As Berelson and his associates put it (1954: 25), "Both social stimulation and social obligation appear to be at the root of interest, that is factors making people both 'want' and 'have' to be interested." These are people who are more likely to be aware of government's impact on their lives (Lipset, 1981: 191-196), to have a greater "stake" in society and politics (Verba and Nie, 1972: 126), to have more skills and resources which make attention to politics both easier and more rewarding (Lipset, 1981: 196-207), and they are more likely to be exposed to normative expectations which impel them toward involvement in public affairs (Lipset, 1981: 207-211).

Among the dimensions of SES, education is regarded as the most important. Indeed, many scholars agree with Campbell (1962: 20) that, "Perhaps the surest single predictor of political involvement is number of years of formal education." Campbell identifies several facets of the educational process that enhance interest. First, exposure to formal schooling widens one's scope of acquaintance with political information. Second, it increases the individual's capacity to perceive

*Demographic and Political Correlates*

personal implications of political events. Third, education enlarges confidence in one's ability to act effectively in politics. In addition, the schools teach the norm of citizen responsibility to pay heed to government and politics (however, see National Task Force on Citizenship Education, 1977). Small wonder, then, that Almond and Verba could write (1963: 381) that, "the educated classes possess the keys to political participation and involvement, while those with less education are less well equipped."

Most of the evidence of formal schooling's impact on political interest comes from cross-sectional surveys of adults, for whom the educational experience is from a few years to several decades past. Thus it is difficult to say whether the normally robust zero-order correlations of formal schooling with interest are due to what happened inside the school itself, or to outside factors that happen to be connected with education. In one direct test of the effects of the number of high school civics classes taken by adolescents, Langton and Jennings (1968: 858) report such "miniscule" results on several basic political orientations, including interest, that they seriously question whether such courses, as then constituted, were worth the expense. One exception to the general findings was that civics courses did lead to increased psychological involvement in politics among black high schoolers from less educated families (Langton and Jennings, 1968: 862). Nonetheless, whether education's effect on interest is direct or not, in the survey setting it is an important predictor.

Another factor consistently found by earlier researchers to be related to political interest is gender (see Sapiro, 1983: 88-92, and the citations therein). Women, especially older, lesser educated ones, are less likely to be politically interested than men. Milbrath and Goel (1977: 48) attribute this to the persistence of traditional gender roles among women raised at a time when politics was still a "man's business" (Merriam and Gosnell, 1924: chap. 5). Although there are substantial gender differences in political interest among children, suggesting that "childhood socialization is responsible for links between gender and political interest" (Sapiro, 1983: 89), others have suggested women's adult roles, especially homemaking and motherhood, lower their attention to public affairs (Lane, 1965: 210-214). However, Sapiro (1983: 89-90) has shown that women's educational achievement, rather than martial status, homemaking, and mother-

*69*

hood, is the strongest predictor of general interest in public affairs. While the "gender gap" in political interest has narrowed recently (Jennings and Niemi, 1974: 305-306; Jennings, 1983), women remain more apathetic, even with education controlled (Bennett, 1984b: 529; see also Jennings and Niemi, 1981: 275-277).

One of the most interesting social factors is age. Over the years, scholars have found a waning of political interest in grade school (Hess and Torney, 1967), a rise during high school (Jennings and Niemi, 1974), a very large drop during young adulthood (Converse, with Niemi, 1971), followed by a rapid and substantial increase which is maintained throughout the mature years (Jennings and Niemi, 1974; Bennett, 1984b), followed by a diminution of interest sometimes after retirement (Converse, with Niemi, 1971; Jennings and Niemi, 1974; Bennett, 1984b; however, see Glenn and Grimes, 1968).

It is generally agreed that young adults are most apathetic, probably due to their preoccupation with establishment of a career and selection of a spouse. After marriage, the arrival of children diminishes political interest, especially among young women (Jennings and Niemi, 1981; however, see Sapiro, 1983). Milbrath and Goel (1977) also suggest that young adults are less likely to be strongly identified with a political party, to be long-term residents of a community, and to have acquired property. Each of these factors is said to produce greater concern with political life.

Lowered interest in public affairs among those over 65 is attributed to several factors, such as the generally lower levels of education among the elderly (Milbrath and Goel, 1977; Verba and Nie, 1972; Bennett, 1985), or to the so-called "disengagement" phenomenon (Converse, with Niemi, 1971). It is also possible that the disproportionate number of women among the elderly, due to differential life expectancy, may also be a factor.

The final social factor to be considered here is race. At the outset it must be noted that, despite a very large number of studies of racial differences in political participation, Guterbock and London (1983: 439) correctly note that findings in this area are "in disarray. Disparate findings and disputatious theoretical perspectives are the norm rather than the exception" (see also Nelson, 1979). It should also be noted that most research on the impact of race on political behavior has dealt, not with psychological involvement *per se*, but participation.

One exception is Matthews and Prothro's (1966: 266-269) study of *Negroes and the New Southern Politics*. They report that, in the early 1960s, southern blacks were somewhat more apathetic than whites from the same region but that, given the vast racial differences in education, income, and status, the relatively small difference was "startling" (1966: 268). In addition, Milbrath and Goel (1977: 47) write that psychological involvement is a more powerful goad to political participation among whites living in Buffalo, New York, while social pressures or group associations are more potent motivations among Buffalo's black community. The only exception to this generalization is engagement in political protest. Unfortunately, they do not report on absolute or comparative levels of interest.

Several studies have found that, once statistical controls are introduced for blacks' lower SES backgrounds, they participate at higher rates than similarly situated whites (Orum, 1966; Olsen, 1970; Verba and Nie, 1972; see, however, Danigelis, 1978). Some scholars have suggested that blacks develop a sense of "group consciousness" (Verba and Nie, 1972) or "ethnic community" (Olsen, 1970) which accounts for their relative over-participation (Shingles, 1981; Guterbock, 1983). Recently, however, the "black consciousness" thesis has been challenged, at least as far as turnout is concerned (Abramson and Claggett, 1984).

The period from 1960 to 1984 has been one of vast changes in racial conditions in America. Especially during the early- and mid-1960s, the "civil rights revolution" changed the conditions of southern blacks from near peonage to almost full citizenship (however, see Salamon and Van Evera, 1973, along with the critique by Kernell, 1973). Thanks both to mobilization by civil rights organizations and the enforcement of the 1965 Voting Rights Act, turnout by southern blacks has been substantially increased. As blacks in the South and elsewhere have come more fully to participate in the governmental process, one would anticipate substantial enhancement in their psychological involvement in public affairs. Given the importance attached to racial differences on other basic political orientations (A. Miller, 1974a; Abramson, 1983), it is well worth while to explore levels of psychological involvement for whites and blacks.

Before turning to assessment of changes in subgroups' political interest between 1960 and 1984, let us briefly consider the American data from the Five Nation Study. This information forms a base line against which later data can be compared.

Recall at the outset that Americans generally were fairly attentive to the political process in the Spring of 1960 (PDI = 26.8). Not surprisingly, the most important social factor shaping interest was socio-economic status, especially educational attainment. While grade schoolers were slightly apathetic (PDI = $-0.7$), high school graduates were substantially engaged in politics (PDI = 41.4), and college graduates were highly interested (PDI = 67.1). As one would also expect, men (36.1) were more attentive than women (18.3), while blacks ($-2.0$) were more apathetic than whites (29.9). Finally, those under 25 years of age (10.8) were least psychologically attuned to public affairs, while those in the prime of life were most concerned (32.1), and interest fell off slightly among those over 60 (22.2). In brief, the evidence from Almond and Verba's data dovetails nicely with what the review of other research leads one to expect.

In what ways have the ensuing decades changed the story? Table 4.2 depicts levels of political interest among several key demographic subgroups from 1960 to 1984.

There are two major stories, and three minor ones, in these data. Certainly one powerful theme is the confirmation they offer to most of the earlier studies' propositions. People from the higher social orders are more politically engaged than those from lower status backgrounds. Also, although bivariate distributions do not establish the fact, education is the dimension of socio-economic status with the strongest effect (see Chapter 5). The data also show that women are generally less politically interested than men, that whites are usually, but not always, more involved than blacks, and that young people are a good deal more apathetic than the elderly and especially the "middle-aged." In this sense, then, the patterns noted in Almond and Verba's data continue on into the mid-1980s.

The "gender gap" in political interest merits a brief note. Over sixty years ago, in their seminal study of nonvoters in Chicago, Merriam and Gosnell (1924: 160) found that, "there was about twice as much general indifference among the women as among the men." Given the recency of women's enfranchisement and the still powerful hold of anti-suffragette opinion, especially among older women of foreign stock, this is hardly surprising. Since the 1920s, and especially after World War II, women's position in American society and norms governing gender roles have changed. Much has been written about the growing politicization of American women since the early 1950s

## Table 4.2:
## Political Apathy by Social Factors, 1960–1984

|  | 1960 | 1962 | 1964 | 1966 | 1968 | 1972 | 1976 | 1978 | 1980 | 1982 | 1984 |
|---|---|---|---|---|---|---|---|---|---|---|---|
| **GENDER:** | | | | | | | | | | | |
| Women | −4.3 (965) | −18.1 (708) | 14.1 (806) | 1.9 (705) | 13.5 (748) | 9.4 (1247) | 18.9 (1390) | −12.0 (1262) | 1.4 (760) | 1.0 (780) | 4.5 (1067) |
| Men | 20.4 (816) | 3.8 (584) | 31.5 (637) | 22.4 (565) | 32.4 (579) | 35.5 (935) | 37.6 (979) | 4.3 (1001) | 20.8 (593) | 12.5 (628) | 21.5 (854) |
| **RACE:** | | | | | | | | | | | |
| Whites | 10.1 (1619) | −6.0 (1170) | 21.1 (1285) | 13.9 (1121) | 24.0 (1170) | 21.6 (1939) | 27.0 (2054) | −2.6 (1939) | 11.4 (1184) | 4.5 (1240) | 13.9 (1661) |
| Blacks | −15.0 (144) | −29.7 (111) | 31.0 (371) | −9.1 (132) | 6.6 (241) | 12.6 (215) | 25.3 (211) | −11.1 (224) | 1.2 (151) | 21.7 (152) | 3.4 (206) |
| **AGE:** | | | | | | | | | | | |
| 18-20 | NA | NA | NA | NA | NA | −17.4 (115) | −19.5 (113) | −37.3 (118) | −27.9 (68) | −42.3 (59) | −25.3 (91) |
| 21-24 | −5.1 (58) | −23.7 (76) | 10.6 (106) | −1.8 (117) | 12.9 (101) | 22.5 (222) | 7.5 (225) | −31.3 (230) | −13.4 (134) | −18.0 (100) | −6.4 (158) |
| 25-34 | −3.9 (382) | −18.2 (259) | 14.0 (306) | 2.6 (229) | 20.4 (265) | 20.4 (460) | 17.8 (560) | −13.7 (546) | −2.2 (313) | −2.6 (339) | 3.1 (479) |
| 35-44 | 5.5 (451) | −3.5 (282) | 29.2 (318) | 17.2 (268) | 24.3 (284) | 28.6 (363) | 30.1 (350) | −3.2 (400) | 11.0 (237) | 10.5 (257) | 14.4 (369) |
| 45-54 | 9.5 (347) | −8.4 (264) | 26.0 (292) | 19.2 (255) | 29.7 (284) | 21.6 (357) | 42.3 (345) | 6.3 (334) | 26.6 (188) | 13.3 (174) | 19.9 (251) |
| 55-64 | 20.5 (281) | 4.5 (197) | 24.6 (211) | 14.8 (175) | 29.7 (186) | 32.7 (306) | 39.7 (352) | 15.9 (302) | 23.1 (182) | 22.1 (218) | 21.9 (237) |
| 67-74 | 11.1 (189) | −6.6 (137) | 24.9 (145) | 7.2 (154) | 17.5 (155) | 22.0 (218) | 42.3 (266) | 12.2 (207) | 27.0 (148) | 21.3 (178) | 33.0 (200) |
| 75+ | 6.6 (73) | −11.5 (70) | 7.6 (65) | 6.6 (61) | −8.6 (70) | −3.9 (129) | 16.3 (150) | 4.2 (116) | 22.2 (81) | 2.5 (81) | 23.4 (124) |

## Table 4.2 (cont.)

| | 1960 | 1962 | 1964 | 1966 | 1968 | 1972 | 1976 | 1978 | 1980 | 1982 | 1984 |
|---|---|---|---|---|---|---|---|---|---|---|---|
| **EDUCATION:** | | | | | | | | | | | |
| Grade School | −14.5 | −36.4 | −9.3 | −19.2 | −11.0 | −10.0 | 7.7 | −30.1 | −12.8 | −22.9 | −15.7 |
| | (540) | (358) | (352) | (330) | (307) | (418) | (361) | (263) | (155) | (153) | (192) |
| Some High School | −9.1 | −20.7 | 9.3 | −13.6 | 4.2 | 1.0 | 8.90 | −21.5 | −19.9 | −19.9 | −10.8 |
| | (330) | (251) | (292) | (227) | (238) | (394) | (342) | (340) | (191) | (156) | (250) |
| High School Graduate | 13.2 | −4.0 | 26.1 | 21.4 | 27.7 | 18.3 | 16.4 | −12.7 | 2.7 | −2.1 | 2.4 |
| | (515) | (368) | (455) | (410) | (411) | (705) | (836) | (851) | (482) | (484) | (674) |
| Some College | 37.3 | 20.7 | 53.7 | 40.8 | 47.6 | 44.5 | 40.9 | 6.1 | 27.0 | 16.5 | 25.9 |
| | (209) | (154) | (175) | (174) | (193) | (368) | (457) | (441) | (286) | (327) | (441) |
| College Graduate | 46.2 | 37.4 | 66.7 | 59.4 | 61.6 | 65.6 | 67.1 | 35.2 | 41.9 | 38.3 | 44.1 |
| | (186) | (155) | (162) | (123) | (177) | (296) | (372) | (361) | (236) | (282) | (360) |
| **FAMILY INCOME:** | | | | | | | | | | | |
| Lowest Quintile | −14.8 | −12.6 | −0.7 | −18.7 | −10.3 | −3.5 | 4.8 | −20.6 | −4.7 | −2.9 | −3.3 |
| | (400) | (270) | (271) | (246) | (205) | (402) | (409) | (391) | (239) | (237) | (342) |
| Second Quintile | −8.5 | −19.5 | 18.6 | 2.2 | 9.8 | 13.1 | 21.8 | −13.8 | 3.9 | 0.0 | 8.9 |
| | (365) | (231) | (253) | (245) | (276) | (372) | (489) | (350) | (232) | (251) | (271) |
| Third Quintile | 17.8 | −4.9 | 17.2 | 15.4 | 24.4 | 15.5 | 23.8 | −7.1 | 6.9 | 5.8 | 10.5 |
| | (298) | (376) | (360) | (274) | (234) | (394) | (401) | (398) | (294) | (242) | (380) |
| Fourth Quintile | 17.9 | 4.4 | 34.0 | 14.9 | 37.3 | 25.1 | 29.4 | −1.4 | 20.6 | 11.7 | 22.3 |
| | (465) | (159) | (218) | (235) | (316) | (507) | (415) | (426) | (190) | (283) | (427) |
| Fifth Quintile | 35.5 | 30.7 | 44.5 | 41.5 | 42.1 | 50.9 | 49.1 | 16.8 | 26.3 | 27.2 | 25.5 |
| | (236) | (189) | (292) | (226) | (264) | (446) | (507) | (409) | (258) | (235) | (311) |

Source: University of Michigan's Survey Research Center/Center for Political Studies' National Election Studies, 1960–1984.

(Baxter and Lansing, 1983). Some students of women in politics have claimed that women have closed the gender gap in turnout and that they now constitute a majority of the voting universe. Generally, increased exposure to higher education and the entry of more women into the work force are the primary reasons cited for their greater political participation.

However, the data in Table 4.2 show a continuing tendency for women to be less politically engaged than men. (Note: This is not to say that women are, on balance, apathetic — 1962 and 1978 excepted.) Moreover, over the quarter-century covered in the table, the size of the "interest gap" between men and women remains basically unaltered. Even with education controlled, men are consistently more politically involved than women, although the differences are less among the highly educated than among the least schooled (see Chapter 5).

Detailed analysis of the "gender gap" in psychological involvement in politics awaits the next chapter. Suffice it here to say that its constancy over 24 years of American politics constitutes one of the more interesting patterns uncovered in Table 4.2. That women have remained less attentive to politics than men while narrowing rates of turnout may require revision of the current theories about their political behavior (see Bennett and Bennett, 1985).

The relation of race to interest is another noteworthy sidelight. In 1960, blacks were considerably more apathetic than whites, and this pattern holds most of the time thereafter. However, this was not the case in 1964 or 1982. Also, in 1976 the difference was less than one could attribute to the races' respective SES characteristics. The discovery that blacks were more emotionally involved in 1964 is very likely due to the dominance of civil rights issues on the national agenda at the time (Funkhouser, 1973; Smith, 1980: 170-171; Carmines and Stimson, 1980).

The even larger difference in the races' political involvement in 1982 may be due to the impact of the Reagan Administration's budgetary cuts and the effect of the recession. Blacks were much more likely that year to say that they had been hurt by the President's economic program, and they were twice as likely to say that they or someone in their household had experienced some reduction in benefits during the previous year or so. While the number of cases is often small, and the strength of the association is modest at best, blacks who felt adversely affected by the Administration's programs were especially politically engaged in 1982.

The 1964 data and especially the 1982 evidence suggest that the presence of a set of group-relevant issues on the national political agenda can stimulate increased emotional involvement in public affairs among a group otherwise disadvantaged by SES background. However, by 1984, blacks were again less politically interested than whites.

A similar phenomenon may be at work among the elderly in 1980 and again in 1984. From 1960 through 1978 (actually through January, 1980), and again in 1982, there is a curvilinear relation between age and involvement. The youngest category is always the least interested, and Converse's (1971: 460-462) explanation for this may still be valid. Normally those most attentive are from 35 to 55 years old. Then, usually after age 75 interest falls off. Perhaps this is a manifestation of the "disengagement" phenomenon. Perhaps it is because, on the whole, the elderly have less formal schooling (Milbrath and Goel, 1977: 114-115; Verba and Nie, 1972: 139-145). Regardless of the reason, the 1980 (from April and June/July as well as later in the year) and 1984 data show that the oldest age categories remain just as attentive as those in the "prime of life."

Determination of the reason for this sudden departure from the normal age-related pattern awaits Chapter 5. Although the 1982 data do repeat the usual curvilinear trend, it is possible that the emergence in the 1980s of age-related political issues such as Social Security, Medicare, and Medicaid has politicized the aged so that they remain more politically concerned at a time when formerly "disengagement" had set in. Certainly the 1984 Continuous Monitoring data from January through June lend support to this contention. For the most engaged age grouping is people between 65 and 74 (PDI = 63.5), and although those over 75 were less attentive, they showed higher levels of interest (PDI = 36.2) than any grouping under 35 years of age. At any rate, the spurt in levels of interest among Americans over 75 during the 1980s cautions against automatic expectations that the very elderly will be politically apathetic.

Another side bar of these data may be relegated to the status of a non-finding. One might have anticipated different patterns in the relations of these social factors and political involvement, depending on the type of election year in question. Some do emerge; the effect of education, in particular, is slightly enhanced in congressional years. But, in the main, the patterns observed for presidential years crop up in virtually the same fashion in off-years. In short, the social factors related to political apathy are the same, regardless of the type of election year.

The final major story in Table 4.2 centers on change in levels of political interest between 1960 and 1984. With the exception of blacks and people who were over 75 at the time of the 1960 and 1984 surveys (not the same persons, of course), virtually every major social grouping was slightly less emotionally engaged in politics at the end of the period than at the beginning.

The changes among income and education categories are especially noteworthy. With regard to income, it is among the highest income quintiles that interest had fallen farthest. These are precisely the sectors of society said to have the greatest "stake" in politics (Verba and Nie, 1972: 126). In an effort to account for the apathy manifested during the 1920s, Lippmann (1927: 22-27) put a share of the blame on the "amazing prosperity" the country experienced after 1922. He wrote (1927: 27) that, "It was obvious that the opportunities to make more money were so ample that it was a waste of time to think about politics."

In the late 1970s and early 1980s, the state of the economy was not so happy as when Lippmann wrote. In the late 1970s, inflation was in double-digits and overall economic growth was lagging. By late 1982, the economy had plunged to depths not recorded since the Great Depression. Ample reasons, if Lippmann were correct, for more concern with politics. And since the well-to-do are supposed to be more politically aware, they should have been under the severest goad to be more emotionally involved than during the halcyon days of the Kennedy-Johnson prosperity. But they were not.

People's reports of their recent financial trends and the expectations for the future show a mixture of support and nonsupport for Lippmann. When asked how their finances have been doing recently, between 1960 and 1972, those who said things had been better were more politically involved than were people who believed either that they had held their own or had experienced financial reverses. From 1976 through 1980, however, those who said they had been experiencing financial declines were the most interested. In 1982 and 1984, there was no relation at all. Also, when asked what they expected in the near future, except for 1982, those who reported they would experience "hard times" were a little bit more interested in politics.

The changes in interest among education categories is intriguing. In absolute terms, of course, the most schooled remained the most interested. However, at every level of education interest was down between the mid-1960s and the early 1980s. Moreover, apathy had risen among precisely those of whom it would have been least expected: people with college experience.

Here is a tale within a story. Between 1960 and 1981, aggregate levels of formal schooling rose substantially (U.S. Bureau of the Census, 1984). Because of the increase in educational opportunities, the public of the 1980s was considerably better schooled than that of the 1960s. Therefore, given the cross-sectional relation of education to interest, there should have been a more politically engaged populace in the 1980s than earlier. But we know this is not so. Part of the reason is that the better-schooled were considerably less politically interested than in the 1960s. Hence, education became a less powerful goad to involvement.

Why? To get some purchase on that question, it is necessary to consider how political factors shape psychological involvement in public affairs.

## Political Factors and Apathy

Several types of political factors are said to influence political interest. A very important one is partisanship (Berelson, Lazarsfeld, and McPhee, 1954: 25-27; Campbell, Gurin, and Miller, 1954: 147; Milbrath and Goel, 1977: 47). The more people are committed to a political party, a candidate, or an issue, the more inclined they are to be emotionally involved in politics. Consequently, as Berelson and his associates note (1954: 27), "anything that weakens partisan feelings decreases interest."

Berelson, Lazarsfeld, and McPhee (1954: 25) also mention "a feeling of potency about affecting political affairs at all. . . ." Their characterization of this basic political disposition sounds much like Campbell, Gurin, and Miller's (1954: 187-188) sense of political efficacy, or Almond and Verba's (1963: 180-181) sense of civic competence. As Berelson and his colleagues put it (1954: 25),

The conviction that things *can* be affected is needed to give people the energy to care. Indeed, it may be such subjective feelings of potency that are responsible for the (alleged) decrease in political interest during the past century or so. The citizen may now feel much less capable of influencing "big government" than his ancestor, who was "closer" to his governors.

Still another political disposition related to political attentiveness is the belief that such is the responsibility of the ordinary citizen in a democracy. Even in colonial times, the belief was evidently widespread that people should be politically interested, aware, and concerned about the "publick" affairs (Dinkin, 1977), and certainly the norm of the "attentive" citizen was firmly held during the revolutionary period (Dinkin, 1982). The requirement of citizen interest has been repeated by educators and politicians ever since. For example, in 1902, President Theodore Roosevelt stated that, "The average citizen must devote a good deal of thought and time to the affairs of the State, . . . and he must devote that thought and time steadily and intelligently" (1958: 73).

Political interest is also said to follow awareness that governmental actions impinge on one's daily existence (Lipset, 1981: chap. 6; Almond and Verba, 1963: chap. 3). If someone believes that what happens in the halls of government affects him personally he is under a stronger goad to keep a "weather eye" on public affairs than is the person who thinks that nothing the government does touches his life directly.

Table 4.3 depicts the changes in political interest between 1960 and 1984 by several political variables. There are two components of partisanship: strength of party identification and relative attraction to the major parties' presidential nominees.[4] As is now common practice (Balch, 1974; Abramson, 1983: 141-144), I have split political efficacy (Campbell, Gurin, and Miller, 1954: 189-194) into its "internal" and "external" components. Two other basic political orientations known to have undergone changes during these years are also depicted: trust in government (A. Miller, 1974a, 1979, 1983; Miller, Miller, and Schneider, 1980: 268-272; Abramson, 1983: 228-

---

4. The measure of candidate preference is simply the respondent's opinion thermometer rating of the Republican presidential candidate subtracted from his O.T. rating of the Democrats' nominee. The measure is not available in 1960 and 1964, and would make no sense in congressional years.

Apathy in America, 1960–1984

### Table 4.3:
### Political Apathy by Political Factors, 1960–1984

|  | 1960 | 1962 | 1964 | 1966 | 1968 | 1972 | 1976 | 1978 | 1980 | 1982 | 1984 |
|---|---|---|---|---|---|---|---|---|---|---|---|
| **STRENGTH OF PARTISANSHIP** | | | | | | | | | | | |
| Apoliticals | −50.1 | −90.2 | −58.8 | −68.8 | 4.2 | −38.7 | −33.8 | −93.7 | −100 | −93.2 | −96.3 |
|  | (56) | (51) | (17) | (16) | (19) | (31) | (30) | (63) | (26) | (29) | (30) |
| Independents | −20.7 | −5.1 | −11.4 | −4.6 | 4.5 | −4.4 | −2.8 | −24.9 | −2.2 | −31.2 | −8.8 |
|  | (164) | (99) | (105) | (154) | (133) | (272) | (337) | (309) | (173) | (154) | (204) |
| Independent Leaners | 7.9 | −12.6 | 22.3 | 21.2 | 40.2 | 28.3 | 26.9 | 2.5 | 14.0 | 3.8 | 9.7 |
|  | (241) | (173) | (207) | (203) | (246) | (470) | (521) | (537) | (300) | (266) | (450) |
| Weak Identifiers | 0.5 | −23.6 | 10.6 | −3.0 | 8.4 | 11.2 | 17.3 | −12.8 | −3.7 | −4.4 | −0.3 |
|  | (671) | (508) | (557) | (544) | (528) | (865) | (931) | (842) | (504) | (539) | (656) |
| Strong Identifiers | 25.9 | 19.2 | 43.2 | 38.0 | 39.5 | 45.0 | 63.5 | 24.4 | 40.2 | 42.2 | 40.5 |
|  | (646) | (453) | (550) | (342) | (400) | (542) | (551) | (505) | (349) | (415) | (575) |
| **CANDIDATE PREFERENCE:** | | | | | | | | | | | |
| Much Prefer Democrat | NA | NA | NA | NA | 20.8 | 58.2 | 49.1 | NA | 40.4 | NA | 40.4 |
|  |  |  |  |  | (24) | (84) | (81) |  | (47) |  | (114) |
| Prefer Both the Same | NA | NA | NA | NA | 27.1 | 27.3 | 40.1 | NA | 11.0 | NA | 18.0 |
|  |  |  |  |  | (303) | (347) | (572) |  | (335) |  | (388) |
| Slightly Prefer Republican | NA | NA | NA | NA | 15.7 | 2.9 | 19.1 | NA | −2.8 | NA | −8.3 |
|  |  |  |  |  | (520) | (682) | (1014) |  | (553) |  | (669) |
| Much Prefer Republican | NA | NA | NA | NA | 35.3 | 27.7 | 34.7 | NA | 29.3 | NA | 23.4 |
|  |  |  |  |  | (397) | (725) | (523) |  | (318) |  | (573) |
|  | NA | NA | NA | NA | 25.0 | 47.5 | 49.4 | NA | 30.8 | NA | 51.6 |
|  |  |  |  |  | (40) | (261) | (79) |  | (65) |  | (118) |

## Table 4.3 (cont.)

| | 1960 | 1962 | 1964 | 1966 | 1968 | 1972 | 1976 | 1978 | 1980 | 1982 | 1984 |
|---|---|---|---|---|---|---|---|---|---|---|---|
| **EXTERNAL POLITICAL EFFICACY:** | | | | | | | | | | | |
| Low | -45.0 (249) | NA | -10.8 (279) | -28.5 (344) | -9.7 (389) | -10.7 (634) | 5.3 (751) | -22.9 (733) | -11.3 (398) | -11.6 (489) | -11.9 (437) |
| Medium | -7.0 (370) | NA | 13.2 (358) | 7.8 (358) | 25.8 (310) | 19.3 (591) | 27.9 (622) | -3.8 (637) | 12.3 (416) | 7.8 (284) | 4.2 (471) |
| High | 27.4 (1094) | NA | 38.9 (753) | 38.2 (560) | 45.5 (585) | 44.7 (902) | 49.0 (848) | 16.0 (749) | 28.5 (459) | 25.9 (556) | 27.1 (987) |
| **INTERNAL POLITICAL EFFICACY:** | | | | | | | | | | | |
| Low | -21.9 (794) | NA | 1.0 (766) | -10.1 (742) | 2.4 (611) | 1.0 (1073) | 12.6 (1039) | -17.4 (1041) | 12. (588) | NA | NA |
| Medium | 29.4 (693) | NA | 43.7 (460) | 33.7 (365) | 33.3 (451) | 30.7 (741) | 30.2 (861) | 3.4 (806) | 15.9 (512) | NA | NA |
| High | 44.5 (251) | NA | 56.8 (187) | 63.3 (155) | 60.5 (236) | 62.6 (340) | 66.1 (383) | 25.2 (336) | 34.0 (191) | NA | NA |
| **TRUST IN GOVERNMENT:** | | | | | | | | | | | |
| Very Trustful | NA | NA | 14.6 (89) | NA | 21.3 (52) | 12.4 (49) | 54.5 (17) | -11.1 (18) | — (9) | 26.3 (19) | 0.0 (27) |
| Slightly Trustful | NA | NA | 19.6 (494) | NA | 20.6 (311) | 29.4 (382) | 23.6 (214) | -0.5 (192) | 11.4 (79) | -3.3 (124) | 12.4 (305) |
| Neutral | NA | NA | 30.4 (371) | NA | 32.8 (369) | 32.9 (471) | 33.0 (418) | 2.5 (316) | 14.6 (198) | 19.6 (168) | 10.7 (451) |
| Slightly Mistrustful | NA | NA | 24.4 (233) | NA | 30.4 (312) | 22.1 (613) | 32.0 (748) | 6.9 (728) | 15.5 (457) | 16.5 (388) | 17.2 (583) |
| Very Mistrustful | NA | NA | 38.4 (133) | NA | 19.2 (151) | 15.7 (418) | 26.4 (651) | -9.3 (640) | 8.7 (459) | 3.8 (534) | 14.9 (349) |

## Table 4.3 (cont.)

| | 1960 | 1962 | 1964 | 1966 | 1968 | 1972 | 1976 | 1978 | 1980 | 1982 | 1984 |
|---|---|---|---|---|---|---|---|---|---|---|---|
| **GOVERNMENTAL ATTENTIVENESS:** | | | | | | | | | | | |
| Very Attentive | NA | NA | 49.1 (422) | NA | 47.1 (293) | 44.1 (338) | 61.7 (197) | 25.9 (243) | 31.9 (75) | NA | NA |
| Slightly Attentive | NA | NA | 27.3 (397) | NA | 31.6 (365) | 35.5 (693) | 36.6 (798) | 8.8 (762) | 18.7 (439) | NA | NA |
| Neutral | NA | NA | 12.2 (197) | NA | 24.8 (218) | 16.9 (467) | 26.3 (428) | −4.8 (467) | 18.2 (259) | NA | NA |
| Slightly Inattentive | NA | NA | 20.8 (159) | NA | 20.3 (192) | 6.4 (402) | 23.8 (559) | −18.0 (428) | 6.2 (352) | NA | NA |
| Very Inattentive | NA | NA | −6.3 (64) | NA | −1.1 (93) | −1.6 (120) | 9.5 (215) | −32.5 (184) | −16.8 (143) | NA | NA |
| **SENSE OF CIVIC DUTY:** | | | | | | | | | | | |
| Very Low | −97.9 (46) | NA | NA | NA | −16.1 (92) | −48.0 (52) | −17.1 (53) | −72.4 (58) | −35.3 (17) | NA | NA |
| Low | −76.6 (50) | NA | NA | NA | 31.7 (180) | −46.8 (94) | −32.0 (75) | −55.9 (102) | −42.0 (50) | NA | NA |
| Medium | −30.3 (109) | NA | NA | NA | 53.8 (724) | −9.0 (178)21. (178) | −12.3 (208) | −22.0 (190) | −26.5 (113) | NA | NA |
| High | 7.7 (647) | NA | NA | NA | 74.2 (2497) | 5 (756) | 22.7 (835) | −1.1 (804) | 4.9 (458) | NA | NA |
| Very High | 24.7 (871) | NA | NA | NA | 78.8 (3340) | 35.9 (1032) | 43.9 (1098) | 11.8 (965) | 25.8 (679) | NA | NA |

Sources: University of Michigan's Survey Research Center/Center for Political Studies' National Election Studies, 1960-1984; for Sense of Citizen Duty in 1968, University of North Carolina's Institute for Research in Social Science's Comparative State Election Project.

232; Lipset and Schneider, 1983a: 16-19, 1983b; Hill and Luttbeg, 1983: chap. 4), and perceptions of governmental attentiveness (Miller, Miller, and Schneider, 1980: 283-287; Bennett, 1984a). Sense of citizen duty (Campbell, Gurin, and Miller, 1954: 194-199) is included not only because it is alleged to affect levels of political interest, but also because it is said to have changed but little since 1960 (Miller, Miller, and Schneider, 1980: 288-292; W. Miller, 1980: 13, 18; Bennett, 1983).

The story that emerges from Table 4.3 is much more complex than that contained in Table 4.2. Several minor themes emerge that could be explored. However, in the interest of space, let us stay with the major ones.

One of the better documented findings of political behavior research has been the decline in the public's attachment to the major political parties (Nie, Verba, and Petrocik, 1979: chap. 4; Hill and Luttbeg, 1983: chap. 2; Abramson, 1983: chap. 7; Wattenberg, 1984). The attenuation in partisan affiliations began sometime between 1964 and 1966, and continued unabated throughout the 1970s. While the data from the 1980s show a small resurgence of partisanship, the contemporary electorate has much weaker party attachments than that of the early 1960s. The reasons for this are not at issue here (see Craig, 1985). Rather, the focus is on the consequences the diminution of partisanship has for political apathy.

First, notice that strength of party allegiance is not linearly related to apathy. Granted, strong partisans are almost always the most involved, pure independents are almost always indifferent, and apoliticals manifest virtually no political interest whatsoever. Indeed, calling oneself an "apolitical" is tantamount to an admission of extreme apathy. However, it is also important to note that weak identifiers are less likely to be politically interested than are the independents who lean toward one of the major parties. Thus, the assertion by Campbell and his associates (1960: 143) that, "the stronger the individual's sense of attachment to one of the parties, the greater his psychological involvement in political affairs", needs to be modified. When apathy is thought of strictly in terms of indifference to the public affairs, independent leaners outstrip partisans whose loyalties are only lukewarm.

Turning to the effect of partisan feelings on apathy over the years, two points should be made. There can be no gainsaying the fact that, as the proportion of strong identifiers has diminished, the result has been a less politically involved populace. This is exacerbated by the fact that, save for strong partisans, between the mid-1960s and the early 1980s, people falling in each of the categories of partisanship became less emotionally involved in public affairs.

The relation of the second component of partisanship — candidate preference — to apathy is also noteworthy. Not only are strong advocates of both parties' presidential candidates more politically involved than their lukewarm supporters, the intense partisans of the candidates in 1980 and 1984 were more emotionally involved in politics than Nixon's and Humphrey's "true believers" had been in 1968 (which is the first year the measure is available).

That is interesting, for Carter's and Reagan's strong adherents in 1980 made up 8.5% of the sample, and Reagan's and Mondale's "true believers" constituted 12.5% of the 1984 sample, compared with a total of 5% of the 1968 sample with very warm feelings about Humphrey or Nixon. In short, had intensity of partisanship been solely responsible for level of political interest, there should have been a more emotionally involved citizenry in 1980 and 1984 than in 1968. But, of course, there was not.

What this means is that partisanship tells only part of the story of changes in emotional involvement in politics. To complete the tale, it is necessary to look at the relations of basic political orientations to political apathy.

Much has been written about changes in the public's trust in political leaders (and perhaps institutions), and in their estimates of their capacity to influence the same (Abramowitz, 1980; Abramson, 1983; Bennett, 1984a; Caddell, 1979; Citrin, 1974, 1981; Converse, 1972; Gilmour and Lamb, 1975; Hill and Luttbeg, 1983; Lipset and Schneider, 1983a, 1983b; A. Miller, 1974a, 1974b, 1979, 1983; W. Miller, 1979, 1980; Sundquist, 1980; J. Wright, 1976). While Almond and Verba (1963: 440-441) found that, in the late 1950s and early 1960s, Americans held very favorable opinions about their political system, throughout the 1970s and into the 1980s scholars and pundits were writing about rising cynicism and declining efficacy. Have these changes had any consequences for emotional involvement in politics?

The answer depends on which basic disposition is considered.

Take the Trust in Government Index[5] as a case in point. Although scholars disagree over what the Trust Index really measures (A. Miller, 1974a, 1974b; Citrin, 1974; Abramson and Finifter, 1981), until recently, there has been no argument about the trends it manifests (A. Miller, 1983; Lipset and Schneider, 1983b). Between the mid-1960s and the early 1980s, no other composite indicator of basic political orientations has shown as profound a change as has the Trust Index (Abramson, 1983: chap. 13).

As political trust has declined, so also has its relation to apathy been altered. In 1964, although the association was not perfectly linear, it was the least trustful citizens who were the most emotionally involved in public affairs. By the 1980s, not only had the ranks of the politically cynical swelled, they were now much less interested than the cynics had been in 1964. More important, however, from 1968 onward the relation of trust to apathy becomes curvilinear, with those in the "neutral" or "slightly mistrustful" categories being the most politically interested. At any rate, given the shape of the association and the amount of variation involved, it is difficult to conclude that declining trust in government *per se* had any substantial effect on changes in political interest.

Should the order to causality be reversed? Nie, Verba, and Petrocik (1979: chap. 15) posit that it was rising political interest (between 1956 and 1960) which led to increased ideological coherence in mass belief systems (beginning in 1964) that in turn led to growing disenchantment with both government and the political parties. They admit that the kind of data at hand does not permit a definitive test of their hypothesis. But they are convinced that, although lack of political interest in the 1950s and 1960s probably meant "neutral apathy," by 1972 disinterest may have come to mean "a positive rejection of politics" (1979: 278-280). They present data (p. 280) which allegedly show that between 1964 and the early 1970s the percentage of the disinterested who were also distrustful rose dramatically. So it did. But the increase in political distrust among the

---

5. The Trust in Government Index is not available for 1960. From 1964 through 1980, I use a four-item version of the standard SRC/CPS index. The "are government people smart" item poses growing technical problems after 1970, and is therefore best not included on the Trust Index at any time. This is also the procedure of Lipset and Schneider (1983a: 16-19). In 1982, only three items, "does government waste taxes," "do you trust the government to do right," and "is government run by a few big interests," were asked. This complicates, but does not preclude, making over-time comparisons.

politically involved was just as striking. Between 1964 and 1972, and into the 1980s, as political distrust rose among the apathetic it increased at almost exactly the same rate among the politically interested.

Whether changes in trust are dependent upon altered interest in public affairs, or the other way around, the evidence in Table 4.3 shows the relationship between the two to be virtually nonexistent. This is surprising. Is not the citizen who is convinced that politicians are "wolves" under a more powerful goad to keep a weather eye on what "the bastards are up to" than is the person who thinks them to be benign? What if, however, in addition to a jaundiced view of elites' trustworthiness, the citizen has also become convinced that nothing he can do will change things? Is it not possible that as citizens become convinced that their opinions do not count in the councils of government and that they are powerless, they will find the political spectacle less engaging? V. O. Key, Jr. thought so. He wrote that (1961: 546), "Attentiveness, with its correlative behaviors will wane unless it is associated with a belief that watchfulness and articulateness have some bearing on what government does and does not do." The data in Table 4.3 are consonant with Key's expectation.

Over the years the SRC/CPS has developed different indicators of perceptions that government is attentive to public opinion and that ordinary people have at least some impact on the governmental process. The best-known is the political efficacy measure (Campbell, Gurin, and Miller, 1954), which has been shown to consist of an "internal" — does the person see himself as politically effective? — and an "external" — is government perceived as receptive to citizens' influence? — dimensions (Balch, 1974; Abramson, 1983: chap. 8).[6] The other measure is the Governmental Attentiveness Index, which is intended to tap beliefs that key democratic institutions are attentive to ordinary people's opinions (Bennett, 1984a).

Since the mid-1960s, both perceptions of governmental attentiveness and belief in the political clout of the average person have waned (Abramson, 1983; Bennett, 1984a). Only internal efficacy has remained essentially unchanged since the early 1960s (Abramson,

---

6. There are major problems with measurement of political efficacy (see Converse, 1972; Asher, 1974; Balch, 1974; McPherson, Welch, and Clark, 1977; Craig, 1979; Craig and Maggiotto, 1982). For reasons of historical continuity, I have followed Abramson's (1983) suggestion to treat both internal and external dimensions as two-item scales.

1983). The reasons for these developments are beyond the scope of this volume. What is of concern is how they may affect political apathy.

Each of these measures is robustly related to emotional involvement in politics, and in the manner Key had anticipated. Over the years, the more people believe they are effective citizens, that government is attentive to their views and amenable to grass-roots influence, the more likely they are to be politically interested. To some degree, of course, these relations are the result of common background factors, such as SES. However, even when such are held constant, the observations still hold, at least in the instances of responsiveness and internal efficacy beliefs.

Two points must be made in this regard. Most obvious is the fact that, as both external efficacy and attentiveness beliefs have ebbed, the result has been a more apathetic populace. More important, the biggest decline in political interest over the years has occurred among those most sanguine about governmental attentiveness and their political clout. This is especially true for internal efficacy beliefs.

The final general political disposition to be considered is sense of civic duty. This "is the feeling that oneself and others ought to participate in the political process, regardless of whether such political activity is seen as worth while or efficacious" (Campbell, Gurin, and Miller, 1954: 194). Over the years, adult Americans have manifested widespread acceptance of the belief that they ought to be politically active (Milbrath and Goel, 1977: 49-52; W. Miller, 1980: 18; Bennett, 1983). Also, this belief has been closely related to the likelihood of voting (Milbrath and Goel, 1977: 49; Erikson, Luttbeg, and Tedin, 1980: 7), but less so with other modes of participation (Bennett, 1983).

The data in Table 4.3 show a robust relation between strength of civic obligation and political interest. The stronger the person's belief in his obligation to be politically active, the more he is inclined to be politically interested. This relation holds even when common background factors, such as education, are taken into account.

Although the period for which data on citizen duty are available is severely truncated, the same pattern detected with governmental attentiveness and political efficacy holds for sense of citizen duty. By 1980, citizens who strongly believed in their duty to participate were somewhat less politically involved than had been the case from the early 1960s through the mid-1970s.

This pattern, which is observed for four of the five basic political orientations depicted in Table 4.3 — trust in government may be the exception — is intriguing. Properly understood, it may point toward an eventual explanation for the slightly lower levels of political interest in the late 1970s and early 1980s.

## Conclusion: The Influence of Political Forces on Political Interest

Immediately it must be admitted that the argument developed here is speculative. Data for a definitive test are lacking in the SRC/CPS archives. Recall that these data were originally collected with primarily cross-sectional analysis in mind. Those seeking to do trend or developmental analyses are often compelled to do post-hoc theorizing to account for the patterns they uncover. Still, the argument makes intuitive sense, and there are some tantalizing tidbits of supportive data in the SRC/CPS's archives.

Could the slightly lower levels of political involvement after 1976 be due to a "period effect?" Several analysts have posited that the 1960s and early 1970s were a time of unusually high political engagement (Beck and Jennings, 1979: 737; Nie, Verba and Petrocik, 1979, *passim*). The events, the issues, the personalities of the time combined to generate a much more politically charged atmosphere than in the immediately preceding era. The spirit of protest and reform was abroad in the land. Huntington (1981) has called the years from 1960 to 1975 "a creedal passion era." Whether or not his analysis is entirely correct, during the period the political process generated much more conflict than had been experienced during most of the 1950s, and the awareness of these cleavages penetrated throughout the populace (Converse, 1975: 90-93; Nie, Verba, and Petrocik, 1979: 106-109; Abramowitz, 1980: 193).

Since the mid-1970s, America has experienced a substantial dampening of the fires of political strife. Most of the events and issues that had generated so much heat in the 1960s and early 1970s (racial conflicts, Vietnam, the youth culture, law and order, Watergate) had been superseded by equally serious but far less explosive ones: the environment, the energy crisis, inflation and unemployment, government deficits. Also, the divisive rhetoric of national political elites during the 1960s and early 1970s, which had played a role in the polarization of the country, was replaced by a much muted style of speech in 1976 (Nie, Verba, and Petrocik, 1979: 358-360) and thereafter. In short, a political period characterized by superheated rhetoric and unusual turmoil was followed by one in which the levels of verbal and behavioral conflict were much lower.

With what results? For present purposes, in the quieter time some people might be less emotionally engaged than in a more tumultuous epoch. Granted, but here the logic of the argument becomes dangerously circuitous: the 1960s and early 1970s must have been more interesting because the public was more involved, while the late 1970s and early 1980s were duller by comparison, because fewer people were interested. To shore up the case, it is necessary to pinpoint the sectors of the populace which would react most sensitively to different political eras.

It would be completely off the mark to expect wide fluctuations in psychological involvement from a superheated to a cooler period. Very likely a substantial segment of the public maintains a fairly constant level of emotional involvement in public affairs, reacting only marginally to variations in the political climate (Campbell, Converse, Miller, and Stokes, 1960: 102). There is a small but detectable minority which probably never manifests any political interest at all (Almond and Verba, 1963: 17-19). Just over two percent of the CPS's New Panel Study was very apathetic in both 1972 and 1976. Probably nothing short of the imminent threat of thermonuclear war would galvanize these people to become attentive to the public affairs. Another, larger minority probably remains constantly interested; 13.6% of the New Panel Study was very involved in 1972 and 1976. It is likely that some people remained alert and attentive through a speech by Calvin Coolidge, who was accused by Lippmann (1927: 21) of deliberately "dampening down" the people's interest in "popular government."

However, other Americans who are at least marginally interested during turbulent times are likely to become inattentive in a more staid era. But, from which segments of the population are such persons likely to come?

One prospective group is young adults. Long known to be less politically involved, the young are also most susceptible to the effects of unusually tempestuous eras. This is the finding of Beck and Jennings (1979), who show that the generation entering the electorate during the late 1960s and early 1970s was unusually politically active. They posit (p. 740) that, "The political events and turmoil of the period most likely drew these young adults into political activism at rates much higher than normal for young people" (see also Jennings and Niemi, 1981: 202-203, 210).

Though Beck and Jennings do not say so, it is reasonable to contend that in a more politically quiescent period (the late 1970s and early 1980s?), young people would not only be much more apathetic than their elders, but also less involved than had been their older brothers and sisters who came of age in the charged atmosphere of the late 1960s and early 1970s. This contention is clearly supported in Table 4.2. The data show that from just the early 1970s to the early 1980s, the youngest members of the electorate (18-20) manifested the largest increases in apathy. If the 21-24 year-olds are considered, data become available for the entire span between 1960 and 1984. For this group, also, the argument holds. Among these young adults the period of peak interest is between 1968 and 1972 — precisely the years of greatest agitation and turmoil — only to be followed in the late 1970s and early 1980s by a much more apathetic cohort. This despite the fact that the young adults of the later period had been more exposed to higher educational opportunities, which Converse (1971: 446-450) argues should have substantially alleviated the proclivity of the young to be politically apathetic.

Another group which might be susceptible to the effects of a superheated political period consists of those without strong partisan ties. Campbell (1960: 399) coined the term "peripheral" voters, *i.e.*, those normally low in political interest, but energized by "high stimulus" (presidential) elections to vote. They do not, however, turn out in "low stimulus" (congressional) contests. According to Campbell (1960: 411), such persons were disproportionately likely to be independents or weak party identifiers.

No great logical leap is required to argue that, just as they react to the vagaries of high or low stimulus elections, so also are those without firm attachments to the parties susceptible to the effects of different political periods. In heated times the independents and weak partisans might become at least marginally interested. In a quieter era they are more likely to be politically apathetic. Strong partisans, however, under the goad of their attachment, are less prone to react differently from one epoch to the next. Again, the data (in Table 4.3) are supportive of the argument.

It would be mistaken to make too much of the political "periods" effect. After all, it is the overall stability of psychological involvement in public affairs that is the most impressive aspect of the data in Table 4.1. Still, after 1976 there is a slight diminution in interest, and the subgroups wherein the decline in interest is most noticeable (the young, political independents and weak identifiers) are precisely those most likely to be susceptible to the effects of different political eras.

Bivariate analysis can be very useful when working with a new measure of a concept such as the Political Apathy Index. However, it does not resolve a main concern of political behavior research: getting a comprehensive understanding of how several factors collectively shape psychological involvement in politics. To do that requires some type of multivariate analysis. Such is the topic of the next chapter.

# CHAPTER 5

# THE CAUSES OF POLITICAL APATHY: A MULTIVARIATE INVESTIGATION

## Introduction

Chapter 4 established that several social and political factors are related to the individual's usual level of interest in the public affairs. Generally speaking, the better educated are considerably more psychologically involved in politics than the least schooled, people in the "prime of life" are more interested than the aged and especially the very young, men are somewhat more attentive to public affairs than women, those who feel a strong sense of civic obligation are more interested than those who do not, and strong partisans of the political parties and presidential candidates are more involved than political independents and lukewarm supporters. Moreover, these relationships persist over a quarter-century of American history marked by rapid and major changes in society and polity.

Unhappily, there are several limitations to the type of bivariate relationships explored in Chapter 4. Foremost, of course, is that bivariate analyses do not rule out the possibility that some of the seemingly robust associations are epiphenomenal, the result of some third (and perhaps fourth) factor(s) hidden in the table(s). After all, a number of the factors now known to be related to apathy are themselves interdependent — e.g., both political efficacy and sense of civic duty are known to be affected by education — and it is possible, nay, likely, that once the effects of one are held constant, seemingly robust associations degenerate toward insignificance. Hence, it is necessary to conduct some type of statistical analysis that has the power to assess the impact of several potential independent variables upon political apathy, while simultaneously holding constant the effects of each of the other putative causal factors.

There are several types of multivariate statistical analysis available that could be profitably employed. One, partition design (Hyman, 1955; Rosenberg, 1968), is straightforward and requires little statistical training. An additional advantage of partition design is that it makes very little demand on the type of data available. On the other hand, as is true of any type of analysis technique, partition design presents several problems to the data analyst. The most serious is the tendency for the technique to become cumbersome to interpret if there are several categories on the dependent, independent, and control variables, making it a relatively inefficient method. Also, it requires a very large number of cases in the sample lest there be many cells in the partial tables with either very few cases or none at all, making conclusions difficult to arrive at. The partition design analyst often finds it necessary to collapse categories on key variables to provide sufficient cases for meaningful analysis, sometimes losing valuable information in the process. Despite these problems, however, the technique has one major advantage not always found with some of the new, more "powerful" types of multivariate statistical analysis: with partition design the effects of the independent variable on the dependent variable can be separately inspected across each of the categories of one or more control variables. This permits the researcher to note variations in the independent variable's impact on the dependent variable from one category of the control variable to the next, thereby rendering a more sensitive interpretation of the results of the control. For this reason, partition design is one useful way to look at the relations of political apathy to several independent variables at the same time.

As implied in the previous paragraph, there are newer, more powerful types of multivariate analysis techniques that are coming into increased use in political science (see, e.g., Kirkpatrick, 1974: chap. 3; Achen, 1983). These more powerful techniques, such as Ordinary Least Squares (OLS) regression analysis, not only require more knowledge of statistics, but make fairly stringent demands upon the data. There is considerable controversy over whether the kind of data usually available from social surveys can satisfy the assumptions of the OLS regression model (Aldrich and Cnudde, 1975; G. Wright,

1976; Luskin, 1978; Downs and Rocke, 1979; Friedrich, 1982; for general, nontechnical treatments of OLS regression, see Lewis-Beck, 1980; Achen, 1982; and Berry and Feldman, 1985). Beyond measurement and specification errors, the most serious problems presented by the regression model are multicollinearity and interaction effects among the independent variables.[1] Nevertheless, despite its stringent assumptions, OLS regression has shown itself to be a robust multivariate analysis technique which, while requiring care in interpretation, can be of great use with the type of research problem under consideration here (Cohen and Cohen, 1975). Moreover, regression forms the basis for causal modeling, which is increasingly being used in political science research (Asher, 1983).

This chapter breaks into three, unequal parts. Part one, which is the longest section, employs cohort analysis and partition design to try to entangle the effects of education, age, and gender. The second section also uses partition design to look at the impact of partisanship, perceptions of governmental responsiveness, while also controlling for age and education. The information gleaned from these analyses is then fed into a series of multivariate stepwise regression analyses to advance the understanding, not only of which factors affect interest in public affairs, but also the relative predictive potency of each. Throughout, one goal is to determine whether the same factors have affected interest over almost a quarter of a century.

In one sense the approach followed in this chapter follows that of Chapter 4. Mainly the goal is to determine the factors that are repeatedly shown to influence attention to politics and government. This means, again, that most of the focus is on variables included on all, or at least most, of the SRC/CPS questionnaires between 1960 and 1984. On another level, however, greater selectivity will be employed. Since it is unnecessary to look at data that merely repeat patterns already known, much of the information that undergirds the conclusions reached below is not shown.[2] Moreover, for reasons discussed in the next section, virtually all the data shown in this chapter come from only four years: 1960, 1968, 1976, and 1984. Finally, in the case of the regression analyses, only four years will be described in any detail: 1960, 1972, 1976, and 1980. Explanation for this is in the last section of the chapter.

---

1. Multicollinearity refers to excessively inter-related predictor variables, while interaction occurs when the effects of independent variables are not simply additive.
2. I will provide additional documentation upon written request.

## Untangling the Effects of Age, Education, and Gender

Among the more interesting findings in Chapter 4 was the curvilinear relation between age and apathy. In every instance between 1960 and 1984, the youngest age grouping was the most apathetic, despite a substantial advantage in educational attainment. Interest rose steadily thereafter, usually peaking some time in the 50s or even 60s, generally followed by subsiding involvement after age 75. The two primary exceptions to the tendency for the very aged to become less politically involved — 1980 and 1984 — can probably be attributed to the importance in those elections of age-related issues.

While there is little doubt about the shape of the relationship between age and interest, disagreement exists as to why the pattern exists. Are the very young steeped in apathy because their lives are wrapped up with the pursuit of careers and the search for "lifemates," or is some other factor at work? It is possible, for example, that the extreme apathy manifested by the very young in the 1970s and 1980s reflects the arrival into the electorate of a new generation of Americans whose political socialization experiences have left them "turned off" the political process. Are the very old politically detached because of their relatively lower levels of formal schooling or due to the onset of senescence and physical infirmities?

Unfortunately, the type of data displayed in Table 4.2 are insufficient to answer these questions. The primary problem is that bivariate displays of the relation of age to some political behavior variable such as the Apathy Index cannot separate the effects of birth cohort (generation), aging *per se*, and the point at which the data are collected (period). Happily, one way to make at least tentative determination of the relative influences of birth cohort, aging, and period is to perform a "cohort analysis" on the data between 1960 and 1984 (Glenn, 1977: 14).

The logic behind cohort analysis is simple enough. To conduct a cohort analysis, one needs two or more cross-sectional surveys over a specified period of time, for which a dependent variable and the respondents' precise age (or birth date) are available at each data point. Then one codes the age variable into birth cohorts that match the length of time between each observation. For example, if there were two surveys conducted ten years apart, one would code the birth cohorts into decades. Then the researcher simply looks at the

## The Causes of Political Apathy

scores of each birth cohort at time one and again ten years later. By constructing what is called a cohort table, it is possible to compare the scores of several birth cohorts at the two periods. By looking down at the columns in the table one checks for the effects (if any) of age at any given time. Glancing across gives evidence for any changes due to the effect of the aging of one or more birth cohorts depicted in the table. While it is never possible to extract simultaneously the definitive effects of birth cohort, aging, and period, the cohort analysis table provides enough information to give a general clue to the relative influence of each.

Given the availability of data on political apathy and age for more than half a dozen surveys over a twenty-four year interval, cohort analysis is an ideal technique. However, one question that needs to be answered is the precise time interval to use. Since it is not possible to construct the Political Apathy Index in either 1970 or 1974, that rules out using a two-year width. Even if data were available for each biennium between 1960 and 1984, dividing the birth cohorts into two-year intervals would provide too few cases for much confidence in the results. Indeed, even if one focuses just on the presidential election years, which would give seven observations at four-year intervals, paucity of cases in some of the older cohorts cautions against placing too much confidence in the results.

The strategy followed here is to look just at four surveys: 1960, 1968, 1976, and 1984. For each data point the age variable is coded into eight eight-year birth cohorts. Since data are available over a 24 year span and given the entry of a new birth cohort at each observation, there are a total of eleven birth cohorts available for analysis. The oldest, born between 1876 and 1883, appears only in 1960; similarly, the youngest, born from 1956 to 1963, appears only in 1984. All of the remainder can be tracked over at least two data points. Those Americans born between 1900 and 1939 can be observed on four separate occasions. The results of the cohort analysis are depicted in Table 5.1. Following the suggestion of Glenn and Grimes (1968), the data are reported separately for men and women.

There are several noteworthy facets of these data. As would be expected, given the fact that the same data are contained in both tables, these data confirm the curvilinear relation of age and interest in public affairs that was depicted in Table 4.2. Now, however, it is possible to see that the diminution of interest associated with the

## Table 5.1:
## Political Apathy[a] by Birth Cohort by Gender, 1960, 1968, 1976, 1984

|  | 1960 Women | 1960 Men | 1968 Women | 1968 Men | 1976 Women | 1976 Men | 1984 Women | 1984 Men |
|---|---|---|---|---|---|---|---|---|
| 1956-63[d] | — | — | — | — | — | — | 21-28[c] −13.0 (178) | 4.0 (151) |
| 1948-55 | — | — | — | — | 21-28 5.6 (291) | 14.0 (203) | 29-36 2.6 (218) | 10.5 (173) |
| 1940-47 | — | — | 21-28 6.5 (123) | 34.3 (96) | 29-36 14.9 (218) | 39.2 (142) | 37-44 4.7 (149) | 32.2 (137) |
| 1932-39 | 21-28 −9.2 (131) | −17.9 (78) | 29-36 7.4 (108) | 37.0 (81) | 37-44 17.3 (139) | 48.6 (137) | 45-52 11.5 (121) | 29.4 (92) |
| 1924-31 | 29-36 −11.3 (185) | 26.4 (148) | 37-44 17.7 (147) | 32.6 (95) | 45-52 37.7 (142) | 51.5 (127) | 53-60 11.5 (79) | 37.8 (90) |
| 1916-23 | 37-44 −17.8 (186) | 28.6 (161) | 45-52 18.0 (116) | 46.9 (94) | 53-60 40.0 (184) | 50.0 (102) | 61-68 25.0 (116) | 28.6 (77) |
| 1908-15 | 45-52 2.0 (151) | 21.4 (136) | 53-60 23.8 (88) | 25.0 (80) | 61-68 29.2 (158) | 43.9 (106) | 69-76 11.0 (82) | 47.6 (65) |
| 1900-07 | 53-60 4.8 (124) | 18.9 (133) | 61-68 32.0 (72) | 31.5 (76) | 69-76 23.6 (106) | 56.7 (79) | 77-84 11.0 (82) | 47.6 (65) |
| 1892-99 | 61-68 16.9 (95) | 54.5 (79) | 69-76 8.4 (59) | 12.8 (39) | 77-84 6.7 (60) | 49.2 (28) | — | — |
| 1884-91 | 69-76 −1.7 (61) | −9.7 (62) | 77-84 −24.1 (29) | 0.0* (13) | — | — | — | — |
| 1876-83 | 77-84 7.4 (27) | 6.3* (16) | — | — | — | — | — | — |

[a]Entries are Percentage Difference Index (PDI) on the Political Apathy Inde3x.
[b]Cohort Birth Dates.   [c]Cohort Ages.   * = Fewer than 20 cases.
Source: University of Michigan's SRC/CPS's National Election Studies.

## The Causes of Political Apathy

aging process has changed over the years. In the 1960s, it tended to occur after age 69.[3] However, in recent years it has not begun until people are in their late 70's and early 80's. Probably two major factors account for the delayed withdrawal of attention to public affairs among the elderly of the 1970s and 1980s: (1) their median level of formal schooling is considerably higher than that of cohorts born prior to the twentieth century (U. S. Census Bureau, 1984: 78); and (2) the emergence, especially since 1980, of age-related issues on the political agenda at election time. In either event, the data in Table 5.1 clearly dispute the claim by Glenn and Grimes (1968: 570-572) that the relation of age to political interest is monotonic.[4]

The data in the table also shed much light on the effects of aging on attention to public affairs. Particularly valuable is the evidence provided by tracking five distinct birth cohorts, born in eight-year intervals between 1900 and 1939, over a twenty-four year span of time. Together, when 1960 is taken as the point of departure, the five cohorts represent Americans ranging in age from newly eligible voters (21) to those born at the dawn of the century (60). Hence, using the four observations it is possible to track the former cohort from youth to the prime of life and the latter from "middle age" to extreme old age.

Looking across the table, and focusing on just the aforementioned cohorts, several patterns emerge. First, one notices a substantial increase in political interest among all five cohorts between 1960 and 1968. This increase is maintained in 1976, only to be followed by diminished interest in almost all cases in 1984. Lest one be tempted to attribute this general trend entirely to a period effect — especially between 1960 and 1968 — it should be recalled that the operationalization of the Apathy Index in the former year is sufficiently different from those at subsequent data points to give some pause. It is likely, then, that at least some of the general increase in interest between 1960 and 1968 is artifactual. Similarly, at least some of the general drop in attention between 1976 and 1984 can be put down to methodological rather than substantive factors (see Chapter 3).

Note, however, that the biggest surge in psychological involvement

---

3. The resurgence of interest among those aged 77 to 84 in 1960 was probably a statistical fluke.
4. Since Glenn and Grimes (1968) used "60 and older" as their oldest age category, it is not surprising that they concluded there was no drop-off in interest due to aging.

in politics between 1960 and 1968 occurred among the youngest birth cohort. Smaller increases were manifested by those cohorts that had already had longer experience with the adult political role by 1960.

Does the very substantial increase in political interest of the 1932-39 cohort between 1960 and 1968 mean that we can always expect such a phenomenon to occur as young adults mature? Not necessarily. Look at the next two birth cohorts to enter the electorate: 1940-47 in 1968, 1948-55 in 1976. Not only was each cohort considerably more politically engaged than the 1932-39 cohort at the time of entry into the electorate,[5] subsequent observations on each — 1976 for the 1940-47 cohort, 1980 for the 1948-55 cohort — show relatively small shifts in interest. In short, it is possible that the unusually low levels of concern with political affairs among the group born from 1932 to 1939 as it entered the electorate between 1956 and 1960 was a carryover from its political socialization experiences as this particular cohort passed through junior and senior high school in the late 1940s and early 1950s. Indeed, it is worth recalling that a substantial portion of this cohort made up the so-called "silent generation" of college students that drove activist faculty to distraction with its indifference to public affairs and pursuit of materialistic self-interests (Altbach and Peterson, 1972: 26-27; Lipset, 1972: 185-187). Whatever the reasons for this cohort's general apathy in 1960, it is worth noting that thereafter it quickly shifted to a more politically engaged stance.[6]

From concern with the youngest cohort in 1960, let us turn to the two oldest: that born from 1908 to 1915 and that born between 1900 and 1907. In the case of the former, it is possible to follow over nearly a quarter of a century people from "the prime of life" — the mid 40's and early "middle age" — the early 50's — to the late 60's to mid 70's. With the latter cohort we can trace changes in interest from middle age to the late 70's and mid 80's. To some degree the two cohorts are noteworthy more for the similarity of the patterns they manifest than for any differences. From 1960 through at least 1976 each shows a continuing growth in attention to the public

---

5. To some degree, there could be an artifact at work here. Recall the discussion in Chapter 3 about the unique problems associated with operationalization of the concept in 1960.

6. Again, one must recall the slight differences in concept measurement after 1960; this could magnify the amount of increased interest measured thereafter.

affairs. Thereafter, however, the two cohorts show slightly different patterns. Among those born from 1900 to 1907, the eight-year span from 1976 to 1984 was marked by a diminished concern with politics, although one could hardly call this group "apathetic" even in 1984, when it was between 77 and 84 years of age. Among those born between 1908 and 1915, one sees a decline in interest only among women from 1976 to 1984. Indeed, among the men of this cohort, there was actually a small increase in interest during this time, making them the only grouping depicted in the table to buck the general trend toward lessened psychological involvement in public affairs between 1976 and 1984. While it would be mistaken to make too much of this, given the small change involved and the paucity of men in the cohort in question (N = 29), the very fact that these individuals showed any enhancement in interest so late in life is noteworthy. Whether this was due to the importance of age-related issues — Social Security, Medicare, Medicaid — on the political agenda in the early 1980s or to the "substitution" of interest in politics "for the activities and concerns that absorbed so much time and energy" before retirement (Glenn and Grimes, 1968: 573) cannot be determined with the data at hand.

In sum, then, looking at the five birth cohorts for which four observations over a twenty-four year span can be had, it is possible to see evidence of period, aging, and, to lesser extent, "generational" effects in Table 5.1. While 1960 clearly stands out as a more politically "quiescent" period, there are good methodological grounds against seizing upon that explanation in its entirety. Certainly there are differences in attention to politics as these cohorts pass through the life cycle. In fact, analysis of all the information in the table underscores the preeminent importance of the aging process in shaping attention to politics and government relative to period and generational effects.

This is not to diminish the significance of generational effects, however. Indeed, turning to the rest of the information in the table, the eye immediately comes to rest upon the cohort born from 1940 to 1947, which entered the electorate sometime between 1964 and 1968. Note especially the levels of interest among the males of this group (about which, more below). Taken together, the men and women of the 1940-47 birth cohort had a Percentage Difference Index of 18.8 in 1968 (N = 219), which makes this the most politically engaged of any group aged 21-28 over the nearly 25 years covered in the table.

What factors account for this particular cohort's unusual level of politicization so early in life? One does not have far to go for putative factors. Young people of this birth cohort would have been between 14 and 21 years of age when John F. Kennedy was inaugurated and set about getting the country "moving again" after the sluggishness of the Eisenhower Era. During adolescence and early adulthood these people would have witnessed such dramatic events as the civil rights revolution, the space program, political assassinations, the Great Society programs, urban riots, and American involvement in Vietnam. So filled were the 1960s with rapid social and political change and so numerous were charismatic leaders that it would be surprising had not the most impressionable segment of the population been attentive to the political process. In addition, the election of 1968 saw two candidates — Eugene McCarthy and Robert F. Kennedy — who especially cast their appeals to the idealism and exuberance of the young, and events throughout the campaign, but especially at the Democrat National Nominating Convention in Chicago, cast young Americans into the center of the political maelstrom. Small wonder, then, for the unusual level of political engagement of the 1940-47 birth cohort in that year.

What is surprising is how quickly the politically engaged cohort of 1940-47 was followed by two less politically involved cohorts. In 1976, the 1948-55 cohort had, in aggregate, a Percentage Difference Index of 8.8 on the Apathy Index (N = 497). In 1984, the entire 1956-63 cohort's PDI value was $-5.2$ (N = 329). (We also know from looking at Table 4.2 that the cohort born between 1964 and 1966 was even more apathetic [PDI = $-25.3$].) A large number of analysts have commented on the phenomenon of youthful apathy since the end of the 1960s. Expressions such as the "me decade" (Wolfe, 1977), or the "culture of narcissism" (Lasch, 1979), are particularly interesting, albeit not necessarily correct, depictions of the tendency for young Americans in the 1970s and 1980s to eschew political interest for self-absorption and the pursuit of private self-interest. 1984 saw the emergence of the "Yuppies" (young, upwardly mobile, urban professionals), who were said to be members of the post-war "baby boom" generation, and were noteworthy primarily for their pursuit of immediate material gratification (Lemann, 1985:

*The Causes of Political Apathy*

264-265). Political commentators went to some length contrasting the political indifference of the Yuppies with the activism of the young during the 1960s.

There is no gainsaying the fact that the birth cohorts which entered the electorate in the 1970s and 1980s have been considerably less politically interested than those born from 1940-47.[7] Less certain is whether the most recent cohorts have been especially apathetic or whether those Americans born from 1940 to 1947 (and possibly 1951) were an unusual generation for their early interest in public affairs. Complicating the determination of the dynamics involved is the possibility that what we see in Table 5.1 is a reflection of the unusual events and personalities of the years from 1961 to 1968 which found especial resonance among the most impressionable segment of the population: the youngest members of the voting-age population.

In any event, the data in the table clearly show the significance of experiences throughout the life cycle for attention to public affairs. Even though older Americans are very often at a serious educational disadvantage *vis-a-vis* the young, it is clear that experiences as one ages amply substitute for lesser formal schooling as a goad to political interest. Moreover, this attention to public affairs is increasingly maintained later in life than was true just a quarter of a century ago.

Thus far, attention has been addressed to the relation of age to political interest irrespective of gender. Closer inspection of Table 5.1 shows that, properly to understand the effects of age, it is necessary to look at men and women separately. Recall the finding in Table 4.2 that women remained less politically interested than men over the entire period from 1960 to 1984, despite changes in their roles in society that should have increased involvement in public affairs. Two are especially significant: their increased exposure to higher education and greater involvement in the work force. In 1960, the median level of formal schooling among American women over 25 years of age was 10.9 years. By 1981, the latest year for which Census Bureau data have been published, the comparable figure was 12.5 (U. S. Census Bureau, 1984: 77). By comparison, men's median level of education rose from 10.3 in 1960 to 12.6 in 1981.[8] In 1960,

---

7. Recall the data in Table 4.2 showing the 18-20 years to be especially apathetic in from the mid-1970s on. These people are not included in Table 5.1.

8. SRC/CPS national election studies data indicate that the increase in educational attainment has continued unabated through 1984.

only 39.2% of the women interviewed by the SRC worked or were seeking employment while 46.1% were housewives, compared with 61.9% of the women interviewed by the CPS in 1984 who worked or were unemployed while only 23.5% were housewives. Again, as a standard, 87.2% of the men in the SRC's 1960 NES worked or were looking for jobs compared with 82.8% of the men contacted by the CPS in 1984.

Students of women in politics have contended that as women became more educated and entered the work force in greater numbers, their engagement in the political process would equal that of men (Andersen, 1975; Welch, 1977). Certainly the historic "turnout gap" between men and women (Merriam and Gosnell, 1924) has been closed since the early 1960s (Poole and Zeigler, 1985: 121-123). The CPS's voter validation study shows that, for the first time, women voted at a slightly higher rate than men in 1984 (68.1% versus 66.9%). On the other hand, women remain less likely to take part in campaign activities that demand more investment of time and energy than "the simple act of voting" (Poole and Zeigler, 1985: 123-127; the phrase is from Lane, 1965: 222). They also continue to be less politically informed than men; in 1984 only 35.7% of women could correctly answer two questions about which political party held more seats in the House of Representatives before the election and which party had won more seats in the election, compared with 54.6% of men.[9]

Similarly, the data in Table 5.1 reveal not only the continuing tendency for women to be less politically interested than men, but also differences in the ways in which age affects men's and women's psychological involvement in public affairs. Not only are young women less politically interested than young men — the sole exception is 1960 — women do not reach a peak level of interest until they are in their 50s and 60s, while men usually reach a zenith of involvement ten to fifteen years earlier. Moreover, the tendency to withdraw attention from public affairs occurs earlier in life among women.

Finally, it should also be noted that, properly to understand the unusually politicized birth cohort of 1940-47, most of this "gener-

---

9. In construction of this index, those who got the answer wrong or said they did not know were coded "0" on each item; those who responded correctly were scored "1" on each variable. Then the two were added together.

ation's" high level of attention to public affairs was among men. Indeed, if one follows this cohort from 1968 to 1984 (*i.e.*, from ages 21-28 to 37-44), the men of this cohort are much more politically involved than the women. It is interesting to speculate that the unusual events and personalities of the 1960s must have galvanized the psychological involvement of the young men who entered the electorate between 1964 and 1968 to an atypical extent.[10] While it is probably a mistake to place most of the weight on the Vietnam War, it is intriguing to note three other birth cohorts of men who are like the 1940-47 cohort in being especially politically interested: 1892-99, 1916-23, 1924-31. These just happen to be the male birth cohorts who were either of military age, or close to it, in previous American wars. Men born between 1892 and 1899 would have been between the ages of 18 and 26 when the United States entered World War I. A male born between 1916 and 1923 would have been from 18 to 25 when the Japanese attacked our bases at Pearl Harbor. And a man born between 1924 and 1931 would have been from 14 to 21 when the Second World War ended. Of course, the boys aged 14 to 17 would have been too young to be drafted, but they would not have been so young as to be untouched by the war's effects. Recall that the armed services accepted volunteers as young as 17. Some of them may have seen service in Korea.

Is it possible that being at or near draft age during a time when the nation's military is engaged in warfare not only stimulates young men to become attentive to the public affairs sooner than otherwise they would, and then leaves a lasting tendency to remain politically attuned? Although the data in the table do not provide a direct answer, they certainly point in that direction. Research by M. Kent Jennings and his associates has marked the "Vietnam generation" *i.e.* those who reached maturity during the mid-1960s as "distinctive" from birth cohorts that came both before and after (Beck and Jennings, 1979; Jennings and Niemi, 1981). The data in Table 5.1 are consonant with that view, but they show that, at least in terms of political interest, the "distinctiveness" of the cohort that came of age between 1964 and 1968 was mostly due to the unusual politicization of the young men.

---

10. If the data are divided into four-year age cohorts, it is not until 1972 that a cohort enters the electorate that is, on balance, apathetic. Perhaps it is just coincidental that this was the first cohort to come of age after the draft had been ended. Then, perhaps it is not.

One has no difficulty accounting for the political indifference of women born before 1900. They grew up before ratification of the 19th Amendment extended the franchise to their sex. As children and even young women, they were no doubt exposed to the cultural norm that politics was "a man's business" (Merriam and Gosnell, 1924). Even after enfranchisement, these women carried the legacy of that cultural norm for the rest of their lives. It is more problematic, however, to account for the continuing "gender gap" in interest among women born in this century. To find women born since 1940 — who have come of age at a time of a growing women's movement that has called for greater political awareness among women — still less politically involved than their male birth cohorts calls for more extended analysis.

There are several possible explanations for the enduring gender difference in political interest. One avenue would explore continuing male-female differences in childhood socialization (Orum, Cohen, Grasmuck, and Orum, 1974; Sapiro, 1983). Are girls trained at home and in the schools to eschew attention to public affairs while boys learn that keeping abreast of political affairs can be rewarding? Such is the thrust of research by Ronald Rapoport (1981, 1985), although elsewhere he shows that there may be generational forces at work to reduce this tendency in the near future (Rapoport, 1982). It is also possible that the tendency for men to be more politically interested follows from their greater educational attainment and from their greater involvement outside the home. As was implied above, women who have entered the work force are more politically active than those who remain in the traditional role of housewife (Andersen, 1975; Welch, 1977; Poole and Zeigler, 1985).

Data necessary for a definitive test of the sex-role socialization hypothesis are not available in the SRC/CPS data archive for the period under consideration here. What can be done, however, is to see how men's and women's educational attainment and work status affect their attention to public affairs. Let us take up the question of education first.

Table 5.2 depicts men's and women's interest in politics by both age and educational attainment in 1960, 1968, 1976, and 1984.[11]

---

11. In order to provide sufficient cases for meaningful analysis, it is necessary to divide the age variable into just four rather large categories. As a result, cohort analysis can no longer be done.

## Table 5.2:
### Political Interest[a] by Gender, Controlling for Education and Age

|  | Grade School Women | Grade School Men | Some High School Women | Some High School Men | High School Graduate Women | High School Graduate Men | Some College Women | Some College Men | College Graduate Women | College Graduate Men |
|---|---|---|---|---|---|---|---|---|---|---|
| | | | | | **1960** | | | | | |
| 21-29 | -83.4* (12) | -100* (10) | -19.5 (36) | -60.0 (20) | 0.1 (70) | 15.8 (38) | 38.4* (13) | 16.7 (24) | -14.2* (14) | — (6) |
| 30-44 | -61.4 (62) | 8.0 (50) | -51.4 (72) | 18.6 (59) | -10.2 (137) | 22.8 (110) | 33.3 (54) | 58.0 (31) | 59.4 (32) | 56.1 (41) |
| 45-64 | -25.4 (114) | 14.5 (139) | 0.0 (48) | 16.6 (60) | 25.0 (68) | 34.4 (61) | 34.0 (47) | 44.0 (25) | 29.9 (37) | 51.8 (29) |
| 65+ | -30.0 (67) | 5.9 (86) | 16.7 (24) | 9.1* (11) | 38.5 (26) | — (5) | 46.1* (13) | — (2) | 52.5* (19) | — (8) |
| | | | | | **1968** | | | | | |
| 21-29 | — (7) | — (4) | -34.8 (23) | -30.0* (10) | 7.4 (54) | 12.2 (33) | 27.3 (33) | 47.6 (42) | 39.1 (23) | 77.8* (18) |
| 30-44 | -26.1 (23) | -16.7 (24) | -20.7 (58) | 45.8 (24) | 25.8 (101) | 20.7 (58) | 50.0 (30) | 76.2 (21) | 34.6 (26) | 65.8 (38) |
| 45-64 | -6.7 (60) | -0.1 (62) | 7.7 (52) | 27.7 (36) | 31.5 (76) | 53.4 (60) | 51.8 (27) | 62.5 (24) | 70.8 (24) | 70.3 (27) |
| 65+ | -21.7 (69) | -5.1 (58) | 34.7 (23) | 0.0* (12) | 27.8* (18) | 63.6* (11) | 8.3* (12) | — (4) | — (8) | 92.3* (13) |

Apathy in America, 1960–1984

**Table 5.2 (cont.)**

|  | Grade School Women | Grade School Men | Some High School Women | Some High School Men | High School Graduate Women | High School Graduate Men | Some College Women | Some College Men | College Graduate Women | College Graduate Men |
|---|---|---|---|---|---|---|---|---|---|---|
| | | | | | 1976 | | | | | |
| 18-29 | — (6) | — (6) | -13.2 (57) | -26.6 (25) | -18.8 (170) | -9.0 (90) | 26.5 (102) | 13.0 (108) | 29.0 (52) | 59.8 (51) |
| 30-44 | -18.5 (14) | 30.3* (17) | -21.2 (50) | 13.7 (22) | 5.5 (155) | 20.7 (85) | 49.1 (53) | 61.8 (51) | 65.3 (59) | 78.5 (75) |
| 45-64 | 17.5 (80) | 24.3 (56) | 23.6 (70) | 42.0 (56) | 35.1 (151) | 47.1 (87) | 47.4 (58) | 61.1 (43) | 68.2 (43) | 82.7 (52) |
| 65+ | -19.2 (104) | 30.3 (80) | -2.6 (40) | 64.2 (20) | 56.2 (65) | 69.3 (31) | 84.4 (32) | — (8) | 88.6* (18) | 90.7* (16) |
| | | | | | 1984 | | | | | |
| 18-29 | — (4) | — (4) | -29.4 (34) | -51.8 (27) | -20.5 (117) | -18.0 (78) | -1.4 (73) | 8.4 (60) | 11.1 (36) | 52.7 (38) |
| 30-44 | -15.4* (13) | — (6) | -35.1 (37) | -11.1 (27) | -18.8 (122) | 0.0 (88) | 14.5 (89) | 42.2 (71) | 40.1 (77) | 42.6 (94) |
| 45-64 | -40.6 (32) | -14.3 (35) | -20.0 (35) | 9.1 (33) | 12.4 (113) | 30.8 (65) | 34.6 (49) | 44.4 (45) | 55.6 (36) | 57.7 (45) |
| 65+ | -16.7 (54) | 11.2 (44) | -6.2 (32) | 56.6 (23) | 41.4 (58) | 63.3 (30) | 55.0 (29) | 70.0 (20) | 44.5* (18) | 57.2* (14) |

[a] Entries are the percentage difference index on the Political Apathy Index.
* = Fewer than 20 cases.

Source: University of Michigan's Survey Research Center/Center for Political Studies' National Election Studies.

*The Causes of Political Apathy*

Before taking up the meaning of these data, however, a brief methodological aside is necessary.

Due to the limitation of cases in the SRC/CPS national election studies, it is necessary to collapse the age variable into only four categories: under 30, 30-44 years of age, 45-64, and 65 and older. At that, under the effects of the simultaneous controls for gender and age, there are several instances in which so few cases were contained in the cells as to preclude meaningful analysis. Fortunately, the consistency with which the results are replicated — both in the years covered in the table and those not presented — lends credence to the analysis.

Several facets of these data are noteworthy. The most important finding, of course, is that education affects political interest among men and women, which is hardly a surprising datum, but should be reassuring to those who have believed that, as women's formal schooling comes to equal that of men, the gender gap in attention to politics will narrow.

Narrow it certainly should, but there is evidence of a continuing gender difference in interest even when education is controlled. Moreover, the "gap" is greater among the younger age categories. The latter fact brings out another aspect of the data in the table: age is a particularly important factor among women. Without regard to any particular educational level, one sees more change in political interest in conjunction with age among women. While age also has an effect among men, it is considerably more muted.

At first blush, one is at a loss to determine why younger well-educated women remain less politically engaged than young men of similar schooling. Perhaps it is because of gender differences in the curricula chosen while in college. Perhaps it reflects underlying career aspirations and achievements. To get at the latter possibility, Table 5.3 shows men's and women's political interest while controlling for age and employment status.[12]

The first thing to note in the table is confirmation of the hypothesis

---

12. To get better purchase on the question, in 1960 and 1984, the respondent's occupation was analyzed, looking at both gender and age (divided into those under 45 and those 45 and older). Occupation was divided into professional and semi-professional, businessmen and managers, clerical and sales, skilled and semi-skilled workers, and unskilled and service workers. In both years, among younger workers, women were more apathetic than men, regardless of occupation. On the other hand, in both years older women who were in professional and semi-professional careers were more politically involved than older men.

*109*

## Table 5.3:
## Political Interest[a] by Gender, Controlling for Employment Status and Age

|  | <30 | 30-44 | 45-64 | 65+ |
|---|---|---|---|---|
|  |  | 1960 |  |  |
| HOUSEWIFE | −27.2 | −10.6 | −4.2 | 8.2* |
|  | (81) | (207) | (141) | (13) |
| WORKING |  |  |  |  |
| Women | 0.9 | −22.2 | 12.4 | 72.9* |
|  | (56) | (135) | (160) | (11) |
| Men | −12.7 | 25.5 | 25.4 | 30.8 |
|  | (94) | (278) | (284) | (39) |
|  |  | 1968 |  |  |
| HOUSEWIFE | 2.8 | 19.4 | 14.7 | 0.0 |
|  | (71) | (119) | (108) | (77) |
| WORKING |  |  |  |  |
| Women | 11.4 | 6.3 | 30.9 | −14.3* |
|  | (61) | (112) | (113) | (14) |
| Men | 28.3 | 34.9 | 42.1 | 15.0 |
|  | (92) | (163) | (176) | (20) |
|  |  | 1976 |  |  |
| HOUSEWIFE | −12.2 | 20.6 | 39.9 | 15.3 |
|  | (115) | (124) | (148) | (131) |
| WORKING |  |  |  |  |
| Women | 3.1 | 16.0 | 34.1 | 48.1* |
|  | (210) | (175) | (178) | (14) |
| Men | 9.4 | 45.6 | 50.1 | 67.3 |
|  | (227) | (227) | (234) | (22) |
|  |  | 1984 |  |  |
| HOUSEWIFE | −6.9 | −4.4 | −15.2 | −6.7 |
|  | (43) | (69) | (72) | (59) |
| WORKING | −17.1 |  |  | 29.4* |
| Women | (164) | 6.2 | 17.7 | (17) |
|  | 1.7 | (236) | (142) | 50.0* |
| Men | (178) | 23.6 | 30.6 | (16) |
|  |  | (2163) | (157) |  |

[a]Entries are percentage difference index on Political Apathy Index. * = Fewer than 20 cases.
Source: University of Michigan's SRC/CPS's National Election Studies.

that entrance by women into the labor force enhances attention to public affairs. In 13 of the 16 comparisons, working women are more politically interested than similarly aged housewives. In short, as more women have begun working over the past 25 years, one consequence has been at least a marginal increase in their attention to political life.

It should also be noted that, with but two exceptions, working women are less politically engaged than similarly aged men who work. However, this does not necessarily mean that entrance into the work force has a different connotation for women than it does for men. With the data at hand, one cannot distinguish women who mean work to be a full-time career from those for whom working does not supplant the more traditional roles of housewife and mother. However, before one accepts the proposition that adoption of such traditional sex roles automatically entails less interest in public affairs, it should be noted that, especially among women under 45 years old, those who are single are more apathetic than those who are married. Moreover, with the exception of 1976, women under 45 who have children under 18 years of age are more politically interested than those who do not.

In sum, then, it appears that even when education and employment status are taken into account, women are still somewhat less likely to be politically involved. Although the data necessary to test the hypothesis are not available, it is reasonable to speculate that this continuing gender gap in interest is part of the same phenomenon Rapoport has identified for women's generally low levels of attempts to influence others' votes. He believes that this phenomenon "is related to the reluctance of female adults to express [political] attitudes, and . . . this reluctance finds its roots in childhood and adolescent socialization" (1981: 35). If this be true, it will take more than just increased levels of formal schooling and greater participation in the labor force to bring American women's psychological involvement in public affairs up to a par with men's.

Before closing this discussion of the relative influences of gender and age, the implications of the findings on marital status and the presence of young children in the home need to be teased out. One of the usual explanations for the political apathy of younger Americans is that they are so preoccupied with the pursuit of a life-mate and establishment of a career that there is little time or psychic energy left for political engagement. When PDI's on the Political Apathy Index are plumbed with gender, age, and marital status simultaneously taken into account, there is no strong or consistent relation between age, marital status, and political involvement. Among men and women under age 45, it makes very little difference whether the individual is single, separated/divorced, or married and living with a spouse. This finding is somewhat surprising, given the tendency for marital status to be a factor in turnout among the young (Wolfinger and Rosenstone, 1980: 44-45). Pursuit of the reasons for this "nonfinding" is beyond our scope; suffice it to say that, once more, it has been shown that the factors behind political interest are not necessarily those related to turnout at the polls on election day.

Another factor often said to diminish general interest in public affairs, again primarily among the young, is the presence of school-aged children in the home (Jennings, 1979: 761). However, Sapiro (1983: 91-92) has contested the traditional assumption, showing that parenthood does not dim attention to political life. Similarly, the PDI's on the Apathy Index show no clearcut and consistent relation between gender, age, the presence of children under the age of 18, and political interest.

Before concluding this section, three things need to be said. First, if two of the three factors usually relied upon to account for youthful apathy show no clear or consistent relation to the Political Apathy Index, this does not mean that marital status and parenthood ought to be entirely dismissed as factors in young people's abysmal participation levels. Second, it is very important to remember that, regardless of their employment and marital statuses and whether or not they are parents, most of the time over almost a quarter-century covered by the data, most young Americans have been indifferent to the public affairs. It is only among the college educated young that one finds much attention to the public affairs.

This observation brings up the third and final point. If education is such an important factor generating political interest, given the very substantial increase in levels of exposure to higher education of the American electorate since 1960, why hasn't attention to government and politics similarly increased? The question is even more intriguing since the strength of the zero-order relationship between education and the Apathy Index is the same in 1984 as it had been in 1960 ($r = .268$ vs. $r = .265$).

The Causes of Political Apathy

The obvious implication is that other factors have come to affect interest in public affairs that offset young people's educational attainment. Two factors are worthy of attention: (1) the strength of people's attachment to the major political parties, and (2) people's perceptions of the extent to which public officials are responsive to public opinion. It is to a consideration of these political factors that attention is now turned.

## The Impact of Partisanship, External Political Efficacy, Education, and Age

Four aspects of partisanship are pertinent here. First, as was pointed out in Chapter 4, one of the more intensively studied phenomena of the last two decades has been the weakening of Americans' attachment to the major parties. Second, it is also a well established finding of political behavior research that young people are generally considerably less likely than the elderly to be strongly attached to a political party. Third, young people who have entered the electorate since the late 1960s have been even less likely than those who had reached maturity in the 1950s and early 1960s to identify with a political party, and have been less likely to take on the attributes of party supporters with the passage of time. (To some extent, this may be a function of the higher levels of educational attainment among young people in the 1970s and 1980s.) Fourth, again as was shown in Chapter 4, while strength of partisanship is not linearly related to psychological involvement in public affairs (see also Abramson, 1983: 91-92), strong partisans are much more likely to be politically interested than are independents. Could it be that the decreased attachment to political parties among the young since the 1960s has contributed to their lessened inclination to pay attention to government and politics? Table 5.4 presents the answer. It depicts political interest by partisanship, controlling for education and age.[13]

Inspection of the table shows that each of the variables, partisanship, education, and age, influences interest in the public affairs.

---

13. Age is divided into less than 45 and 45 and older. To secure sufficient cases for analysis, the education variable was collapsed into three categories: those who did not complete high school, high school graduates, and those with at least some college experience. In each year, people who were apolitical were excluded from the analysis.

## Table 5.4:
## Political Interest[a] by Partisanship, Controlling for Education and Age

|  | Independent | | Independent Leaner | | Weak Identifier | | Strong Identifier | |
|---|---|---|---|---|---|---|---|---|
|  | <45 | 45+ | <45 | 45+ | <45 | 45+ | <45 | 45+ |

### 1960

| | | | | | | | | |
|---|---|---|---|---|---|---|---|---|
| <H.S. Grad. | −68.5 | −34.1 | −14.9 | −1.8 | −32.5 | −4.5 | −11.1 | 12.0 |
|  | (38) | (47) | (47) | (56) | (114) | (202) | (99) | (225) |
| H.S. Grad. | −12.9 | −46.1* | −6.0 | 0.0* | −1.4 | 16.6 | 26.0 | 69.6 |
|  | (31) | (13) | (66) | (17) | (147) | (60) | (100) | (69) |
| College | 50.0* | 52.7* | 77.1 | 20.0 | 23.6 | 33.8 | 43.0 | 58.1 |
|  | (16) | (19) | (35) | (20) | (85) | (62) | (79) | (74) |

### 1968

| | | | | | | | | |
|---|---|---|---|---|---|---|---|---|
| <H.S. Grad. | −32.2 | 16.2 | 20.0 | 20.0 | −30.2 | −20.5 | 33.2 | 18.5 |
|  | (31) | (31) | (25) | (25) | (63) | (156) | (48) | (151) |
| H.S. Grad. | 4.4 | 38.5* | 26.7 | 66.8 | 10.7 | 24.7 | 40.0 | 54.0 |
|  | (23) | (13) | (52) | (30) | (112) | (69) | (55) | (50) |
| College | 13.0 | 16.7* | 50.5 | 78.2 | 48.6 | 56.6 | 64.7 | 70.7 |
|  | (23) | (12) | (81) | (32) | (72) | (53) | (54) | (41) |

### 1976

| | | | | | | | | |
|---|---|---|---|---|---|---|---|---|
| <H.S. Grad. | −32.4 | −6.4 | −10.5 | 24.0 | −27.6 | −2.9 | 49.3 | 54.8 |
|  | (37) | (47) | (38) | (65) | (76) | (225) | (34) | (156) |
| H.S. Grad | −21.1 | 8.9 | −14.1 | 39.3 | −0.6 | 43.2 | 40.3 | 76.0 |
|  | (124) | (34) | (117) | (56) | (184) | (136) | (75) | (105) |
| College | 27.2 | 41.0 | 39.0 | 80.8 | 43.0 | 59.9 | 69.5 | 81.0 |
|  | (74) | (20) | (180) | (66) | 208) | (91) | (86) | (92) |

### 1984

| | | | | | | | | |
|---|---|---|---|---|---|---|---|---|
| <H.S. Grad. | −46.2 | −24.4 | −43.5 | −5.2 | −38.3 | −28.6 | 18.4 | 18.3 |
|  | (26) | (35) | (39) | (39) | (47) | (77) | (36) | (131) |
| H.S. Grad. | −36.3 | 0.0 | −17.9 | 34.6 | −14.2 | 20.6 | 24.6 | 48.0 |
|  | (55) | (22) | (112) | (58) | (155) | (86) | (65) | (100) |
| College | 24.6 | 58.3* | 26.3 | 44.3 | 9.2 | 37.9 | 54.8 | 63.3 |
|  | (53) | (12) | (137) | (61) | (206) | (82) | (137) | (101) |

[a]Entries are the percentage difference index on the Political Apathy Index. * = Fewer than 20 cases.
Source: University of Michigan's SRC/CPS's National Election Studies.

*The Causes of Political Apathy*

Moreover, the nature of the relationships among all four factors remains essentially the same over the 24 years covered by the data. It is also apparent that education and age have stronger relationships to psychological involvement in public affairs than does partisanship.

Still, it is interesting to note the type of impact partisanship does have. It is strongest, as would be expected, among those who have not had any university exposure. It is especially important among people who have not graduated from high school. In this sense, strength of partisanship works the same for both young and old.

Closer inspection, however, reveals that partisanship is most important among the young, and it is to those under age 45 that especial attention should be focused. Young people who have had at least some college experience are politically interested, regardless of partisanship. On the other hand, among those who have not gone to college, only strong identifiers are politically interested. In short, among Americans under age 45, education and, to a lesser degree, partisanship, both affect interest in public affairs.

As noted above, it is precisely among the young that partisanship has waned most since the mid-1960s. Interestingly, the marginals in Table 5.4 show that it is among those who have not gone to college that identification with the two major parties has fallen most. In 1960, 31% of young people whose education stopped at or before the 12th grade were strong identifiers, 41% were weak partisans, 18% were independent leaners, and 11% were Independents. Thirty-seven percent of the young with college background were strong identifiers, 40% were weak identifiers, 17% were independent leaners, and only eight percent were Independents. In 1984, only 19% of young people without any exposure to college were strong partisans, 38% were weak identifiers, 28% were independent leaners, and 15% were Independents. Twenty-six percent of young persons who had gone to college were strong partisans, 38% were weak identifiers, 26% were independent leaners, and ten percent were Independents. In short, if one is looking for the growing education-based disparity in political interest among young people, the loosened ties to the major political parties of those with less than college education is one significant factor.

Another factor is perceptions of governmental elites' responsiveness to public opinion. Recall V. O. Key, Jr.'s point that, unless people believe that there is reason to believe political leaders pay at

*115*

least some attention to what the people think, it is bootless to keep abreast of what is happening in the political arena (1961: 546). One indicator of people's beliefs about governmental responsiveness is the SRC's "External Political Efficacy Index" (Balch, 1974; Abramson, 1983). Abramson has shown that between 1960 and 1980 there was a substantial decline in the public's belief that government would be responsive to ordinary folk (1983: 175-176; see also Bennett, 1984a). While there was an increase in external efficacy beliefs in 1984, perceptions of governmental responsiveness remained well below the halcyon days of 1960. According to Abramson and Aldrich (1982), the decline in the public's belief that governmental leaders will do what the people want them to is one of the major reasons for the turn-down in turnout since 1960.[14]

In Chapter 4 it was established that, as perceptions of governmental responsiveness have waned, the result has been a more apathetic populace. However, it was also pointed out that external political efficacy beliefs are related to educational attainment (Abramson, 1983: 179), just as is political interest. What would be the impact on political interest of both education and external political efficacy beliefs? Table 5.5 shows the answer. In keeping with the thrust of the chapter, age is also brought into the analysis.

Five aspects of these data merit comment. First, attention to public affairs is affected by both educational attainment and external political efficacy beliefs. Second, education appears to have the stronger impact.

Third, there have been some important changes in the patterns of the relationships. Particularly noteworthy is the tendency in 1984, especially among younger people, for those without college backgrounds to be apathetic regardless of external efficacy beliefs. In 1960, young high schoolers who were sanguine about governmental responsiveness were politically interested, while in 1968 and 1976 all those with less than university exposure who were "high" on the External Efficacy Index were attentive to public affairs. Among young persons with college experience in 1984, on the other hand, those who take a dim view of governmental responsiveness are only marginally interested in politics while those who are sanguine are considerably more attentive. Prior to 1984, young people with college

---

14. They contend that the other major factor is the decline in attachment to the major political parties.

## Table 5.5:
## Political Interest[a] by External Political Efficacy, Controlling for Education and Age

|  | Low |  | Medium |  | High |  |
|---|---|---|---|---|---|---|
|  | ‹45 | 45+ | ‹45 | 45+ | ‹45 | 45+ |

### 1960

| ‹H.S. Grad. | −62.1 | −42.6 | −25.3 | −14.9 | −18.8 | 28.8 |
|---|---|---|---|---|---|---|
|  | (66) | (129) | (87) | (120) | (159) | (267) |
| H.S. Grad. | −41.6 | −12.5* | −15.7 | 31.3 | 20.3 | 38.2 |
|  | (24) | (16) | (64) | (32) | (252) | (110) |
| College | — | — | 28.1 | 10.7 | 49.5 | 56.0 |
|  | (4) | (9) | (39) | (28) | (170) | (136) |

### 1968

| ‹H.S. Grad. | −39.1 | −22.5 | 2.5 | 18.1 | 14.1 | 40.5 |
|---|---|---|---|---|---|---|
|  | (69) | (177) | (40) | (94) | (57) | (84) |
| H.S. Grad. | 0.1 | 25.7 | 7.8 | 45.5 | 32.9 | 51.4 |
|  | (48) | (39) | (64) | (44) | (128) | (74) |
| College | 28.9 | 31.3* | 50.0 | 58.7 | 54.9 | 69.0 |
|  | (38) | (17) | (38) | (29) | (153) | (87) |

### 1976

| ‹H.S. Grad. | −22.3 | −0.5 | −14.9 | 38.1 | 21.6 | 44.3 |
|---|---|---|---|---|---|---|
|  | (92) | (235) | (47) | (129) | (33) | (93) |
| H.S. Grad | −20.7 | 27.3 | −0.7 | 41.6 | 12.3 | 62.4 |
|  | (158) | (97) | (153) | (77) | (160) | (140) |
| College | 34.0 | 65.0 | 45.1 | 53.3 | 48.7 | 82.2 |
|  | (125) | (39) | (145) | (69) | (261) | (152) |

### 1984

| ‹H.S. Grad. | −43.7 | 10.9 | −38.1 | −15.5 | −14.4 | 20.6 |
|---|---|---|---|---|---|---|
|  | (55) | (110) | (42) | (84) | (49) | (78) |
| H.S. Grad. | −40.0 | 9.6 | −18.0 | 32.5 | −1.4 | 36.1 |
|  | (95) | (62) | (94) | (80) | (212) | (122) |
| College | 1.3 | 47.2 | 19.9 | 31.7 | 33.3 | 59.9 |
|  | (72) | (36) | (106) | (63) | (358) | (154) |

[a]Entries are the percentage difference index on the Political Apathy Index. * = Fewer than 20 cases.
Source: University of Michigan's SRC/CSP's National Election Studies.

experience were generally quite interested regardless of external political efficacy perceptions.

It is also interesting to note that, between 1960 and 1984, external political efficacy beliefs fell most among young people with less than college background. In 1960, 14% of those under age 45 who had not gone to college were "low" on the External Political Efficacy Index, 23% were "medium," and 63% were "high." By comparison, only two percent of those with college experience were "low," 18% were "medium," and 80% were "high." In 1984, 27% of those without university training were "low," 25% were "medium," and 48% were "high." Thirteen percent of the university educated were "low," 20% were "medium," and 67% were "high." The reasons for the more substantial decline in external efficacy beliefs among lesser educated young Americans is beyond the scope of this volume. It is clear, however, that one consequence has been less attention to politics among these people.

Finally, the data shed interesting light on the interrelation of external efficacy beliefs and age. Perceptions of governmental responsiveness or unresponsiveness make more difference among the young. For the most part, people who are 45 years of age or older are more politically interested than the young at all combinations of education and external efficacy perceptions. In several cases, the differences are truly astounding. The impact of age is clearly the strongest among those who completed high school, and weakest among people who had at least some college experience.

In sum, the data in Table 5.5 show all three variables, age, education, and external political efficacy beliefs, affect interest in politics. These data also reveal one of the main weaknesses of partition design as a method for analyzing several factors at once. It is very difficult to assess the relative effects of two or more independent variables. Yet, this is precisely the information needed to complete a multivariate analysis of political interest. To obtain such information, another data analysis technique is needed.

## The Results of OLS Regression Analysis

As indicated at the beginning of the chapter, there are several multivariate statistical analysis techniques that are employed by contemporary political scientists faced with problems similar to the one here. Three of the most widely used are ordinary least squares (OLS) linear regression (Lewis-Beck, 1980; Achen, 1982; and Berry and Feldman, 1985), discriminant analysis (Klecka, 1980), and logit and probit analysis (Aldrich and Nelson, 1984). While each has advantages and disadvantages (see Aldrich and Cnudde, 1975), the one to be employed here is multiple step-wise regression. Not only is OLS regression analysis sufficiently robust to handle most of the problems encountered with the type of data in use, it is among the most widely used multivariate analysis techniques in political science and other social science disciplines such as economics and sociology.

Basically, multiple regression assumes that it is possible to "regress" a dependent variable — *i.e.* the Political Apathy Index — on a set of independent variables by the following equation:

$$\hat{Y} = a + B_1X_1 + B_2X_2 + B_3X_3 + \ldots B_nX_n + E.$$

In the equation, $\hat{Y}$ is the estimated value of the dependent variable, $X_1, X_2, \ldots, X_n$ are the independent variables included in the model, $B$ is the partial slope coefficient, or the slope of the relation between each independent variable and the dependent variable, once the effects of all other independent variables are taken into account, $a$ is the intercept value, or the point on Y where the values of all the independent variables are zero, and $E$ is the "error term."

As indicated above, OLS regression analysis makes some very stringent demands upon the data (Lewis-Beck, 1980: 26-30; Berry and Feldman, 1985: 10-11). For example, not only must all the variables be measured at the interval level, there must be no specification error (*i.e.*, no relevant independent variables have been left out of the model and no irrelevant ones have been included), no measurement error, and the relationships amongst all the variables must be linear. Several assumptions focus on the error term: the mean value of the error term across the independent variables must be 0, the variance of the error term must be constant (homoscedasticity) and there must be no autocorrelation among the error terms of the independent variables. There must be no perfect collinearity, which means that no independent variable is perfectly linearly related to any other independent variable, or combinations thereof, in the model. Finally, OLS multiple regression also assumes the effects of the independent variables are additive and not multiplicative.

At the outset, it must be admitted that no set of survey data totally

*119*

meets all these assumptions. Certainly those in use here do not. The question, then, is what happens to the results of regression analysis when data violate the model's assumptions. While some statisticians claim that the regression technique is robust enough to handle most cases (Pedhazur, 1982), others are less certain (Blalock, 1979). Social scientists are increasingly learning ways at least partially to off-set most of the common violations of the regression model. There is general agreement in any case that specification error — failure to include a key relevant independent variable — is a most serious mistake.

The approach followed here is as follows. First, in order to be certain that as many key independent variables as possible are included in the regression analyses, only four years are selected for analysis: 1960, 1972, 1976, and 1980. In these years, the SRC/CPS included a wide variety of demographic and political factors hypothesized by previous researchers to affect psychological involvement in politics. Unfortunately, the SRC did not include the Citizen Duty Index in 1964, 1968, and 1984; hence these years must be eliminated. At that, two variables — the Trust in Government and Governmental Attentiveness indices — were not available for 1960, but it was so important to at least look at the factors affecting political interest in that year that their absence was an affordable price to pay.

Once the four years had been chosen, the Political Apathy Index was recomputed in order to produce a result closer to an interval scale.[15] Similarly, each of the independent variables was either recoded or recomputed to come as close as could be to discrete numbers rather than mere categories (see the appendix to this chapter). Next, a multiple regression run was done for each year in which "all" relevant independent variables were included in the model.

Immediately, it must be admitted that "all" is relative, since one goal was to include predictor variables that were available over the entire 24-year span under consideration here. Hence, it must be said that all the regression models looked at here are "under-specified." If the goal was to achieve maximum predictive capability, such would be a grievous mistake. However, as the primary purpose is to see whether there are predictor variables that remain relatively potent over nearly a quarter of a century of American history, the problem becomes less critical.

---

15. Instead of collapsing the index into five categories, the results of adding the campaign interest and general interest variables were left raw (see the Appendix to this chapter).

Finally, once the first set of regression analyses was complete, those factors found to be statistically unimportant as predictors of apathy were eliminated,[16] and the regression analyses were redone using just those independent variables established as important predictors of political interest even in the multivariate context.[17] These are the results that will be discussed.[18]

Only three aspects of the regression analyses will be covered. First, which independent variables are consistently the most important predictors of apathy? Second, are there any changes over the years in the factors that shape psychological involvement in politics? Third, how much variance in political interest can be explained by the combined effects of a small set of independent variables?

Only a small set of predictors consistently emerges as at least relatively potent predictors of interest in public affairs: sense of citizen duty, partisanship/attraction to presidential candidates, perceptions of governmental responsiveness/attentiveness, perceptions of political competence (internal political efficacy), educational attainment, age, and gender. (It is also interesting to note that race, family income, marital status, employment status, trust in government, and region are not important determinants of apathy.) The consistency with which the same demographic and political factors emerge year after year as important predictors of political interest is impressive. Another noteworthy point is that political interest seems to be influenced more by political factors than by demographic attributes. Other than education, which is among the strongest predictors of interest, age and gender are the only demographic factors to emerge as consistently strong predictors.

Among the political factors, the best consistent predictors are sense of citizen duty, internal political efficacy, and either strength of partisanship or candidate preference. The relative potency of citizen duty and perceptions of personal political competence may at least partially explain why interest in public affairs has not fallen more than it has since the late 1960s and early 1970s, since it has been shown that both citizen duty and internal political efficacy have changed but little since 1960 (Bennett, 1983; Abramson, 1983).

---

16. No predictor which added less than one percent of additional explained variance was left in the regression model. This is a crude, but workable, criterion (see Oldendick and Bennett, 1978).

17. Of course, I will supply the results of the original analyses upon written request.

18. The tables are not depicted to save space. I will supply a summary of the final regression analyses upon request.

How much variance in political interest can be explained by the combined effects of political and demographic factors? On average, a parsimonious set of predictors accounts for just over 25 percent of the variance in the Political Apathy Index. The range is from 23% in 1972 to 28% in 1960. The lion's share of explained variance is accounted for by sense of citizen obligation, perceptions of personal political competence, education, partisanship/attraction to presidential candidates, perceptions of governmental responsiveness /attentiveness, and age.

Of course, this means that a daunting three-quarters of the variance in the Political Apathy Index is left unexplained. Undoubtedly, one can point to measurement error in the dependent and independent variables and to an under-specified regression model as the key explanations. Still, the fact that a small sub-set of predictors can account for a quarter of the variance in the Political Apathy Index is an impressive accomplishment, given the norm in political behavior research.

## Conclusion

The purpose of this chapter was to extend the findings of Chapter 4 by ascertaining the most important factors behind the ordinary citizen's psychological involvement in public affairs. The data presented in the first and second sections elaborate upon previous research and specify more carefully than heretofore the interrelationships among important demographic and political factors that shape people's attention to public affairs. It should now be apparent that the most important factors are political: sense of citizen duty, perceptions of personal political competence, partisanship, and, to a lesser degree, perceptions of governmental responsiveness/attentiveness. While it should occasion no surprise to find a political disposition such as attention to public affairs is heavily dependent upon other basic political orientations, it is interesting to note that most previous research has focused primarily on the social factors responsible.

Among the demographic factors, education is clearly the most important predictor. Nonetheless, fully to understand the dynamics behind interest in public affairs, it is necessary to take the effects of both age and gender into account. No other social factor is consistently an important predictor of interest.

The next question to consider is what difference political interest makes to the citizen and to the polity. That topic is taken up in Chapter 6.

## Appendix

The following are the codes used for each of the variables entered in the regression analyses for this chapter:

Gender: "0" = women; "1" = men.

Race: "0" = black; "1" = white.

Age: actual age coded; range from 17 to 99+.

Region: "0" = Nonsouth; "1" = South.

Marital Status: "0" = not married; "1" = married.

Employment Status: "0" = not working; "1" = working now.

Education: actual final year completed coded; range from 0 years to 17+ years.

Family Income: coded to mid-point of SRC/CPS codes for each year (in actual dollars); *e.g.*, 11.5 = between $11,000 and $12,000 per year.

Partisanship: "1" = Apolitical; "2" = Independent; "3" = Independent Leaner; "4" = Weak Identifier; "5" = Strong Identifier.

Attachment to Presidential Candidate: Opinion Thermometer Rating of Democrat-Opinion Thermometer Rating of Republican; absolute value taken; range from 0° to 100°.

Sense of Civic Duty Index: "0" = Very Low; "1" = Low; "2" = Medium; "3" = High; "4" = Very High.

Internal Political Efficacy Index and External Political Efficacy Index: "0" = Low; "1" = Medium; "2" = High.

Trust in Government Index: range from "4" to "22"; low value = very trusting.

Governmental Attentiveness Index: range from "4" to " 20"; Low value = strong perception of governmental attentiveness.

Political Apathy Index: range from "2" to "10"; low value = very interested.

# CHAPTER 6

# THE CONSEQUENCES OF APATHY

## Introduction

As established in Chapter 4, somewhere between 30% and 45% of the American public is politically interested while between 25% and 35% is indifferent (see Table 4.1). And, since the mid-1970s psychological involvement in American politics has declined somewhat. So what?

Such is the question this chapter seeks to answer. What are the implications of interest/apathy for the individual citizen? And what are the consequences for the American polity? In the attempt to answer the first query, several avenues offer themselves: (1) Is the politically interested citizen a different political actor, qualitatively as well as quantitatively, than the apathetic one? Posing the question thusly opens several lines of inquiry; here we shall focus on whether the psychologically involved citizen exposes himself to more information about public affairs and thus is better informed about government and politics than is his indifferent neighbor. (2) In addition we also want to know how much more active the politically interested person is in the public arena than the apathetic one. (3) Finally, is this activity limited to "the simple act of voting" (Lane, 1965: 222), or does it carry over to more demanding activities?

As important as the preceding questions are, the implications of interest/apathy for the democratic political system are even more basic. Throughout the history of America, citizen indifference has been castigated as being inimical to popular government (Dinkin, 1977, 1982; Roosevelt, 1958; Bryce, 1913). While some observers could defend the individual who eschewed political attentiveness (Dewey, 1927; Lippmann, 1925, 1927), and a few brave souls could see a silver lining in apathy's "clouded sky" (Munro, 1928; Wilson, 1930, 1936; Berelson, 1952), most writers on political indifference have put a decidedly negative "spin" on the phenomenon. Whether the implications of lack of citizen interest be merely the balance of power between contending partisan forces in American politics (Schattschneider, 1960) or the putative fate of democracy itself (Bryce, 1913), citizen political inattention was viewed as unfortunate, to say the very least.

In the effort to deal with the systemic implications of interest/apathy, the focus will be on the potential implications for the American political system of lack of attention to politics. From 1960 to 1984, are Americans who profess interest in the public affairs different from those who abjure psychological involvement in terms of their respective basic orientations toward the political system? In particular, are the indifferent more or less likely to see the system as responsive to their opinions, and worthy of their trust?[1] Finally, in the long run, are these three orientations, in combination, related to lack of citizen participation?

This chapter has three parts. The first section looks at whether political interest is related to how much the individual uses the mass media for political purposes, and whether it influences how well informed the citizen is about public affairs. The second explores the impact of psychological involvement in public affairs on several different types of political activity: reported turnout in national elections, a validated measure of voting, engagement in campaign activities, participation in non-electoral activities on the local and national levels, and reports of taking part in protest demonstrations. The third section investigates whether political apathy interacts with other basic political orientations, such as political efficacy and trust in government, to influence how active people are in the democratic process.

Several aspects of the approach followed here need elaboration. First, the focus is primarily on how political interest/apathy is related to facets of political involvement and participation over time. Hence, one criterion in the selection of topics was the presence on SRC/CPS

---

1. As is already known (see Table 4.3), there is a substantial relation between the Political Apathy Index and External Political Efficacy, but only a weak association between the Apathy measure and Trust in Government.

questionnaires of comparable items over the time span covered in the book. The price to be paid for this approach is, of course, that short shrift must be given to topics which the SRC/CPS has not seen fit to plumb over the years.

As important as it is to assess the consequences of interest/apathy over time, a few topics warrant departure from this approach. Foremost is the analysis of the impact of psychological involvement on non-electoral modes of political activity. According to Verba and Nie (1972: chap. 4), voting and participation in campaign activities constitute separate "dimensions" of grassroots political activity, and are only modestly related to other nonelectoral "modes" of political action. Given the strategic importance to the democratic polity of citizen participation (see Almond and Verba, 1963; Pateman, 1970; Thompson, 1970; Verba and Nie, 1972; Barber, 1984), it is important to look at the impact of the Political Apathy Index on activity outside the electoral arena. Unfortunately, this can be done only in 1976, for that is the only year the CPS included a number of activities beyond voting and campaign participation.

We will also look in more detail at both how the individual's psychological involvement in public affairs affects usage of the mass media for news about government and politics, and how interest and a measure of political "alienation" interact to affect turnout in a presidential election. In the former case, data are available for two years, 1980 and 1984. In the latter instance, 1976 is the only instance in which a suitable indicant of "alienation" and a measure of validated vote are available for the same survey.[2]

One last introductory point needs to be made. In the main, the analyses for this chapter are bivariate: scores on the Political Apathy Index are cross-indexed with various indicators of participation and involvement in politics. This approach has the beauty of simplicity; no special training in arcane statistics is required. Unfortunately, however, bivariate methodology has two glaring faults: (1) it is impossible to determine whether seemingly robust relationships between the Apathy Index and indicators of political participation are actually spurious, because some factor (education, for example) that affects both psychological involvement in public affairs and partici-

---

2. The measure of "alienation" is a two-item index based on whether people felt "proud" of their system of government and whether they thought major changes should be made in it, or it should be kept as it was. For more information, see pages 156-158.

pation is hidden in the data; and (2) it is also not possible to determine how well the Political Apathy Index would "predict" various modes of participation and involvement if other factors known to be related to political activity were also brought into the analysis.

In some measure, of course, detailed exploration of each problem is beyond the scope of this volume. However, some pursuit of these questions is necessary, first to assure against presenting spurious relationships, and second to ascertain the relative potency of the Apathy Index as a predictor of various modes of participation in politics in a multivariate context.

The first problem (spuriousness) can be dealt with quickly. Before assessing whether and how political interest affects people's exposure to political information, knowledge about public affairs, and participation in public affairs, it is necessary to relieve concern that some other factor accounts for both interest *and* these factors. Although several socio-political factors could be involved, the only one explored here is level of educational attainment. Education is the strongest test case to check for spuriousness of the relations between political interest and various modes of political behavior, for it has been repeatedly shown to have the strongest impact on the entire range of activities under consideration here (Campbell, 1962: 20; Almond and Verba, 1963: 379-382; Converse, 1972: 324-325). As Converse (1972: 324) puts it:

> There is probably no single variable in the survey repertoire that generates as substantial correlations in such a variety of directions in political behavior material as level of formal education. . . . [T]he true domain of education as predictor has to do with the large class of indicators of popular involvement and participation in politics. . . . [E]ducation is everywhere the universal solvent, and the relation is always in the same direction. The higher the education, the greater the "good" values of the [participation] variable. The educated citizen is attentive, knowledgeable, and participatory, and the uneducated citizen is not.

Given the importance of education as a predictor of political interest, knowledge, and participation, the best way to determine whether the associations between psychological involvement and various modes of political participation is spurious is to introduce a control for formal schooling. The question, then, is to determine the most appropriate method to achieve this end. Recall the data in Table 3.4 (p. 57). They showed the Pearsonian correlation coefficients between the Political Apathy Index and several modes of political involvement and participation: self-reported vote, a measure of validated turnout, an index of campaign activism, one of usage of the mass media for political purposes, and an indicant of political information. Basically, these data showed the Apathy Index to be moderately associated with each of the measures of turnout and the Campaign Activism Index, and robustly related to the indicants of media usage, and political knowledge.

What would happen to these relationships if a control for educational background were introduced? Table 6.1 shows the product moment correlation coefficients for the relations of the Political Apathy Index to each of these modes of involvement and participation with formal schooling partialled out.[3] To ease reading the table, the zero-order correlations originally displayed in Table 3.4 are reproduced in truncated form above the diagonal, while the first-order coefficients under the education control are shown beneath the same.

For present purposes, the key information in the table is the first-order partial coefficients. These data show clearly that the relations between the Political Apathy Index and several modes of political involvement and participation do not "wash out" when the "universal solvent" — education — is applied. Indeed, on average, just under 90% of the potency of the original relationships is retained even under the effect of the education control. Of course, it is always possible that if some other "third factor" were introduced as a control the relations of the Apathy Index to political participation measures would be either seriously attenuated or even entirely washed out. Nevertheless, for the present the central point is that one can have a good deal of confidence that the relationships between political interest and actual participation in public affairs are not epiphenomenal.

The second concern — how potent a predictor of participation activities the Political Apathy Index is once other factors also known to affect them are brought into the analysis — is a more complicated matter. Not only is some form of multivariate analysis required to

---

3. The entries to the left of the diagonal are the zero-order coefficients and are the same as the figures presented in Table 3.4. The figures to the right of the diagonal are the first-order partials with education controlled. The technique used is partial correlation.

## Table 6.1:
## Zero-Order and First-Order Partial (Education Controlled) Correlations[a] between the Political Apathy Index and Forms of Political Participation

|      | Reported Vote | Validated Vote | Campaign Activism | Media Usage | Political Information |
|------|---------------|----------------|-------------------|-------------|-----------------------|
| 1960 | .35/.30       | NA             | .47/.46           | .47/.41     | .41/.34               |
| 1962 | .36/.32       | NA             | .37/.34           | NA          | NA                    |
| 1964 | .27/.20       | .22/.18        | .39/.32           | .46/.50     | .41/.36               |
| 1966 | .41/.37       | NA             | NA                | NA          | .44/.36               |
| 1968 | .41/.37       | NA             | .37/.33           | .49/.43     | .29/.31               |
| 1972 | .36/.27       | NA             | .36/.30           | .47/.43     | .42/.38               |
| 1976 | .35/.31       | .26/.23        | .37/.33           | .56/.51     | .44/.40               |
| 1978 | .39/.36       | .35/.33        | .37/.32           | .55/.51     | .42/.37               |
| 1980 | .39/.36       | .32/.28        | .32/.29           | .50/.45     | .35/.30               |
| 1982 | .46/.42       | NA             | .40/.37           | .57/.54     | .41/.36               |
| 1984 | .34/.30       | .33/.28        | .36/.33           | .48/.43     | .37/.31               |

[a] Entries above the diagonal are the zero-order coefficients; those below are the first-order partials with education controlled.

Source: University of Michigan's Survey Research Center/Center for Political Studies' National Election Studies.

resolve the question, given the nature of the several types of political participation considered here different methods of statistical analysis must be used. For example, while multiple stepwise regression would be appropriate for the Campaign Usage Index, which has five discrete categories, the same method would not work on a dichotomous dependent variable such as turnout. In that instance, an alternative technique such as discriminant analysis is preferred.

Moreover, the attempt to depict the results of multivariate analysis procedures for each of the participation variables in every year from 1960 to 1984 requires such a volume of tables as to become needlessly long and confusing. Instead, at strategic points in the chapter a brief consideration of how well the Apathy Index predicts political behavior relative to other independent variables will be entertained, normally without recourse to presentation of the supporting data.[4]

Before assessing the implications of interest/apathy for citizen political involvement and participation, a brief word is in order about the criteria by which particular activities were chosen. Basically two considerations governed the selections. One, there had to be previous research linking interest in public affairs with the behavior in question (Milbrath and Goel, 1977: 36, 39-40, 46-47). Second, the activities had to be available on SRC/CPS questionnaires with virtually identical operationalizations over the entire 24 years between 1960 and 1984. The only exceptions to the second criterion are those mentioned above..

## Exposure to Political Information and Knowledge About Public Affairs

An obvious consequence of interest in public affairs ought to be greater attention to accounts of government and publics in the mass media. According to Milbrath and Goel (1977: 39-40), a number of studies have shown that *"Persons who are attracted to politics* (interested, concerned, curious, intense preferences) *expose themselves more to stimuli about politics than those not so attracted."* In America, this means primarily following accounts of government and politics in various organs of the mass media (TV, newspapers, radio,

---

4. Naturally, if anyone wishes to see the data, I will supply the information upon request.

and newsmagazines). Table 6.2 shows the effect of political interest on an index of media usage for political purposes[5] from 1960 to 1984.

Essentially, these data show that the Apathy Index has a very potent impact on the average number of media organs people have relied upon for information about election campaigns over the 24-year span of time. Moreover, the pattern of the relation is remarkably stable over time, and it varies but little depending upon whether the information comes from a presidential year or an off-year. On average, people who are very apathetic report using just over one medium for information about campaigns, while the very involved say they use three-plus media. In short, the relationship between the Political Apathy Index and the Mass Media Usage Index is very robust throughout the period. Indeed, this is the strongest association depicted in Table 6.1 (see also Table 3.4). And, even with education controlled, the relationship retains 90% of its original potency. Thus, the data in Table 6.2 confirm the finding by earlier research that the politically interested citizen employs a variety of mass media for political information, while the apathetic one either avoids political communications entirely or pays but scant heed.

Moreover, even when several demographic and political factors known to be related to media usage are entered along with the political Apathy Index into multiple stepwise regression analyses, the latter emerges as the strongest predictor in every year.[6] The Apathy Index has by far the strongest impact on the Media Usage Index, explaining from 19% to 29% of the variance in media usage even

---

5. The particular questions used are as follows:

> We're interested in this interview in whether people paid much attention to the election campaign this year. Take newspapers for instance—did you read about the campaign in any newspaper?
> How about radio—did you listen to any speeches or discussions about the campaign on the radio?
> How about television—did you watch any programs about the campaign on television?
> How about magazines—did you read about the campaign in any magazines?

The answers to each question were coded "0" if the answer was "No," and "1" if the respondent said "Yes". Then the answers were simply summed to create an additive index.

6. The particular variables included the Political Apathy Index, education, gender, race, age, a measure of strength of partisanship, sense of citizen duty, and measures of internal and external political efficacy. If someone wishes to see the precise indicants used, I will supply the information upon request.

## Table 6.2:
## Mass Media Usage[a] by Political Apathy Index, 1960-1984

|      | Very Apathetic | Slightly Apathetic | Neutral | Slightly Involved | Very Involved |
|------|------|------|------|------|------|
| 1960 | 1.60 | 2.15 | 2.58 | 2.88 | 3.04 |
|      | (302) | (320) | (385) | (266) | (488) |
| 1964 | 1.29 | 2.14 | 2.48 | 2.80 | 3.17 |
|      | (107) | (241) | (425) | (390) | (273) |
| 1968 | 1.24 | 1.88 | 2.36 | 2.67 | 3.02 |
|      | (112) | (203) | (386) | (319) | (289) |
| 1972[b] | 1.01 | 1.69 | 2.11 | 2.55 | 1.91 |
|      | (72) | (195) | (354) | (275) | (207) |
| 1976 | 1.03 | 1.79 | 2.44 | 2.95 | 3.25 |
|      | (171) | (335) | (719) | (534) | (592) |
| 1978 | 0.93 | 1.54 | 2.35 | 2.66 | 3.04 |
|      | (284) | (478) | (757) | (411) | (259) |
| 1980 | 1.13 | 1.80 | 2.46 | 2.70 | 3.12 |
|      | (120) | (239) | (488) | (273) | (221) |
| 1982 | 0.99 | 1.53 | 2.34 | 2.79 | 3.18 |
|      | (146) | (262) | (473) | (291) | (206) |
| 1984 | 1.20 | 1.84 | 2.50 | 2.83 | 3.07 |
|      | (174) | (310) | (712) | (411) | (307) |

[a] Entries are the mean number of media used for political purposes.
[b] In 1972, the mass media variables were included on only Form 1 of the questionnaire.

Source: University of Michigan's Survey Research Center/Center for Political Studies' National Election Studies

when the effects of other predictors of media utilization such as education, sense of citizen duty, strength of partisanship, race, gender, political efficacy, and age are taken into account.

To assess fully how psychological involvement in public affairs affects one's exposure to information about government and politics, it would be helpful if one had a measure of the latter. Unfortunately, the index depicted in the table focuses solely on whether or not people report following accounts of the election campaign in various organs of the media. Given that Americans are seldom more politically engaged than during the national election season (Bryce, 1891, II: 324; Lane, 1965: 141), it is possible that the data displayed in the table exaggerate usage of media organs for political purposes.

While there are no data available on this question over the 24-year span under consideration, a few tantalizing tidbits are available that suggest any bias in the table is probably small. For example, in 1980 and again in 1984, the CPS asked: "How often do you watch the national network news on early evening TV — every evening, three or four times a week, once or twice a week, or less often?" On average, somewhere between three-fifths and three-quarters of the very interested reported watching TV news every night, compared with only a little over one-in-five of the very apathetic. Moreover, just about 13% of very apathetic persons volunteered "never" watching TV news, compared with between one and five percent of those who were very involved.

Of course, this tells little about whether either the apathetic or the interested citizenry actually pays any attention to news of government and politics while watching the network programs. Fortunately, in 1980 and 1984, the CPS followed up its initial question with this: "When you watch the news on TV, do you pay a great deal of attention to news about government and politics, do you pay some attention, or don't you pay much attention to news about government and politics?" Among the very apathetic, between two-fifths and three-fifths said they don't pay much attention to news about public affairs, while only about one-in-twenty reported paying "a great deal" of heed. Among the very involved, between 82.8% and 90.5% reported paying a great deal of attention to news about government and politics, while only about one percent claimed not to watch news of public affairs. Indeed, the association between scores on the Apathy Index and people's reports of how much attention they gave

*The Consequences of Apathy*

to news about politics was very robust; the Pearsonian product moment correlation coefficients were .568 in 1980 (N = 1277) and .577 in 1984 (N = 1851). Finally, even with education controlled, the relation held 97% of its original strength in both years.

As would be expected, the one medium most relied upon by the apathetic is television. In 1980, the CPS asked: "In general, which do you rely on *most* for news about politics and current events — television, newspapers, magazines, or radio?" Among the very apathetic, 74.8% said TV was the medium used most, 8.4% said newspapers, 1.7% said magazines, and 15.1% said radio. On the other hand, 58.9% of people who were very involved on the Apathy Index said TV was the most used medium, 39.6% said newspapers, 11.2% said magazines, and 6.6% said radio.[7]

The message derived from Table 6.2 and the information described just above is that only a small percentage of Americans who are very uninterested in public affairs is completely out of contact with information about government and politics, while only a trace element among those who are very psychologically involved gets no political information. The obvious question becomes whether and how well utilization of mass media converts to retention of knowledge about public affairs. This is the next topic: Is the interested citizen more knowledgeable than his apathetic neighbor and, if so, how much more so?

Immediately the topic of knowledge about public affairs is broached problems emerge. First, it is very difficult to design an "adequate" test of citizens' knowledge about government and public affairs (see Hyman, Wright, and Reed, 1975; Gallup, 1977). Second, even if such were not so, there is no battery of questions tapping knowledge of government and politics on SRC/CPS questionnaires over the entire period from 1960 to 1984. All that is available are the following questions:

> Do you happen to know which party had the most Congressmen in Washington before the election (this) (last) month? [If yes] Which one?
> Do you happen to know which party elected the most Congressmen in the elections (this) (last) month? [If yes] Which one?

---

7. In this instance the figures sum to more than 100% because a number of the "very involved" listed more than one medium.

Despite its obvious weaknesses, a cumulative index was built so that each respondent could be placed depending on whether he answered incorrectly (or did not know) both items, answered one right, or got both correct.[8] Table 6.3 presents the relations between scores on the Political Apathy Index and the "Political Information" Index between 1960 and 1984.

Three facets of these data merit comment. First, and most important, the data show a close linkage between level of psychological involvement in politics and political knowledge over almost a quarter of a century. Second, as the information in Table 6.1 confirms, the relation of interest to information is robust, and remains so even with formal schooling controlled. Indeed, the Political Apathy Index is always the best predictor of performance on the Political Information Index, even when other factors such as education, gender, race, age, political efficacy, sense of citizen duty, and strength of partisanship are taken into account.[9] Third, unlike the relations of the Apathy Index to the other factors considered in this chapter, the patterns of the association change rather significantly over time. The unusual character of this relationship merits extended comment.

Note that, over the 24 year span, the very apathetic seldom do well on the "Political Information Index;" only once (1968) do 20% of the very apathetic answer both questions correctly, and only on two other occasions (1964, 1984) do more than 15% of the very disinterested qualify as "well informed." It is not unusual for those who eschew all interest in the public affairs to do very poorly on the test of their political information.

On the other hand, there is much greater variance in the "knowledge" scores of people who express interest in politics. Take those who are very interested as a case in point. While they generally do well on the knowledge test, on two occasions (1966, 1980) only about one-third were "well informed." Although one is tempted to put the relatively poor performance of psychologically engaged citizens in 1966 down to the fact that political information is more sparsely available in congressional election years than in presidential ones (Stokes and Miller, 1966), the better performances of the very

---

8. In creating the Political Information Index, people who got an answer correct were coded "1"; those who either missed the answer or said they didn't know were coded "0". Then the two answers were simply summed together.

9. Again, if someone wishes to see the results of the regression analyses, I will supply the information upon request.

## Table 6.3:
## Political Information Index[a] by Political Apathy Index, 1960-1984

|  | Very Apathetic | Slightly Apathetic | Neutral | Slightly Involved | Very Involved |
|---|---|---|---|---|---|
| 1960 | 13.9 | 39.1 | 52.1 | 51.9 | 64.9 |
|  | (310) | (322) | (392) | (262) | (488) |
| 1964 | 17.8 | 41.9 | 57.8 | 71.8 | 81.0 |
|  | (107) | (241) | (422) | (390) | (274) |
| 1966 | 3.0 | 11.7 | 17.3 | 25.8 | 31.9 |
|  | (169) | (205) | (376) | (252) | (260) |
| 1968 | 20.3 | 26.6 | 42.4 | 51.5 | 65.2 |
|  | (118) | (203) | (387) | (324) | (290) |
| 1972[b] | 8.1 | 30.3 | 46.5 | 59.3 | 70.0 |
|  | (74) | (195) | (355) | (275) | (207) |
| 1976 | 10.3 | 26.7 | 42.5 | 58.5 | 75.7 |
|  | (170) | (337) | (727) | (538) | (595) |
| 1978 | 11.1 | 21.4 | 37.9 | 49.6 | 66.8 |
|  | (297) | (491) | (778) | (417) | (265) |
| 1980 | 3.3 | 7.1 | 10.1 | 17.9 | 31.5 |
|  | (120) | (241) | (494) | (273) | (222) |
| 1982 | 4.0 | 15.0 | 19.9 | 35.0 | 54.8 |
|  | (151) | (267) | (477) | (294) | (208) |
| 1984 | 16.8 | 24.9 | 40.8 | 59.0 | 67.8 |
|  | (173) | (313) | (713) | (410) | (307) |

[a]Entries are the percentage "well informed," i.e., answered both questions correctly.
[b]Questions on "Information" appeared only on Form 1 of the CPS questionnaire.

Source: University of Michigan's Survey Research Center/Center for Political Studies' National Election Studies.

interested in both 1978 and 1982 caution against this explanation alone. Also, 1980 was a presidential year, and one in which the public as a whole did very poorly on the Political Information Index. What happened?

Recall that in 1980, for the first time since the early 1950s, the Republicans captured control of the U. S. Senate. Remember also that the second query included in the Information Index asks people which "party elected the most Congressmen in the elections (this) (last) month." Although the data are lacking to test it, a good guess is that while people knew the Republicans had won control of one house of Congress, they were confused as to just which one it was. Hence, many people, including those who were very involved in public affairs, guessed wrongly that it was the House of Representatives. (Since voters are more likely to be aware of the Senate and senators [Hinckley, 1981: 21-24; Jacobson, 1983: 86-92], it is not surprising that so many people got confused.) By 1982 and especially by 1984, the initial confusion on this score had been cleared up, at least among those who pay a good deal of attention to government and politics.

The implication is that people's performance on the test of "political knowledge" depicted in Table 6.3 may depend as much or more on factors outside the individual, such as the results of Senate and House elections and the amount of time devoted in the mass media to these races, than on how much attention the citizenry pays to government and politics *per se*. It would be helpful, therefore, if another test of political information were available that plumbs knowledge of a different character.

Happily, one such can be had, but only for 1972. In that year, the CPS included on Form 1 of its questionnaire the following three questions:

> Do you happen to know how many times an individual can be elected President?
> Do you know how long the term of office is for a United States Senator?
> How long is the term of office for a member of the House of Representatives in Washington?

These questions, although hardly difficult enough to tax anyone who has gone through a junior high school civics class, are part of the backlog of political information the ordinary citizen is supposed to possess. Responses to the three were combined to form a second "Political Knowledge Index,"[10] and the resulting indicant was cross indexed with the Political Apathy Index. As might be expected, there is a connection between how much attention Americans pay to public affairs, and how much they know about basic "nuts and bolts" facts of American government. Among the very apathetic, for example, 50% missed all three questions, and another 41.9% missed two; only 1.4% of the politically indifferent knew all three questions. Among the very interested, on the other hand, 28.3% passed the test "with flying colors" — *i.e.*, got all three correct — while 35.6% got two right, and only 8.3% missed all three.

As can be surmised from the data above, the relation between the Apathy Index and the second "Political Knowledge" test is far more perfect.[11] The Pearsonian correlation coefficient is $r = .342$ ($N = 1098$), indicating the two indicants are, at best, only modestly articulated. However, the first-order partial coefficient falls only to .272 when education is controlled, indicating that most of the strength of the relation between psychological involvement and knowledge cannot be attributed to educational background.

While it would be very helpful if more information were available, the data on the relations between psychological involvement in public affairs and exposure to political communications and knowledge about government indicate that the interested citizen *is* a qualitatively different political actor than the apathetic one. The former is three times as likely to utilize all four of the major media organs for political purposes, and he is many, many times more likely to be politically informed. Moreover, these patterns remain virtually unchanged over nearly a quarter of a century of American history.

Now the question arises, is the politically involved American also a quantitatively different political actor than his apathetic neighbor? That is the topic of the next section.

---

10. The procedure used to create the second "Political Knowledge Index" is the same as that used to build the first. If the respondent answered correctly he was coded "1"; if he either missed or said he didn't know, he was coded "0". Then the three items were summed together.

11. In large measure this is because Americans did so poorly on the "test." Twenty percent missed all three, 38% missed two, 27% missed one, and only 15% got all three correct. In this sense, the scores of the very interested look pretty good.

## Political Interest and Political Activity

In their compendious review of research on political participation, Milbrath and Goel (1977: 46) observe that, "At least a dozen studies spread over different cultures . . . have shown that *persons who are more interested in and concerned about politics are more likely to be activists. . . .*" Milbrath and Goel also point out that "the relationship is so regular that many authors do not bother to report it."

Although it is easy to understand the temptation to take the relation of psychological involvement in public affairs and participation in politics for granted, Milbrath and Goel also indicate why such can be a mistake. They report (1977: 46-47) that data from both the work by Verba and his associates (Verba, Nie, and Kim, 1971) and the "Buffalo Study" show that psychological involvement in public affairs articulates more closely with some "modes" of political activity than others. Political interest is most closely associated with participation in election campaigns, participation in community activities, and political protest, but is less directly tied to voting and so-called "patriotic" activities and contacts with public officials. Thus, before concluding there is an automatic link between interest and participation in politics, it is wise to look closely at different types of activity.

In addition, it is also a good idea to look for possible changes in the relation of interest to participation over time. As has been noted at several points, between the early 1960s and the mid-1980s turnout in national elections has fallen almost ten percent, while psychological involvement in public affairs has fallen much less. Thus, it is well worth the time to look at the implications of interest in politics for political activity over the period from 1960 to 1984.

As has been common since publication of Verba and Nie's, *Participation in America* (1972), several different "modes" of political participation will be treated separately: turnout in national elections, participation in other forms of campaign activities, involvement in non-electoral activities at the local and national levels, engagement in political protest, and writing letters to public officials and newspaper/magazine editors. One need not necessarily subscribe to Verba and Nie's specific characterization of the multi-dimensional nature of political activity to recognize that the relations of psychological involvement to diverse forms of action require individual treatment (Milbrath and Goel, 1977; Barnes, Kaase, *et al.*, 1979; Olsen, 1982; Bennett and Bennett, 1986).

## The Consequences of Apathy

The first form of political participation considered is turnout in national elections. In many ways, voting is the most fundamental of all political activities; it is at once the only one undertaken by more than half the population (Bennett and Bennett, 1986), and the form of activity most closely linked with democratic government in contemporary theories of politics (Pennock, 1979; Pomper, with Lederman, 1980; Margolis, 1983). The relation of interest in public affairs to reported turnout in national elections between 1960 and 1984 is depicted in Table 6.4.

Several aspects of these data are worthy of attention. First, as has been shown in political behavior research over the decades, people who claim to be politically interested report participating in national elections at two to three-and-one-half times the rate of those who are most indifferent. Second, this holds true for the entire span of time covered in the table, despite the fact that these years saw a significant decline of turnout in national elections. Third, as one would expect, the disparity in turnout between the very apathetic and the very involved is greater in congressional elections than in presidential elections. This is very likely because the excitement and media coverage attached to the latter bring in "peripheral" voters, who abstain in "low stimulus" contests, to join with "core" voters, thus enlarging the electorate (Campbell, 1960, 1964).

Closer inspection of the table, however, reveals some interesting changes in the pattern of the relation over the years. While there is very little change in the rate of reported turnout among those who are very involved in public affairs, there has been a substantial drop in turnout between the 1960s and 1980s among those who are "very apathetic," "slightly apathetic," and "neutral" on the Political Apathy Index. The 20.8 percent drop in reported turnout among the "slightly apathetic" is especially noteworthy.

Another point worth noting is that the strength of the relation between the Apathy Index and reported turnout changed but little in presidential years, but increased slightly in off-years. In either case, these relationships are significantly stronger than those reported by Milbrath and Goel (1977: 47), probably because the data in Table 6.4 come from a composite index of psychological involvement in politics rather than from a single indicator of general political interest, as was the case with the Buffalo Study.

Having said this, however, it should be mentioned that the relation

## Table 6.4:
## Reported Turnout[a] by Political Apathy Index, 1960-1984

|  | Very Apathetic | Slightly Apathetic | Neutral | Slightly Involved | Very Involved |
|---|---|---|---|---|---|
| 1960 | 47.2 | 76.7 | 82.7 | 89.5 | 93.1 |
|  | (309) | (322) | (392) | (266) | (491) |
| 1962 | 31.5 | 54.0 | 61.4 | 69.6 | 81.3 |
|  | (279) | (263) | (311) | (255) | (182) |
| 1964 | 46.3 | 65.7 | 77.8 | 85.9 | 88.3 |
|  | (108) | (242) | (428) | (391) | (274) |
| 1966 | 24.3 | 41.7 | 65.6 | 73.1 | 87.4 |
|  | (169) | (206) | (378) | (253) | (261) |
| 1968 | 42.9 | 60.2 | 74.4 | 85.5 | 90.3 |
|  | (119) | (206) | (387) | (324) | (290) |
| 1972 | 35.6 | 51.8 | 71.6 | 83.5 | 90.7 |
|  | (163) | (357) | (690) | (528) | (443) |
| 1976 | 33.9 | 50.7 | 69.9 | 80.6 | 88.6 |
|  | (171) | (337) | (731) | (542) | (595) |
| 1978 | 22.9 | 36.0 | 58.8 | 72.8 | 84.2 |
|  | (297) | (405) | (782) | (419) | (266) |
| 1980 | 34.7 | 48.5 | 73.5 | 84.7 | 93.7 |
|  | (121) | (241) | (494) | (274) | (222) |
| 1982 | 20.4 | 33.8 | 63.6 | 80.7 | 89.0 |
|  | (152) | (266) | (475) | (295) | (210) |
| 1984 | 40.2 | 55.9 | 75.9 | 84.5 | 93.2 |
|  | (174) | (313) | (715) | (412) | (307) |

[a]Entries are the percentage of each category that reported voting in the election.

Source: University of Michigan's Survey Research center/Center for Political Studies' National Election Studies.

*The Consequences of Apathy*

between interest in politics and reported turnout is generally weaker than those for the measures of media usage, political information, and campaign activism (see Table 6.1). The reason for this is not hard to find. As Milbrath and Goel put it (1977: 46), "many individuals vote because of patriotic sentiments, traditional commitments, and group pressure rather than personal involvement."

At that, one must admit to a certain degree of skepticism concerning the potency of the relation between political interest and reported turnout. Could it be that, for a significant percentage of people, the relation is artifactually heightened by the natural tendency for someone who claims interest in politics to feel it necessary to report voting, even though he went nowhere near the polls? There is a well-known tendency to survey respondents to report participating in national elections when in fact they did no such thing (Clausen, 1968-1969; Traugott and Katosh, 1979; Katosh and Traugott, 1981; Sigelman, 1982; Hill and Hurley, 1984). Could it be that there is some systematic relation between the Political Apathy Index and what people tell survey interviewers about their turnout in elections?

Fortunately, beginning in 1964, the SRC/CPS has conducted several voter validation studies. To determine whether there is some systematic connection between the Index and turnout, scores on the Political Apathy Index were cross-indexed with the SRC/CPS's measure of "validated turnout" for the elections of 1964, 1976, 1978, 1980, and 1984. The data are displayed in Table 6.5.

At the outset it should be noted that the concern about artificial inflation of the relation between the Apathy Index and reported turnout was, for the most part, overblown. While there is some diminution in the strength of the association between the Index and validated vote (see Table 6.1), the decline is, with but one exception (1976), very slight. As has been repeatedly established by political behavior studies, people who are more psychologically involved in public affairs are two to three times as likely to vote in national elections as those who are apathetic. Moreover, although data from other congressional elections are needed, it appears that political interest is a slightly better predictor of turnout in off-years than during presidential contests. There is also some indication of a slight increase in the values of the associations between the Index and validated turnout over the twenty years in which validation studies have been done. Finally, the results of discriminant analyses show that the Po-

*143*

## Table 6.5:
## Validated Turnout[a] by Political Apathy Index, 1964-1984

|      | Very Apathetic | Slightly Apathetic | Neutral | Slightly Involved | Very Involved |
|------|----------------|--------------------|---------|-------------------|---------------|
| 1964 | 42.9           | 62.1               | 68.9    | 78.1              | 82.4          |
|      | (84)           | (195)              | (334)   | (329)             | (227)         |
| 1976 | 36.6           | 39.3               | 60.1    | 67.1              | 76.0          |
|      | (157)          | (371)              | (708)   | (528)             | (578)         |
| 1978 | 16.4           | 27.0               | 44.3    | 70.9              | 71.9          |
|      | (287)          | (478)              | (758)   | (409)             | (260)         |
| 1980 | 28.3           | 42.1               | 64.1    | 72.9              | 81.2          |
|      | (106)          | (214)              | (443)   | (255)             | (197)         |
| 1984 | 33.9           | 49.3               | 69.5    | 77.5              | 88.8          |
|      | (165)          | (282)              | (681)   | (373)             | (286)         |

[a] Entries are the percentage certified as having actually voted as established by the SRC/CPS's "Voter Validation Studies."

Source: University of Michigan's Survey Research Center/Center for Political Studies' National Election Studies.

litical Apathy Index is the best predictor of validated turnout over the years, even when the effects of education, age, gender, race, region, strength of partisanship, and political efficacy are taken into account.[12]

Having said all this, however, one must admit that the strength of the relationship between interest in public affairs and turnout is, relatively speaking, muted. As students of voting have repeatedly shown (Campbell, Converse, Miller, and Stokes, 1960; Lipset, 1981; Verba and Nie, 1972; Wolfinger and Rosenstone, 1980), a variety of factors enter the decision to vote or abstain. Many have little relation to the individual's degree of emotional involvement in politics. He may feel he has a moral obligation to vote, to show his allegiance to his country. He may feel duty-bound to back a party or a candidate. He may even be virtually "dragooned" by one of the parties' or candidates' organizations. Each of these factors is probably orthogonal to whether the individual is politically interested or not.

If, therefore, it must be admitted that the Apathy Index is but modestly related to "the simple act of voting" (Lane, 1965: 222), how does it relate to other modes of political activity that require more personal initiative and time? Table 6.6 begins to answer that question.

Three facets of these data need comment. First, those who are interested in public affairs are considerably more likely to engage in campaign activity than are the apathetic. Indeed, among the latter, engagement in some form of campaign activity is so rare as to be virtually undetectable. Second, the consistency of the pattern shown in the table, regardless of either the type of election during which the information was collected or the passage of nearly 25 years, is especially noteworthy. For each of the categories on the Apathy Index, changes in the average number of activities undertaken are virtually nil. Third, the Apathy Index is not only a significant predictor of campaign activism, its potency is virtually unchanged when education is controlled. Moreover, the Index remains the most potent predictor of campaign activity, even when such variables as sense of citizen duty, strength of partisanship, political efficacy, education,

---

12. The goal in these analyses was not to maximize discriminatory power, but to compare the Apathy Index with predictors known to be related to turnout. At that, even with only eight or nine variables in the equation, the average was better than 65% of the cases correctly classified.

*145*

## Table 6.6:
## Campaign Activism[a] by Political Apathy Index, 1960-1984

|      | Very Apathetic | Slightly Apathetic | Neutral | Slightly Involved | Very Involved |
|------|---------------|--------------------|---------|-------------------|---------------|
| 1960 | 0.08          | 0.14               | 0.37    | 0.55              | 0.99          |
|      | (308)         | (319)              | (391)   | (266)             | (485)         |
| 1962 | 0.03          | 0.19               | 0.15    | 0.61              | 0.71          |
|      | (279)         | (260)              | (310)   | (253)             | (181)         |
| 1964 | 0.03          | 0.17               | 0.30    | 0.55              | 0.97          |
|      | (107)         | (241)              | (428)   | (389)             | (274)         |
| 1968 | 0.07          | 0.18               | 0.32    | 0.59              | 0.89          |
|      | (118)         | (204)              | (383)   | (323)             | (284)         |
| 1972 | 0.06          | 0.15               | 0.35    | 0.60              | 0.84          |
|      | (163)         | (357)              | (688)   | (528)             | (441)         |
| 1976 | 0.08          | 0.22               | 0.34    | 0.57              | 0.58          |
|      | (171)         | (335)              | (726)   | (540)             | (595)         |
| 1978 | 0.07          | 0.11               | 0.32    | 0.62              | 0.92          |
|      | (298)         | (492)              | (781)   | (418)             | (267)         |
| 1980 | 0.05          | 0.27               | 0.43    | 0.60              | 0.82          |
|      | (120)         | (242)              | (490)   | (274)             | (222)         |
| 1982 | 0.03          | 0.11               | 0.28    | 0.55              | 0.96          |
|      | (152)         | (267)              | (476)   | (294)             | (207)         |
| 1984 | 0.09          | 0.21               | 0.38    | 0.54              | 0.94          |
|      | (174)         | (312)              | (714)   | (411)             | (305)         |

[a]Entries are the average number of campaign activities reportedly undertaken.

Source: University of Michigan's Survey Research Center/Center for Political Studies' National Election Studies.

## The Consequences of Apathy

gender, race, and age are entered in multiple stepwise regression analyses. Even after the effects of all the other predictors have been taken into account, the Political Apathy Index explains anywhere from 10% to 21% of the variance in the Campaign Activity Index.

Having said this, however, one must point out that even the very interested average less than one campaign act. It is only that participation in campaigns among the very apathetic is so seldom seen that the very involved appear, by comparison, to be "activists." From the very first, students of political participation in America have remarked about the general paucity of engagement in political activity by ordinary citizens. Aside from voting in national elections, no type of political action is undertaken by even half the adult population, and most activities are performed by a tiny fraction of the public (Bennett and Bennett, 1986). The observation by Woodward and Roper (1950: 875) that, "in America the few act politically for the many," remains sound. If even the very interested engage in so few campaign activities, what must be the situation when attention is shifted to nonelectoral modes of participation in politics?

To some degree, the effort to look at the impact of political interest on engagement in nonelectoral modes of political participation is frustrated by a general absence of relevant data. Given the nature of the SRC/CPS's National Election Studies, it is not surprising that virtually all the information extant on political participation consists of activities related to campaigns. Fortunately, all is not lost, for the SRC/CPS has occasionally cast a broader net. On four occasions (1964, 1968, 1972, 1976) the SRC/CPS asked two questions about nonelectoral political action:

> Aside from this particular election campaign, here are some other ways people can be involved in politics. Have you ever written a letter to any public officials giving them your opinion about something that should be done?
>
> Have you ever written a letter to the editor of a newspaper or magazine giving any political opinions?

As one would expect, there is a relation between one's interest in public affairs and one's proclivity for writing to public officials and newspaper/magazine editors. Between 1964 and 1976, on average only four percent of those who were very apathetic had ever written to public officials to express their political opinions, compared to an

*147*

average of almost 42% among the very interested. The strength of this relation ranged from r = .261 in 1964 to r = .296 in 1972, and most of the relationship's potency remained intact even with formal schooling controlled.

There is also an association between the Apathy Index and having written to a newspaper/magazine editor to express opinions on political issues, although it is generally weaker. This is primarily because so few people report writing to editors. One thing is clear: the very apathetic almost never write to editors! In two of the years for which the variable is available (1964 and 1972) not one person among the very apathetic had ever communicated with an editor to express a political opinion. Among the very involved, the situation was somewhat better; on average just over eleven percent of the most interested had at some time written to an editor. The strength of the relationship ranged from r = .095 in 1968 to r = .220 in 1972. Most of its potency was maintained even with education taken into account.

There are two ways to look at the relation of the Apathy Index to writing letters to public officials and editors. One is to point out that, especially with regard to writing to editors, the very interested are not *all* that active. The other view notes that letter writing occurs about ten times more often among the very interested than among the very apathetic. To help determine whether the glass is half empty or half full, let's look at other modes of nonelectoral participation.

While many may consider an analysis of just the two letter writing items to be "slim pickin's," the CPS's 1976 National Election Study contains a treasure trove of questions about participation in nonelectoral activities at both the national and local levels. A total of five activities dealt with the national level, and six were centered on local politics. Two of the questions probed engagement in protests and demonstrations. To determine how political interest affects participation in nonelectoral activity, three separate additive indices were created: (1) a National Participation Index,[13] (2) a Local Partic-

---

13. The National Participation Index is an additive index of the following items: [During the past two or three years, have you. . . .]

> Written a letter to the editor of a magazine or newspaper about some national problem?
> Worked with others or joined an organization trying to do something about some national problem?
> Spoken to or written your congressman or some other national leader?
> Signed a petition either for or against action by the national government?

People who said "Yes" were coded "1" while those who said "No" were coded "0".

## The Consequences of Apathy

ipation Index,[14] and (3) a Demonstration Participation Index.[15] Table 6.7 depicts the relations between the Political Apathy Index and the three indicants of nonelectoral participation.

Looking at these data it would appear that, indeed, the glass is half full. People who are more psychologically involved in public affairs are considerably more likely than the apathetic to engage in nonelectoral activities, be they "elite challenging" modes such as engaging in demonstrations and protests, or non-elite challenging at both local and national levels. Depending upon the type of activity in question, those who are very interested are from 3.75 to ten times more likely than the very apathetic to be politically active. The Pearsonian product moment correlation coefficients range from $r = .095$ for the relation of the Apathy Index to the Demonstration Participation Index to $r = .280$ and $r = 281$ for the Index's respective associations with the Local Participation and National Participation indices. Moreover, when the Apathy Index is included in multiple stepwise regression analyses with such factors as education, gender, race, age, sense of citizen duty, strength of partisanship, and internal and external political efficacy, it is by far the strongest predictor of participation at the national level, is second only to education at the local level, and virtually ties age as a predictor of engagement in demonstrations. In short, there is ample evidence to show that one's level of psychological involvement in public affairs is a strong and consistent

---

14. The Local Participation Index is an additive index of the following activities: [During the past two or three years, have you. . . .]

> Attended meetings of city council or school board?
> Written a letter to the editor of the local newspaper about some public problem?
> Worked with others or joined an organization in your community to do something about some community problem?
> Spoken to or written an official about some local problem?
> Signed a petition for or against action by the local government?

Those who said "Yes" were coded "1" and those saying "No" were coded "0".

15. The Demonstration Participation Index is the sum of the replies to two questions: [During the past two or three years, have you. . . .]

> Taken part in a sit-in, demonstration, or protest concerned with some national problem?
> Taken part in a sit-in, demonstration, or protest concerned with some local problem?

An individual who replied "Yes" was coded "1"; someone who said "No" was given a score of "0".

## Table 6.7:
## Non electoral Political Participation by Political Apathy Index, 1976

|  | Very Apathetic | Slightly Apathetic | Neutral | Slightly Involved | Very Involved |
|---|---|---|---|---|---|
| National Part.[a] | 0.08 (171) | 0.16 (337) | 0.33 (730) | 0.44 (541) | 0.81 (592) |
| Local Part.[b] | 0.36 (171) | 0.38 (335) | 0.78 (727) | 0.97 (541) | 1.35 (592) |
| Demonstrations[c] | 0.9% (171) | 1.2% (337) | 1.8% (728) | 4.0% (542) | 5.9% (594) |

[a] Entries are the mean number of activities performed. The National Participation index is an additive index of four activities: contacting a congressman/national political leader; signing a petition regarding a national problem; working with others on a national problem; and writing to an editor regarding a national problem.

[b] Entries are the mean number of activities performed. The Local Participation Index is an additive index of five activities: signing a petition regarding a local problem; working with others on a local problem; contacting a local official; attending a school board/local city council meeting; and writing to an editor regarding a local problem.

[c] Entries are the percentage that had engaged in at least one demonstration. The Demonstrations Index is an additive index of two items: demonstrating regarding a national problem and demonstrating regarding a local problem.

Source: University of Michigan's Center for Political Studies' 1976 National Election Study.

## The Consequences of Apathy

predictor of his/her proclivity to engage in various forms of nonelectoral political activity.

However, as was the case with participation in campaign activities and writing letters to public officials and editors, the data in Table 6.7 show that those who are very involved in politics can be considered to be political "activists" only by comparison to the dearth of activity among the apathetic. The relatively low rates of political activity among even the very interested become even more apparent when one recalls that the questions on letter writing ask the respondent if he "has ever" written to a public official or editor, while the nonelectoral activity items in 1976 ask people if they have done any of these activities "during the last two or three years." Since stretching the time frame of performance of a political activity generally increases the likelihood that people will reply in the affirmative (Bennett and Bennett, 1986), it is remarkable that the rates of reported participation among the very involved are not higher than they seem to be.

The discovery that many more people claim interest in the public affairs than actually engage in political action recalls Dahl's (1961: 280) observation that "it is easier to be merely interested than to be active. Considering the psychic economy of the individual, interest is cheap, whereas activity is relatively expensive." Dahl's point is well taken, but the context within which he frames it may miss something important. It is one thing if people who say they pay a great deal of attention to public affairs refrain from active engagement in the political arena because they choose not to pay the price of admission in terms of the time, emotional and physical energy political participation costs. Archie Bunker was certainly interested in government and politics, but he seldom stirred from his battered old chair other than to go to the kitchen to "rent" an occasional beer.

But, what if Bunker's political inactivity stemmed from a deep-seated conviction that, based on what he had "learned" by paying heed to politics, the political system was so loaded against him and his kind that any effort on his part would have small chance of success? What if there are citizens "out there" in substantial numbers who maintain abiding interest in politics but are politically passive because they think the leadership of the American political system cannot be trusted and that the system is unresponsive to their efforts at influence? Are people who are interested but politically inactive more like Charles Hadley's (1978: 39-40) "positive apathetics," *i.e.* people who do not vote "because their lives are going so well that voting seems irrelevant?" Or are there more people out there like Gilmour and Lamb's (1975: 107-109): "Abstainers," *i.e.* politically interested, but also passive *and* alienated? This is the question taken up in the final section.

## Apathy, Basic Political Orientations, and Political Activity

From the beginning, students of American political behavior have been concerned about the ramifications for the political system of grassroots political indifference. If the citizen is politically apathetic because he has more pressing personal or family concerns and is basically satisfied with things as they are, psychological detachment from the political order is unlikely to pose a significant threat to the established order. But, take the opposite case: someone who keeps abreast of political happenings but is convinced politicians can't be trusted and the system is loaded against him. Surely the friends of democracy cannot but look upon such a combination of basic political dispositions without at least mild trepidation.

Much as these concerns have exercised political behavior researchers, they have seldom been in position to present data relevant to the problem. Now, at least, such are available. Using the Political Apathy Index as the centerpiece, what are the behavioral consequences of apathy and indifference in conjunction with the beliefs that (a) political leaders are either trustworthy or not, and (b) the American system is either responsive to the ordinary citizens or not. The particular behavior in question is voting, as established by the SRC/CPS's voter validation studies.

Little justification is needed for looking at voting in national elections. According to Richard Rose (1980: 1): "Elections are the central institution for popular participation in government. Without elections, the mass of the population has no means to influence the choice of a nation's governors." Moreover, as has been mentioned, voting is the sole form of political action undertaken by more than half the citizenry.

Selection of the two basic political orientations — trust in government and external political efficacy — requires a more extended consideration. Certainly it is fairly easy to understand why "external political efficacy" — "the belief that the authorities or regime are responsive to influence attempts" (Balch, 1974: 24), would be included in a study of the implications of apathy for democratic politics. As V. O. Key puts it (1961: 547; see also Almond and Verba, 1963: 479-481):

> . . . if a democracy is to exist, the belief must be widespread that public opinion, at least in the long run, affects the course of public action. In a technical sense that belief may be a myth, an article of faith, yet its maintenance requires that it possess a degree of validity. It seems that those clerics who most successfully perpetuate their myths are those who can turn up a miracle for their communicants now and then.

Inclusion of a measure of ordinary people's trust in political leaders may be a bit more problematic. While most students of democratic government believe that public confidence and trust in political leaders and institutions is an essential ingredient of the system's legitimacy (Easton, 1965, 1975; A. Miller, 1974a, 1974b; J. Wright, 1976; Caddell, 1979; Lipset and Schneider, 1983a), a few writers maintain that public distrust of elites is a healthy thing in a democracy (Hart, 1978). For present purposes, attention is centered on Gamson's (1968: 46-48) formulation of the implications of trust or cynicism for political action or inaction. Are people who are cynical of political leaders more likely to be politically indifferent and inactive or is distrust a goad to pay attention to public affairs and to "throw the bums out?" The well-documented decline of public confidence and trust in political leaders since the mid-1960s adds another reason for focusing on this dimension (A. Miller, 1974a; Abramson, 1983; Hill and Luttbeg, 1983; Lipset and Schneider, 1983a).

Over the years there has been sufficient analysis of the impact of external political efficacy beliefs and trust in government upon popular participation in government. Belief that political elites are unresponsive to ordinary citizens contributes to abstention from the polls (Campbell, Gurin, and Miller, 1954; Almond and Verba, 1963; Gilmour and Lamb, 1975; J. Wright, 1976; Reiter, 1979; Abramson and Aldrich, 1982; Abramson, 1983; Lipset and Schneider, 1983a), while cynicism appears to be unrelated to turnout (Citrin, 1974; Lipset and Schneider, 1983a). It has also been established that, contrary to Gamson's (1968) expectation, those who are politically efficacious and cynical vote less than those who are efficacious but trusting (Fraser, 1970; Hawkins, Marando, and Taylor, 1971).

What has not been plumbed, however, is how these two basic political orientations interact with citizen political interest/apathy to affect participation. However, before commencing the analysis, three points need to be made, one substantive, two methodological. First, it has already been established in Chapter 4 that psychological involvement in politics is related to perceptions of governmental responsiveness but only tenuously connected to trust in government. Second, for present purposes no assumptions need be made concerning the causal ordering of citizen political interest and other basic political orientations such as efficacy and trust. Regardless of whether one thinks interest "causes" efficaciousness and/or trust, or the other way around, the data necessary to test such hypotheses do not exist in the SRC/CPS archives.

The final methodological point deals with the necessity to recompute the operationalization of some concepts. In order to secure sufficient cases for analysis, the Political Apathy Index was recomputed and collapsed into a dichotomy.[16] Similarly, the Trust in Government Index had to be recalculated into just three categories: Trustful, Neutral, and Cynical. Fortunately, the External Political Efficacy Index could be left unchanged.

Table 6.8 presents the relations between validated turnout and the Political Apathy and External Political Efficacy indices from 1964 to 1984. As can be readily seen, both measures combine to influence the person's likelihood of voting. People who are both politically interested and perceive government to be responsive to influence attempts are from 25 to 40 percentage points more likely to have voted in national elections than those who are both indifferent and believe efforts to influence government will be bootless. (It should be noted in passing that political interest and external political efficacy both contribute to turnout, with the former the more potent predictor.[17]) Moreover, the disparity in turnout rates among the two "extreme" groupings in the table became more pronounced after

16. The Index was cut at precisely the midpoint.
17. Such could have been inferred from the results of the multiple discriminant analyses described above. Indeed, these data show the Apathy Index to be a much more potent predictor than external efficacy beliefs.

## Table 6.8:
## Validated Vote[a] by Political Apathy Index and External Political Efficacy, 1964-1984

|  | Apathetic Lo Exteff | Apathetic Med Exteff | Apathetic Hi Exteff | Involved Lo Exteff | Involved Med Exteff | Involved Hi Exteff |
|---|---|---|---|---|---|---|
| 1964 | 54.1 | 56.4 | 62.7 | 71.2 | 77.8 | 79.0 |
|  | (111) | (117) | (150) | (104) | (185) | (461) |
|  | [8.5][b] | [8.9] | [11.4] | [7.9] | [14.1] | [35.1] |
| 1976 | 35.5 | 42.5 | 56.1 | 58.4 | 71.5 | 76.7 |
|  | (320) | (186) | (160) | (403) | (414) | (669) |
|  | [14.9] | [8.6] | [7.4] | [18.7] | [19.2] | [31.1] |
| 1978 | 26.3 | 24.8 | 31.2 | 53.5 | 56.21 | 64.3 |
|  | (419) | (303) | (285) | (286) | (315) | (451) |
|  | [20.3] | [14.7] | [13.8] | [13.9] | [15.3] | [21.9] |
| 1980 | 36.5 | 49.0 | 53.0 | 65.9 | 73.0 | 81.5 |
|  | (197) | (147) | (132) | (167) | (226) | (276) |
|  | [17.2] | [12.8] | [11.5] | [14.6] | [19.7] | [24.0] |
| 1984 | 36.4 | 58.5 | 58.2 | 70.5 | 77.7 | 82.3 |
|  | (228) | (195) | (273) | (176) | (247) | (634) |
|  | [13.0] | [11.1] | [15.6] | [10.0] | [14.1] | [36.2] |

[a] Entries are the percentage certified as having actually voted, as established by the SRC/CPS's "Voter Validation Studies."

[b] Entries inside the brackets are the percent of the total sample in each year.

Source: University of Michigan's Survey Research Center/Center for Political Studies' National Election Studies.

1964. Whereas just over half those who were apathetic and inefficacious nonetheless voted in the Johnson-Goldwater contest, in the 1970s and 1980s only a little over a third of such people voted in presidential elections and just over a quarter cast ballots in 1978.

It should also be noted that the combination of apathy and political inefficaciousness increased to become a larger portion of the total public, from 8.5% of the total in 1964 to somewhere between 13% and 20% in the 1970s and 1980s. Commensurately, the combination of political interest with strong belief in governmental responsiveness declined from 35% of the total public in 1964 to somewhere between one-fifth to one quarter of the electorate between 1976 and 1980. 1984 saw a resurgence of the combination of involvement and strong perceptions of governmental responsiveness, without, however, a shrinkage of the percentage of people who were both apathetic and low on external political efficacy. Small wonder, then, that turnout in national elections declined from 61.9% of the eligible electorate in 1964 to just over 53% in 1984. Those factors that undermine people's belief that attempts at political influence will be successful and corrode interest in the public affairs undercut the likelihood that citizens will partake of democracy's most fundamental act.

If a combination of apathy and low external efficacy diminishes the probability that citizen will vote, what are the consequences of the interaction of citizen political interest with trust in government? Table 6.9 supplies the answer. Inspection of the data reveals that, unlike the clear patterns in Table 6.8, the various combinations of the Apathy Index and the Trust in Government Index do not produce straightforward consequences for turnout. There is no gainsaying the fact that political interest has by far the stronger impact on voting. The relation of trust/cynicism to turnout is much more complex. Generally speaking those who do not believe politicians can be trusted are slightly more likely to vote than citizens who are trustful. However, the differences are usually so small as to fall well within statistical error. Such small differences simply reinforce the contention of those who discount any relation of trust to turnout.

It is interesting to note that, at least in recent presidential elections, apathetic citizens who are cynical are somewhat more likely to have voted than those who are confident of political leaders. At that, however, more than half of such people abstained between 1976 and 1980, and almost half were abstainers in 1984. Moreover, be-

## Table 6.9:
## Validated Vote[a] by Political Apathy Index and Trust in Government Index, 1964-1984

|  | Apathetic Trustful | Apathetic Neutral | Apathetic Cynical | Involved Trustful | Involved Neutral | Involved Cynical |
|---|---|---|---|---|---|---|
| 1964 | 55.1 | 62.5 | 55.6 | 77.8 | 78.7 | 79.1 |
|  | (176) | (75) | (90) | (315) | (225) | (196) |
|  | [16.3][b] | [7.0] | [8.4] | [29.2] | [20.9] | [18.2] |
| 1976 | 36.4 | 41.0 | 44.8 | 72.7 | 71.5 | 70.4 |
|  | (70) | (106) | (418) | (156) | (295) | (933) |
|  | [3.5] | [5.4] | [21.1] | [7.9] | [14.9] | [47.2] |
| 1978 | 29.0 | 29.9 | 29.2 | 55.9 | 61.7 | 59.0 |
|  | (100) | (144) | (631) | (102) | (167) | (702) |
|  | [5.4] | [7.8] | [34.2] | [5.5] | [9.1] | [38.0] |
| 1980 | 38.7 | 41.3 | 47.3 | 71.8 | 79.5 | 73.0 |
|  | (31) | (63) | (357) | (39) | (117) | (477) |
|  | [2.9] | [5.8] | [32.9] | [3.6] | [10.8] | [44.0] |
| 1984 | 52.4 | 48.0 | 53.4 | 81.0 | 78.8 | 79.1 |
|  | (124) | (177) | (343) | (189) | (274) | (549) |
|  | [7.5] | [10.7] | [20.7] | [11.4] | [16.6] | [33.2] |

[a]Entries are the percentage certified as having actually voted, as established by the SRC/CPS's "Voter Validation Studies."
[b]Entries inside the brackets are the percent of the total sample in each year.

Source: University of Michigan's Survey Research Center/Center for Political Studies' National Election Studies.

tween 1964 and the early 1980s, the combination of apathy with cynical orientations increased from only eight percent of the total public to one-third.[18] Thus, the data in Table 6.9 indicate that there is a sizable number of Americans who are at once cynical, indifferent, and politically inert.

Does such a large group constitute a potential threat to democratic politics in America? In large measure, the answer depends upon what it "means" to be cynical in American politics in the 1970s and 1980s. For some observers, the cynical constitute a corpus of citizens profoundly alienated from politics as usual in the United States (A. Miller, 1974a, 1974b; Caddell, 1979). Other writers demur, claiming that, at least in the context of contemporary American political culture and the particular measuring instrument employed by the SRC/CPS, to be cynical means little more than ritualistic expression of fashionable cliches (Citrin, 1974) or, at most, partisan disgruntlement with the latest electoral outcome (W. Miller, 1979). In all likelihood, the last view comes closest to the truth (Sniderman, 1981; Abramson and Finifter, 1981).

What is needed is an indicant more clearly related to political "alienation" as conceived in terms of "estrangement" from the established order in American politics (Lane, 1962). Fortunately, one is available in the SRC/CPS National Election Studies, albeit only for 1976.[19] In that year, the CPS asked its respondents two questions:

> Some people believe a change in our form of government is needed to solve the problems facing our country, while others feel no real change is necessary. Do you think a big change is needed in our form of government, or should it be kept pretty much as it is?
> I'm going to read you a pair of statements about our form of government, and I'd like you to tell me which one you agree with more. Would you say . . . "I am proud of many things about our form of government," or "I can't find much in our government to be proud of"?

For present purposes, someone who believes that big changes are needed in the American "form of government" and cannot find much

---

18. The size of the group with this combination of dispositions fell by almost twelve percentage points between 1980 and 1984.

19. Actually, the same two questions were asked on Form 2 of the 1972 questionnaire, but there is no validated vote available for the entire 1972 sample.

*The Consequences of Apathy*

to feel proud of will be classified as "Alienated." Someone who is proud of our system of government and wants it kept pretty much as is will be termed "Allegiant." And people with other combinations of replies will be said to have "Mixed" orientations.

Table 6.10 depicts validated turnout by the Political Apathy Index and the "Political Alienation Index" for 1976. In some ways, these data echo those in Table 6.9. In both, the Political Apathy Index has clearly the stronger impact on turnout. The effects of either the Trust in Government Index or the "Political Alienation Index" are much less.

However, it is also clear that the latter has more effect on the probability of voting, at least in 1976, than the former. Indeed, the "Allegiant" are considerably more likely to have voted than the "Alienated," regardless of whether they are involved or apathetic. Persons with "Mixed" orientations who are apathetic are just a bit less likely to vote than the "Alienated," but slightly more likely to vote if they are interested.

Perhaps the most interesting information in the table is the fact that

### Table 6.10:
### Validated Vote[a] by Political Apathy Index and Political Alienation Index, 1976

Political Alienation Index

| Alienated | | Mixed | | Allegiant | |
|---|---|---|---|---|---|
| Apathetic | Involved | Apathetic | Involved | Apathetic | Involved |
| 37.7 | 55.4 | 35.1 | 61.5 | 51.8 | 75.4 |
| (96) | (135) | (280) | (356) | (222) | (735) |

[a] Entries are the percentage certified as actually having voted as established by the CPS's 1976 "Voter Validation Study."

Source: University of Michigan's Center for Political Studies' 1976 National Election Study.

Americans who are "allegiant" vote regardless of whether they are politically interested or not, while their fellow citizens who are "alienated" are most likely to abstain if apathetic, and only slightly more likely than not to vote even if psychologically involved in public affairs. It is also noteworthy that there is a relationship between the two measures: 41.7% of the "alienated" are politically apathetic, compared with only 23.2% of "allegiant" Americans. (It should also be noted that 44.1% of those with "mixed" orientations are also politically indifferent.)

The data in Table 6.10 suggest that those who have worried about the political consequences of apathy for the democratic process may have exaggerated the problem, but they haven't entirely "missed the boat." In 1976, at least, 12.6% of the adult electorate could be classified as disenchanted with "our system of government," and yet 59% of these people maintained some emotional involvement in public affairs. Moreover, just over half these people voted.

In short, in 1976 there was a small but significant proportion of the American citizenry which, although disenchanted with "our form of government," nonetheless maintained an interest in government and politics and was marginally involved in the electoral process. Whether such people constitute a potentially mobilizable public on behalf of a leader or movement committed to substantial alterations in the American form of government cannot be determined. Also, in the absence of more information over time, it cannot be ascertained whether this group is waxing or waning.[20] All that can be said for the moment is that in the mid-1970s there was a sizable minority of Americans who were both politically involved and yet alienated from their government. While they constitute but a fragment of the American public, their presence must be a source of concern for those who worry about the consequences of political indifference or interest for democratic politics.

## Conclusion

The purpose of this chapter was two-fold. First, it sought to determine whether the apathetic citizen is qualitatively different from

---

20. If the data from Form 2 of the 1972 CPS's National Election Study are any indication, the size of the alienated group grew somewhat by 1976.

his interested neighbor. He is. The citizen who is very interested is both more likely to pay attention to a variety of media, and to be politically informed. Whether the interested American is a more "rational" political actor than the indifferent one cannot be determined with precision, but he brings a better backlog of politically relevant information to bear in his decision making.

Second, Americans who maintain interest in the public affairs are also much more likely to be politically active, at least in terms of voting. When it comes to other forms of participation in politics, be it campaign activities or nonelectoral modes, the very interested are much more active than the very apathetic. But in absolute terms, they engage in political action only occasionally.

It is also clear that citizen political interest/apathy has both real and potential implications for the democratic process. From 1964 to 1984, Americans who were both apathetic and convinced they had little or no clout in the political process abstained from voting. Thus, as the numbers of both the indifferent and the politically inefficacious swelled after 1964, it is not surprising that turnout likewise fell. Finally, it is also clear that the combination of indifference with political disenchantment has detrimental consequences for voting in national elections. If the 1976 data are to be believed, there is a small but important percentage of the mass public which is alienated from the American form of government, but still pays attention to the public affairs. Whether such a combination of basic political orientations constitutes a serious problem for democracy in America cannot be determined with the data in hand. But certainly the existence of even a small proportion of politically involved but alienated citizens must be a worrisome thing.

# CHAPTER 7

# SUMMARY AND CONCLUSIONS

In the beginning, the question was posed whether the citizenry had become more apathetic. If Almond and Verba's (1963) characterization of an involved electorate in the early 1960s was accurate, how do Americans fare now?

Between the year that saw the razor-thin victory of John F. Kennedy and that witnessing the overwhelming re-election of Ronald Reagan, turnout in national elections fell nearly ten percent. The decline in voting led many politicians, pundits, and professors to worry that American were turning away from politics and governmental affairs.

However, as shown here, the public has not become as apathetic as many observers have feared. If "apathy" is defined as an individual's characteristic degree of indifference to public affairs, the American people are about as politically attentive in the 1980s as they had been in the early 1960s, although slightly less so than in the late 1960s and early 1970s. Moreover, despite the momentous changes that have occurred in American society and politics over the last quarter of a century, levels of political apathy have fluctuated within a fairly narrow range.

Moreover, the same factors that shaped political interest in the early 1960s continue to do so today. Evidence from the SRC/CPS's national election studies indicates that people are attentive to public affairs because they believe they ought to be, they are strongly committed to a major political party or candidate, they are well-educated, they are over 30 years of age, and they believe the federal government is attentive and responsive to public opinion. Such information permits us to sketch a profile of the apathetic American over the past quarter of a century. The indifferent person is young, with limited education and lower socioeconomic status, unattached to either major political party, uncommitted to political candidates, and unwilling to believe either that he has any moral obligation to pay heed to public affairs or that there would be any likely positive benefits from doing so.

As a result of his disinclination to be interested in what happens in political life, the apathetic American tends either to avoid following accounts of public affairs in the mass media entirely, or to catch just an occasional glance at the evening news shows on TV. Moreover, he tends to be innocent of even the least taxing information about public affairs; more demanding "tests" of standard "civics books" knowledge escape him entirely. The indifferent citizen may turn out from time to time in presidential elections, probably driven to the polls by a sense of citizen duty. However, he almost never shows up at the polls in off-year elections, and he is certainly unlikely to take part in any more demanding electoral activities. Finally, to borrow a term from an earlier age, he is definitely a "slacker" (Munro, 1928) when it comes to engagement in political activity outside the electoral arena.

In the course of outlining this profile of the apathetic American, several propositions derived from previous research were tested at some length. Some of the most interesting deal with age and aging. A particularly important finding is the discovery that there is a drop-off in interest late in life. Whether this is due to the so-called "disengagement" phenomenon cannot be directly determined with the data at hand. However, an intriguing discovery is that the diminution in interest occurs later in life during the 1980s than had been the case in the 1960s. Two factors may explain this: the increased schooling among the very aged of the 1980s and, even more so, the rise of age-related issues into the political agenda since 1980. Since it is unlikely that the physiological and psychological changes associated with aging have changed much since the 1960s, the fact that the onset of diminished political interest has been delayed by about ten years during the past two decades militates against the assumption that increased apathy is a "natural" by-product of retirement from active involvement in the work force.

Another important discovery is the necessity to look at the effects of age on political interest separately for men and women. During

*Summary and Conclusions*

the late 1960s, when young men, no doubt concerned about the Vietnam War, became unusually attentive, young women remained basically indifferent to politics. Despite having finally equalled men's rates of turnout in national elections, women continue to be less psychologically involved in public affairs. They are slower to pick up an interest in political life as they age, and they withdraw attention to politics earlier than men. While it cannot be determined using just SRC/CPS data, it is likely that the continuing "gender gap" in political interest is a function of gender differences in socialization during childhood and adolescence (Rapoport, 1981).

One important change over the past quarter of a century has been the increased exposure of the young to more formal schooling (Converse, 1972; Bennett, 1985). It was once assumed that a better educated populace would be a more politically engaged one. However, despite their significant advantages in terms of years of educational attainment, young Americans during the 1970s and 1980s have been even more politically indifferent than young people had been in the mid- and late-1960s. The very low levels of political interest among the very young during the late 1970s and early 1980s is one of the more noteworthy findings of this volume.

Increased exposure to higher education is not the only advantage accruing to young people who entered the electorate during the past dozen years or so. They are the first generation of Americans to grow up with access to the type of televised coverage of political news begun by the major networks in 1963. Yet despite having more years of formal schooling and "easier" access to news about government and public affairs, young adults in the early 1980s remain steeped in political apathy, especially if they have not gone to college.

The obvious question is why. Two factors appear responsible. One is young people's decreased attachment to the major political parties since the mid-1960s. The reasons for the decreased identification with the established parties among those who have entered the electorate during the past ten to fifteen years are beyond our scope (see Beck, 1974; Wattenberg, 1984). Suffice it to recall Berelson, Lazarsfeld and McPhee's (1954) warning that that which undermines partisanship likewise diminishes political interest. Interestingly, some early assessments of voting behavior in 1984 have identified a growing attachment among the young to the Republican Party (Ladd, 1985; Pomper, 1985). While that development did not have an immediate impact on young people's attention to public affairs, it may have ramifications in the future.

The second factor is the perception by the young, especially those who have not had college exposure, that government does not respond to public opinion. Many years ago, V. O. Key, Jr. (1961) warned that a corollary of decreased belief in governmental attentiveness and responsiveness to ordinary citizens would be less attention to public affairs. In the 1980s, at least among those young people who have not gone to college, Key's warning has come home to roost.

The time at which a less politically interested "generation" of young Americans began entering the electorate — the early 1970s — is noteworthy. The rapidity with which a politically engaged — at least the male — youth cohort was supplanted between the late 1960s and early- to mid-1970s by apathetic ones corresponds with the findings of Jennings and Niemi (1981) in their comparison with the political orientations of the high school senior classes of 1965 and 1973. While the former had been characterized as unusually politicized (Jennings and Niemi, 1974; Beck and Jennings, 1979), based on its impressions of the qualities of "the good citizen," the latter was much, much different. As Jennings and Niemi (1981: 225) put it, "We can categorize the 1973 cohort as distinctly less imbued with the traditional virtues associated with civic training. Politics was less central in their lives and the participant culture was less valued. Indeed, one sees signs of a withdrawal, of a turning inward." Obviously, the 1973 apathetic senior class has been followed into the voting-age population by almost a dozen more.

Jennings and Niemi (1981: 226) point to several possible explanations for the increased apathy among the class of '73. One was the fallout of an image of "dirty politics" associated with Watergate. But there were two more fundamental factors as well. Perhaps the seniors of 1973 were convinced that Americans were sufficiently politically attentive and active that "the country had nothing to be ashamed of on that score." Or, possibly they felt that, "compared with other evils, the lack of political activity . . . [was] not serious, that there . . . [were] other shortcomings far more crucial."

Perhaps. At any rate, the tendency for the very young to be extremely apathetic has continued throughout the 1970s and into the 1980s. While their decreased attachment to the major parties and

*Summary and Conclusions*

weakened belief — at least among those who have not attended college — that government is attentive and responsive to people like themselves doubtlessly account for a goodly portion of the increased apathy among the young in recent times, there are other factors also at work. For example, throughout the late 1970s and early 1980s, there were signs of a lessened belief among the very young that they had a moral obligation to be politically active (Bennett, 1983). Evidently that also carried over into their willingness even to pay attention to what went on in politics and government.

The continued entry into the electorate over a dozen years of extremely indifferent young people who are otherwise advantaged by greater exposure to higher education and easier access to news about government and public affairs is one of the main reasons for the slightly diminished political interest among the public as a whole in recent years. The deeper apathy the very young have brought with them upon attainment of majority status, along with a delayed emergence of attention to politics as they have passed through the third decade of life, have slightly off-set the delayed diminution of interest among the elderly and the normal awakening of interest associated with aging among cohorts who had entered the electorate before the 1970s.

It is unfortunate that these and other changes in young people's basic political orientations have occurred at a time when scholarly interest in the process of political socialization has waned. Most of the major studies of childhood and adolescent political socialization (*e.g.* Greenstein, 1965; Hess and Torney, 1967; Easton and Dennis, 1969; Langton, 1969; see also Sigel, ed., 1970; Dennis, ed., 1973) were based on data collected in the late 1950s and early 1960s. While there was a voluminous literature on student politics in the late 1960s and early 1970s, considerably less attention has been given to the topic recently (for one exception, see Sigel and Hoskin, 1981). Perhaps it is symptomatic of the lessened commitment to the study of childhood and adolescent political socialization that, although the multi-volume *Handbook of Political Science* (Greenstein and Polsby, eds., 1975), published a decade ago, contained a chapter on the topic (Sears, 1975), the American Political Science Association's recent collection of essays assessing *The State of the Discipline* (Finifter, 1983) does not. Perhaps the time has arrived for a renewed emphasis on the subject.

Basic to the study of psychological involvement are its consequences both for the citizen and the state. In terms of the former, there is no question that the apathetic person differs qualitatively and quantitatively from his interested neighbor. It would be going too far to equate the apathetic individual with Almond and Verba's (1963: 17-19) "parochical" orientation to politics. While the parochial *is* indifferent to public affairs, his apathy stems from a hidebound lack of awareness of how his daily existence is influenced by what politicians and the state do. A quarter of a century ago, Almond and Verba (1963: 99) found less than ten percent of the public fit their characterization of the parochial. Today, it is highly likely that a smaller percentage of the adult populace would qualify.

No, while there is a relationship between awareness of government's impact on one's existence and the degree of attention paid to political life (see below), today's apathetic individual is simply *indifferent* to what politicians and bureaucrats do. But he pays a price for his inattention. Said cost stems not just from the fact that he seldom casts a vote or that his visage is almost never seen performing other forms of political activity. That politicians pay greatest heed to those who are perceived as most actively supportive of them is a truism in American politics, but one that contains more than a kernel of truth (Fenno, 1978: chap. 1). Thus, to the degree that the political opinions of apathetic Americans differ from interested and active ones — which is only partly so (Shaffer, 1982) — and to the extent that decision-makers take only the wishes of the latter into consideration — a little more likely — the wages of political inattention amount to a form of "taxation without representation."

But there is an even greater price for political inattention. It is, bluntly put, ignorance. The individual who pays no heed to public affairs is so seldom armed with relevant and up-to-date information about political events, issues, and personalities, that even if he were suddenly to become interested and concerned, it is highly unlikely that his response would be timely, appropriate, or effective. So much time and psychic energy would be required to acquire a relevant backlog of accurate information in order to "catch on" to a political situation, the previously indifferent individual, even if he sorely wished to do so, would probably prefer to retire to his normal inattentive state. For this reason, if no other, it is not surprising to find people who are apathetic at one time will remain so later, while

*Summary and Conclusions*

those who are politically involved at $t_1$ find it easier to remain so at $t_2$. When one considers that, at least in the 1980s, the typical apathetic American is young, of limited educational background and without strong commitment to a political party, the psychic "price" to be paid for trying to overcome past indifference becomes truly burdensome.

An equally serious question is what apathy means for the democratic process. The traditional view has held it to be inimical to the health and well-being of democracy. Typical of this notion is the sentiment expressed by Robert Maynard Hutchins (1954): "The death of democracy is not likely to be an assassination from ambush. It will be a slow extinction from apathy, indifference, and undernourishment." Juxtaposed is the position of Bernard Berelson (1952) who views apathy as a positive good for the democratic system by giving elites room to maneuver and seek the middle way between the hot-eyed rigidity of extreme partisans.

In large measure it is impossible to reconcile such conflicting views. Moreover, as one reads the conceptions of democracy which undergird Berelson's argument and those of his critics (Duncan and Lukes, 1963; Davis, 1964; Walker, 1966; Pateman, 1970), it is obvious that they mean very different things indeed. Although he does not clearly say so, it appears that Berelson's conception of the democratic process is cast in the mold of Joseph Schumpeter (1975: 269), who defines "the democratic method" as "that institutional arrangement for arriving at political decisions in which individuals acquire the power to decide by means of a competitive struggle for the people's vote." According to Schumpeter and those who have followed in his footsteps, "the role of the people is to produce a government" or at least an intermediate body from which a government will eventually be chosen. This view places great weight on democratic leaders and commensurately little upon popular involvement in the process of government.

On the other hand, the conception of democracy among those who view apathy as a detriment is closer to the traditional approach taken by theorists such as Rousseau and John Stuart Mill. For example, Duncan and Lukes (1963) quote approvingly Mill's (1958: 55) statement that, "the only government which can fully satisfy all the exigencies of the social state is one in which the whole people participate. . . ." Obviously, in this conception that which hinders popular involvement in any aspect of government prevents the fullest development of democracy. Small wonder, then, that theorists who call for the greatest possible participation by the ordinary citizenry in government would see political indifference as a threat. Such was what Hutchins had in mind.

But there is another sense in which apathy has been viewed as at least a potential threat to the established democratic order. Here, the concern is with why people are politically indifferent, and what that could entail if they should suddenly become politically energized. If the citizen pays no heed to public affairs because he is fundamentally pleased with the way things are going and thus would find it an inefficient use of his time and psychic energy to maintain interest in a system that produces outputs to his liking anyway, apathy is, at worst, a cipher (Wilson, 1936). However, if there should be a substantial portion of the public which is apathetic because it is alienated from the established order, that is quite another thing.

Part of the problem is that, until recently, adequate measures of both political apathy and political alienation were unavailable. Fortunately, the SRC/CPS national election studies contain not only a useful indicant of psychological involvement in public affairs — the Political Apathy Index — but also several indicators of political trust and alienation. The best-known of the latter — the SRC's "Trust in Government Index" (Miller, Miller, and Schneider (1980: 253) — has been used as a surrogate for "alienation" (A. Miller, 1974a, 1974b), but has also been attacked as inadequate to that task (Citrin, 1974; see also Abramson and Finifter, 1981). In Chapter 6, a different measure of "alienation" was employed in conjunction with the Apathy Index. Unfortunately, the two-item indicator of alienation was included only on the CPS's 1972 and 1976 national election studies, and only the latter had a measure of validated vote.

While the data base is limited, the evidence suggests that those who have worried about the co-variation of apathy with alienation may have slightly exaggerated the problem, but they were on the right track. In the 1970s, those Americans who could not find much in our political system to feel proud about and who called for major changes in our way of government were twice as likely to be politically apathetic as were their "allegiant" fellow citizens. At that, however, almost three-fifth of the "alienated" Americans maintained at least some degree of interest in politics and government.

## Summary and Conclusions

The measure of "alienation" described in Chapter 6 sheds useful light on the relationship between political apathy and alienation. It would be helpful, however, if additional evidence could be adduced. Happily, an interesting tidbit comes from the CPS's 1972 national election study. Respondents to both national samples conducted that year were asked: "(How do you feel about) what our national government is doing?" Respondents were given a range of replies: "delighted, pleased, mostly satisfied, mixed (about equally satisfied and dissatisfied), mostly dissatisfied, unhappy, and terrible." The CPS also allowed the respondent to state either that "I never thought about it," or "I can't answer that question." This indicant provides the handle needed to get some purchase on whether people are apathetic because they are satisfied with the status quo, or because they are unhappy with the way things are going.

When the question on how people feel about what "our national government is doing" is cross-indexed with the Political Apathy Index, there is only a very weak relationship. Granted, those who said they were satisfied were more politically interested than those who were dissatisfied. For example, those who were either "delighted" or "pleased" had a PDI of 32.0 on the Apathy Index (N = 100), compared with a value of 22.7 for those who felt either "terrible" or "unhappy" (N = 206). Indeed, the only group which was politically apathetic was that which either had not thought about how it felt about what the national government was up to, or could not answer the question (PDI = $-52.0$) [N = 100]). In short, at least in 1972, it could be said that there were almost as many Americans who were apathetic because they were unhappy with the status quo as there were who were satisfied.

If the analysis in Chapter 6 and the information described above suggest anything, it is that those who worry about a possible interrelation between apathy and alienation have a point. But perhaps it is only a small one. Recall that only about 12% of the public could be classified as "alienated" in 1976 (Chapter 6), and only 9.6% of the CPS's respondents said they felt either "unhappy" or "terrible" about what the national government was doing in 1972.

It is important to recall that the 1970s were a period of especially high public discontent with national political leaders (Abramson, 1983; Hill and Luttbeg, 1983; Lipset and Schneider, 1983a). There is evidence that public confidence in national leaders has improved in the early 1980s (A. Miller, 1983; but also see Lipset and Schneider, 1983b). If so, there would be even fewer people who are politically indifferent because they are unhappy with the status quo in the 1980s than a decade earlier. Still, it must still be a worrisome thing to some students of democracy that even a small group of such people exists.

Before closing, consider one last point. According to Nunn, Crockett, and Williams, 1978: 164), a 1973 national survey found a fairly strong relationship between interest in public affairs and a measure of tolerance for nonconformity. In 1973, 66% of those who were more interested in national politics were politically tolerant, compared with only 33% of the apathetic. While the measure of tolerance relied upon by Nunn and his associates can justly be criticized (see Sullivan, Piereson, and Marcus, 1982: 31-33), their data raise an important question. If it were to be found that apathetic citizens are also less likely to be tolerant of unpopular political grounds, and/or less inclined to support democratic principles, would it necessarily be advantageous to democracy if such persons were suddenly to become politically energized? Perhaps some of the concerns expressed by scholars such as Lipset (1981: chap 6) were not so far-fetched after all.

## The Future Study of Apathy: What Is to Be Done?

No matter how detailed, a single analysis of a phenomenon cannot cover all of its facets. So it is here. Much remains to be done to advance our understanding of political apathy, its causes and consequences. It is appropriate, therefore, to end this work with a brief review of what needs to be done in future work.

One topic given very short shrift here is the psychological underpinnings of interest in politics. Morris Rosenberg's (1954-1955, 1962) research has indicated that persons with weak egos avoid attention to public affairs because of possible further damage to their sense of self-esteem (see also Milbrath and Goel, 1977: 41). The SRC/CPS included a four-item measure of "Personal Efficacy" on its 1960, 1968, 1972, and 1976 National Election Studies. In each year, those who score "very low" on this indicant are much less politically involved than those who score "very high." However, the relationship between the personality measure and the Apathy Index is never

*Summary and Conclusions*

robust, and somewhere between 24% and 37% of its strength is eroded when education is controlled. Still, these data, limited as they are, indicate that more work is needed on the personality bases of political interest.

Another question mentioned only in passing is the relation between the individual's economic condition and his attention to public affairs. It has long been contended that those who are forced by adverse economic circumstances to invest most of their waking hours to keeping body and soul together have neither the time nor the psychic energy left over for the "luxury" of following political life (Brody and Sniderman, 1977: 346). Rosenstone (1982: 41) has found that, "Economic adversity reduces voter turnout." What impact do reversals in one's economic fortunes have on his political interest?

On several occasions between 1968 and 1984, the SRC/CPS asked people whether they and their family were faring better, the same, or less well than they had been a year before. They were also asked to extrapolate their expectation of their financial condition a year hence. In every year except 1978, people who said they were doing better financially now than they had a year ago and expected to be even better off next year were more politically involved than those who had suffered economic reversals and projected even harder times next year. 1978 reversed the usual pattern. However, and this is the important point, even those undergoing economic downturns and anticipating worse times were politically interested. Economic adversity may indeed reduce voting, but it does not necessarily make people politically apathetic. More work needs to be done to explore this relationship in greater depth.

Another factor passed over is how one's awareness that what government does affects him influences attention to public affairs. Presumably, someone who perceives that his daily existence is significantly affected by what goes on in the halls of government will be under a more severe goad to pay heed to public affairs than Almond and Verba's (1963) parochial (see also Lipset, 1981: chap. 6). The Five Nation Study and the 1968 Comparative State Election Project contained the same question: "Thinking about the national government in Washington, about how much effect do you think its activities, the laws passed and so on, have on your day-to-day life? Do they have a great effect, some effect, or none?" In 1966, the SRC asked, "How much difference do you think it makes to people like you what the government in Washington does: a good deal, some, or not much?" In each year, those who perceived the national government as having a substantial impact on them were much more politically interested than those who did not.

Unfortunately, a question probing people's awareness of how much impact the national government has on their lives has not been included on an SRC/CPS national election study since 1966. The 1960s witnessed a significant growth of the federal government's power over people's lives; that development continued throughout the 1970s, and has not been reversed even with Ronald Reagan in the White House. Have people become more aware of the national government's effect upon them, and does such perception stimulate interest? Or, could the arrow of causality run the other way? Are those who are politically attentive more likely to be aware of how government touches them? The question is important, and needs an answer.

There is also the question of how psychological involvement in public affairs should be measured. Despite its weaknesses, the Political Apathy Index has served us well. It is unidimensional, stable over time, and appears to be valid as well. Still, there is a need for better measurement of social science concepts (Blalock, 1982), and the study of political apathy is no exception.

For example, the general political interest variable has, as Jennings and Niemi (1981: 28) note, "few concrete referents." What might happen to political interest if people were given greater specificity? In 1968, the SRC asked, in addition to the general interest question, questions about interest in international and world affairs, national affairs, state affairs, and local affairs (V431, V432, V433, V434). The 1968 data show people paid about the same amount of attention to national, local, and state affairs, and slightly less to international and world affairs. This, despite the fact that at the time Vietnam was considered to be the nation's most pressing problem.

There were, however, some interesting differences in the demographic factors related to interest at the different levels. For example, while women were considerably less likely than men to be very interested in international, national, and state affairs, they were just as likely to follow local matters.

It would be interesting to see how interest at each governmental level has changed since 1968 (see, for example, Jennings and Niemi,

## Summary and Conclusions

1974, 1981). It would also be worthwhile to determine whether one could use the four indicants to develop an even better measure of psychological involvement than the Apathy Index.

The effort should also be taken to explore other avenues toward measurement of apathy. One possible approach has been used by the National Opinion Research Center (NORC). In its Spring, 1982 General Social Survey, NORC included the following:

> On these cards are various aspects of life. We would like to know how important each of these aspects of life is for you. On each of these cards you see on the right hand side a scale with seven points. The lowest point with number 1 indicates that this aspect of life is unimportant to you. Point 7 at the top indicates that particular aspect of life is very important to you. The numbers in between indicate varying degrees of importance.

Fortunately, one of the aspects of life was "politics and public affairs." It is interesting to note that, in 1982, 13.4% of the American public placed "politics and public affairs" at scale position 1, *i.e.*, "unimportant," and another 9.8% put them at scale position 2. On the other hand, 9.8% placed public affairs at position 7, or "important," and an additional 12.2% placed it at position 6.

Some might view the NORC's 1982 indicant as a slightly more sensitive index for classifying people's concern with politics and public affairs than the SRC/CPS's usual general political interest indicator. The two are related, a little. In 1982, NORC included the 1966 version of the SRC's standard measure. While only 27.4% of those who placed "politics and public affairs" on scale position 1 with the NORC measure also said they followed what goes on in government and public affairs "most of the time," 56.6% of those who put "politics and public affairs" at scale position 7 gave the more interested reply to the SRC's standard question.

However, the relation between the two variables is weak at best. The Pearsonian product moment correlation coefficient for the association between them is $r = .211$ ($N = 1476$). There are, in short, many people who think "politics and public affairs" are important to them who nonetheless are indifferent on the SRC's traditional measure, and many who think political life is unimportant who still say they regularly follow what happens in that sphere of life.

There are two ways of looking at NORC's indicant. One views it as another way of getting at people's awareness of how government affects them. The other sees it as a surrogate for general political interest. Each has merits. What is needed is further work with the NORC measure employing additional indicators such as measures of media usage, political knowledge, turnout, and political participation generally. Until such is done, the NORC measure's potential as an alternative or addition to the SRC's general interest item must remain unknown.

There is also the question of the timing of people's interest in public affairs. Long, long ago, Bryce (1891) noted that the public's interest peaked at election time and was lower otherwise. If the CPS's 1980 special election studies and its 1984 Continuous Monitoring Survey from January through June are to be believed, there is a tendency for people's interest to vary significantly throughout the course of an election year. More work should be done to determine how the public's attention to public affairs fluctuates with the political calendar.

Finally, there is one last point. Survey methodology is an excellent technique for the study of grassroots political phenomena such as apathy. But, it has its limits. The survey analyst often finds himself at a loss to probe much beneath the surface of his topic, to plumb the deeper reasons behind why people say and do the things they do. An alternative is to employ Robert Lane's (1962) technique of in-depth interviews with a small group in order the better to understand the psychological dynamics underneath people's political behavior. To follow in Lane's footsteps is the path the study of grassroots political interest needs to trod.

In trapsing that road or in additional work on cross-sectional surveys, several points should be kept in mind. First, students of politics ought not be surprised when ordinary people indicate they are only mildly politically interested. Most people most of the time do not "eat, breathe, and sleep politics." Save in times of national or international emergency or travail, and unless some politically relevant event touches directly upon him, the typical citizen's life is too preoccupied with personal, family, work, or recreational affairs to give more than a modicum of concern to public affairs.

Second, there is, however, some cause for concern for those who support democratic politics. While many Americans are apathetic because they are fairly satisfied with the status quo, there is also a small minority that is discontented with the way things are, but still regularly pays heed to government and politics. Could these people become mobilizable on behalf of a movement uncommitted to normal democratic politics? Many of George Wallace's devotees in the late 1960s and early 1970s came close to the profile of the alienated but attentive minority described in Chapter 6 (Oldendick and Bennett, 1978). One wonders whether there might be others of similar and different ideological and partisan proclivities. The evidence suggests there are (Gilmour and Lamb, 1975; Sniderman, 1981).

Finally, what will happen to Americans' political interest in the future? In particular, will the recent entrants into the electorate who have been especially apathetic become more psychologically involved as they go through the life cycle? Evidence from almost a quarter of a century suggests they will. But, at least among those who have not gone to college and remain unattached to a major political party and disinclined to think government listens to them, it is unlikely they will ever become particularly interested. Still, there are signs of a reawakened partisanship among some of the young, and more people are gradually coming to believe that government does pay them at least some heed. If true, the prospects for citizen political interest in America's future are rosier than they seemed just a few years ago.

Nevertheless, one must not expect a restoration of citizen involvement to the degree seen during the last three decades of the 19th century. Not only have political cleavages been essentially disconnected from ethnoreligious affiliations, there are too many other distractions — professional sports, entertainment, etc. — for politics to be the sideshow it once was. Perhaps that's not such a bad thing after all.

# References

Abramowitz, Alan I. 1980. "The United States: Political Culture Under Stress." In Gabriel A. Almond and Sidney Verba, eds. *The Civic Culture Revisited*. Boston: Little, Brown & Co., pp. 177-211.

Abramson, Paul R. 1983. *Political Attitudes in America: Formation and Change*. San Francisco: W. H. Freeman & Co.

Abramson, Paul R., and Aldrich, John H. 1982. "The Decline of Electoral Participation in America." *American Political Science Review*, 76 (September): 502-521.

Abramson, Paul R., Aldrich, John H., and Rohde, David W. 1983. *Change and Continuity in the 1980 Elections*. Revised ed. Washington, DC.: Congressional Quarterly Press.

Abramson, Paul R., and Claggett, William. 1984. "Race-related Differences in Self-reported and Validated Turnout." *Journal of Politics*, 46 (August): 719-738.

Abramson, Paul R., and Finifter, Ada W. 1981. "On the Meaning of Political Trust: New Evidence from Items Introduced in 1978." *American Journal of Political Science*, 25 (May): 297-307.

Achen, Christopher H. 1982. *Interpreting and Using Regression*. Sage University Paper series on Quantitative Applications in the Social Sciences, series no. 07-029. Beverly Hills, CA.: Sage Publications.

Achen, Christopher H. 1983. "Toward Theories of Data: The State of Political Methodology." In Ada W. Finifter, ed. *Political Science: The State of the Discipline*. Washington, DC.: American Political Science Association, pp. 69-93.

Adamany, David, and Shelley, Mack C., II. 1980. "Encore! The Forgetful Voter." *Public Opinion Quarterly*, 44 (Summer): 234-240.

Adorno, Theodore, *et al.* 1950. *The Authoritarian Personality*. New York: Harper & Row, Inc.

Aldrich, John, and Cnudde, Charles. 1975. "Probing the Bounds of Conventional Wisdom: A Comparison of Regression, Probit, and Discriminant Analysis." *American Journal of Political Science*, 19 (November): 571-608.

Aldrich, John, and Nelson, Forrest D. 1984. *Linear Probability, Logit, and Probit Models*. Sage University Paper series on Quantitative Applications in the Social Sciences, series no. 07-045. Beverly Hills, CA.: Sage Publications.

Almond, Gabriel A. 1954. *The Appeals of Communism*. Princeton, NJ.: Princeton University Press.

Almond, Gabriel A. 1960. *The American People and Foreign Policy.* New York: Frederick A. Praeger, Inc.

Almond, Gabriel A., and Verba, Sidney. 1963. *The Civic Culture: Political Attitudes and Democracy in Five Nations.* Princeton, NJ.: Princeton University Press.

Altbach, Philip G., and Peterson, Patti M. 1972. "Before Berkeley: Historical Perspectives on American Student Activism." In Philip G. Altbach and Robert S. Laufer, eds. *The New Pilgrims: Youth Protest in Transition.* New York: David McKay Co., Inc. pp. 13-31.

Andersen, Kristi. 1975. "Working Women and Political Participation." *American Journal of Political Science,* 19 (August): 439-454.

Aristotle. 1962. *The Politics.* Ed. & Trans. Ernest Barker. New York: Oxford University Press.

Asher, Herbert, B. 1974. "The Reliability of the Political Efficacy Items." *Political Methodology,* 1 (Spring): 45-72.

Asher, Herbert B. 1983. *Causal Modeling.* Second ed. Sage University Paper series on Quantitative Applications in the Social Sciences, series no. 07-003. Beverly Hills, CA.: Sage Publications.

Bachrach, Peter. 1967. *The Theory of Democratic Elitism: A Critique.* Boston: Little, Brown & Co.

Balch, George I. 1974. "Multiple Indicators in Survey Research: The Concept 'Sense of Political Efficacy.' " *Political Methodology,* 1 (Spring): 1-43.

Barber, Benjamin. 1984. *Strong Democracy: Participatory Politics for a New Age.* Berkeley, CA.: University of California Press.

Barnes, Samuel H., Kaase, Max, et al. 1979. *Political Action: Mass Participation in Five Western Democracies.* Beverly Hills, CA.: Sage Publications.

Baxter, Sandra, and Lansing, Marjorie. 1983. *Women and Politics: The Visible Majority.* Revised ed. Ann Arbor, MI.: University of Michigan Press.

Beck, Paul A. 1974. "A Socialization Theory of Partisan Realignment." In Richard G. Niemi, et al. *The Politics of Future Citizens.* San Francisco: Jossey-Bass, Inc., pp. 199-219.

Beck, Paul A., and Jennings, M. Kent. 1979. "Political Periods and Political Participation." *American Political Science Review,* 73 (September): 737-750.

Bell, Daniel, ed. 1963. *The Radical Right.* Garden City, NY.: Doubleday Anchor Books.

Benello, C. George, and Rousopoulos, Dimitrios, eds. 1971. *The Case for Participatory Democracy.* New York: Grossman Publishers.

Bennett, Linda L. M., and Bennett, Stephen E. 1985. "Gender Differences in Political Interest, 1960-1984." A paper prepared for delivery at the Southern Political Science Association's Annual Meeting, Nashville, TN. (November).

Bennett, Stephen E. 1973. "Consistency Among the Public's Social Welfare Policy Attitudes in the 1960s." *American Journal of Political Science,* 17 (August): 544-570.

Bennett, Stephen E. 1983. "Sense of Citizen Duty, 1952-1980: Change Admist Constancy?" A paper prepared for delivery at the Southern Political Science Association's Annual Meeting, Birmingham, AL. (November).

# References

Bennett, Stephen E. 1984a. "Changes in the Public's Perceptions of Governmental Attentiveness, 1964-1980." *Micropolitics*, 3(3): 309-348.

Bennett, Stephen E. 1984b. "Apathy in America, 1964-1982: A New Measure Applied to Old Questions." *Micropolitics*, 3(4): 499-545.

Bennett, Stephen E. 1985. "The Education-Turnout 'Puzzle' in Recent National Elections." Unpublished MS. Cincinnati: University of Cincinnati.

Bennett, Stephen E., and Bennett, Linda L. M. 1986. "Political Participation." In Samuel Long, ed. *Annual Review of Political Science*. Norwood, NJ.: Ablex Publishing Corp. Vol. 1 (forthcoming).

Benson, Lee. 1967-1968. "An Approach to the Scientific Study of Past Opinion." *Public Opinion Quarterly*, 31 (Winter): 522-561.

Berelson, Bernard, R. 1952. "Democratic Theory and Public Opinion." *Public Opinion Quarterly*, 16 (Fall): 313-330.

Berlson, Bernard R., Lazarsfeld, Paul F., and McPhee, William N. 1954. *Voting*. Chicago: University of Chicago Press.

Berry, William D., and Feldman, Stanley. 1985. *Multiple Regression in Practice*. Sage University Paper series on Quantitative Applications in the Social Sciences, series no. 07-050. Beverly Hills, CA.: Sage Publications.

Bishop, George F., Oldendick, Robert W., and Tuchfarber, Alfred J. 1982. "Political Information Processing: Question Order and Context Effects." *Political Behavior*, 4(2): 177-200.

Bishop, George F., Oldendick, Robert W., and Tuchfarber, Alfred J. 1984. "Interest in Political Campaigns: The Influence of Question Order and Electoral Context." *Political Behavior*, 6(2): 159-169.

Black, Merle, Kovenock, David M., and Reynolds, William C. 1974. *Political Attitudes in the Nation and States*. Chapel Hill, NC.: Institute for Research in Social Science, University of North Carolina.

Blalock, Hubert M., Jr. 1979. *Social Statistics*. Revised second ed. New York: McGraw-Hill Book Co.

Blalock, Hubert M., Jr. 1982. *Conceptualization and Measurement in the Social Sciences*. Beverly Hills, CA.: Sage Publications.

Broder, David S. 1980. *Changing of the Guard: Power and Leadership in America*. New York: Simon & Schuster.

Brody, Richard A. 1978. "The Puzzle of Political Participation in America." In Anthony King, ed. *The New American Political System*. Washington, DC.: American Enterprise Institute, pp. 287-324.

Brody, Richard A., and Sniderman, Paul. 1977. "From Life Space to Polling Place: The Relevance of Personal Concerns for Voting Behavior." *British Journal of Political Science*, 7 (March): 337-360.

Bryce, James. 1891. *The American Commonwealth*. Two volumes. Second ed., revised. London: MacMillan Co., Ltd.

Bryce, James. 1913. *Promoting Good Citizenship*. Boston: Houghton Mifflin Co.

Bryce, James. 1921. *Modern Democracies*. Two volumes. New York: The Macmillan Co.

Burnham, Walter Dean. 1965. "The Changing Shape of the American Political Universe." *American Political Science Review*, 59 (March): 7-28.

Burnham, Walter Dean. 1971. "Communication." *American Political Science Review*, 65 (December): 1149-1152.

Burnahm, Walter Dean. 1974. "Theory and Voting Research." *American Political Science Review*, 68 (September): 1002-1023.

Burnham, Walter Dean. 1981. "The System of 1896: An Analysis." In Paul Kleppner, et al. *The Evolution of American Electoral Systems*. Westport, CT.: Greenwood Press, pp. 147-202.

Burke, Edmund. 1959. *Burke's Politics: Selected Writings and Speeches of Edmund Burke on Reform, Revolution, and War*. Eds. Ross J. S. Hoffman and Paul Levack. New York: Alfred A. Knopf, Inc.

Caddell, Patrick H. 1979. "Crisis of Confidence, I: Trapped in a Downward Spiral." *Public Opinion*, 2 (October/November): 2-8, 52-55, 58-60.

Campbell, Angus. 1960. "Surge and Decline: A Study of Electoral Change." *Public Opinion Quarterly*, 24 (Fall): 397-418.

Campbell, Angus. 1962. "The Passive Citizen." *Acta Sociologica*, 6 (fasc. 1-2): 9-21.

Campbell, Angus. 1964. "Voters and Elections: Past and Present." *Journal of Politics*, 26 (November): 745-757.

Campbell, Angus, Gurin, Gerald, and Miller, Warren E. 1954. *The Voter Decides*. Evanston, IL.: Row & Peterson.

Campbell, Angus, Converse, Philip E., Miller, Warren E., and Stokes, Donald E. 1960. *The American Voter*. New York: John W. Wiley & Sons.

Carmines, Edward G., and Stimson, James A. 1980. "The Racial Reorientation of American Politics." In John C. Pierce and John L. Sullivan, eds., *The Electorate Reconsidered*. Beverly Hills, CA.: Sage Publications, pp. 199-218.

Carmines, Edward G., and Zeller, Richard A. 1979. *Reliability and Validity Assessment*. Sage University Paper series on Quantitative Applications in the Social Sciences, series no. 07-017. Beverly Hills, CA.: Sage Publications.

Cassel, Carol A., and Hill, David B. 1981. "Explanations of Turnout Decline: A Multivariate Test." *American Politics Quarterly*, 9 (April): 181-195.

Cavanagh, Thomas E. 1981. "Changes in American Voter Turnout, 1964-1976." *Political Science Quarterly*, 96 (Spring): 53-65.

Chambers, William N., and Davis, Philip C. 1978. "Party Competition and Mass Participation: The Case of the Democratizing Party System, 1824-1852." In Joel H. Silbey, Allan G. Bogue, and William M. Flanigan, eds. *The History of American Electoral Behavior*. Princeton, NJ.: Princeton University Press, pp. 174-197.

Citrin, Jack. 1974. "Comment: The Political Relevance of Trust in Government." *American Political Science Review*, 68 (September): 973-988.

Citrin, Jack. 1981. "The Changing American Electorate." In Arnold Meltsner, ed. *Politics and the Oval Office*. San Francisco: Institute for Contemporary Studies, pp. 31-61.

Claggett, William. 1981. "Turnout and Core Voters in the Nineteenth and Twentieth Centuries: A Reconsideration." *Social Science Quarterly*, 62 (September): 443-449.

Clausen, Aage. 1968-1969. "Response Validity: Vote Report." *Public Opinion Quarterly*, 32 (Winter): 588-606.
Connelly, Gordon M., with Field, H. H. 1944. "The Non-Voter—Who He Is, What He Thinks." *Public Opinion Quarterly*, 8 (Summer): 175-187.
Converse, Philip E. 1964. "The Nature of Belief Systems in Mass Publics." In David E. Apter, ed. *Ideology and Discontent*. New York: The Free Press, pp. 206-261.
Converse, Philip E. 1972. "Change in the American Electorate." In Angus Campbell and Philip E. Converse, eds. *The Human Meaning of Social Change*. New York: Russell Sage Foundation, pp. 263-337.
Converse, Philip E. 1974. "Comment on Burnham's 'Theory and Voting Research.'" *American Political Science Review*, 68 (September): 1024-1027.
Converse, Philip E. 1975. "Public Opinion and Voting Behavior." In Fred I. Greenstein and Nelson W. Polsby, eds. *Handbook of Political Science*. 8 Volumes. Reading, MA.: Addison-Wesley Publishing Co., Vol. 4: pp. 75-169.
Converse, Philip E., and Markus, Gregory B. 1979. "Plus ca Change . . . : The New CPS Election Study Panel." *American Political Science Review*, 73 (March): 32-49.
Converse, Philip E., with Niemi, Richard G. 1971. "Non-voting among Young Adults in the United States." In William J. Crotty, Donald M. Freeman, and Douglas G. Gatlin, eds. *Political Parties and Political Behavior*. Second ed. Boston: Allyn & Bacon, pp. 443-466.
Cohen, Jacob, and Cohen, Patricia. 1975. *Applied Multiple Regression/Correlation Analysis for the Behavioral Sciences*. Hillsdale, NJ.: Lawrence Erlbaum Associates, Publishers.
Craig, Stephen C. 1979. "Efficacy, Trust, and Political Behavior: An Attempt to Resolve a Lingering Conceptual Dilemma." *American Politics Quarterly*, 7 (April): 225-239.
Craig, Stephen C. 1985. "The Decline of Partisanship in the United States: A Reexamination of the Neutrality Hypothesis." *Political Behavior*, 7(1): 52-78.
Craig, Stephen C., and Maggiotto, Michael. 1982. "Measuring Political Efficacy." *Political Methodology*, 8(3): 95-109.
Dahl, Robert A. 1961. *Who Governs?* New Haven, CT.: Yale University Press.
Danigelis, Nicholas L. 1978. "Black Political Participation in the United States." *American Sociological Review*, 43 (October): 756-771.
Davis, Lane. 1964. "The Cost of Realism: Contemporary Restatements of Democracy." *Western Political Quarterly*, 17 (March): 37-46.
Dean, Dwight G. 1960. "Alienation and Political Apathy." *Social Forces*, 38 (March): 185-189.
DeNardo, James. 1980. "Turnout and the Vote: The Joke's on the Democrats." *American Political Science Review*, 74 (June): 406-420.
Devine, Donald J. 1970. *The Attentive Public: Polyarchical Democracy*. Chicago: Rand McNally & Co.
Dennis, Jack, ed. 1973. *Socialization to Politics*. New York: John W. Wiley & Sons.
Dewey, John. 1927. *The Public and Its Problems*. New York: Henry Holt & Co.

Dinkin, Robert J. 1977. *Voting in Provincial America*. Westport, CT.: Greenwood Press.

Dinkin, Robert J. 1982. *Voting in Revolutionary America*. Westport, CT.: Greenwood Press.

Di Palma, Guiseppe. 1970. *Apathy and Participation*. New York: The Free Press.

Downs, George W., and Rocke, David M. 1979. "Interpreting Heteroscedasticity." *American Journal of Political Science*, 23 (November): 816-828.

Duncan, Graeme, and Lukes, Steven. 1963. "The New Democracy." *Political Studies*, 11(2): 156-177.

Easton, David. 1965. *A Systems Analysis of Political Life*. New York: John Wiley & Sons.

Easton, David. 1975. "A Re-Assessment of the Concept of Political Support." *British Journal of Political Science*, 5 (July): 435-457.

Easton, David, and Dennis, Jack. 1969. *Children in the Political System: Origins of Political Legitimacy*. New York: McGraw-Hill Book Co.

Erikson, Robert S., Luttbeg, Norman R., and Tedin, Kent L. 1980. *American Public Opinion: Its Origins, Content, and Impact*. Second ed. New York: John Wiley & Sons.

Fenno, Richard E., Jr. 1978. *Home Style: House Members in Their Districts*. Boston: Little, Brown & Co.

Ferejohn, John A., and Fiorina, Morris P. 1979. "The Decline of Turnout in Presidential Elections." A paper prepared for delivery at the National Science Foundation Conference on Voter Turnout, San Diego, CA.

Finifter, Ada W., ed. 1983. *Political Science: The State of the Discipline*. Washington, DC.: American Political Science Association.

Finley, M. I. 1983. *Politics in the Ancient World*. Cambridge: Cambridge University Press.

Forrest, W. G. 1969. "The Realities of Athenian Government." In Frank J. Frost, ed., *Democracy and the Athenians*. New York: John W. Wiley & Sons, pp. 131-149.

Fraser, John. 1970. "The Mistrustful-Efficacious Hypothesis and Political Participation." *Journal of Politics*. 32 (May): 444-449.

Friedrich, Robert J. 1982. "In Defense of Multiplicative Terms in Multiple Regression." *American Journal of Political Science*, 26 (November): 797-833.

Funkhouser, G. Ray. 1973. "The Issues of the Sixties: An Exploratory Study in the Dynamics of Public Opinion." *Public Opinion Quarterly*, 37 (Spring): 62-75.

Gallup, George. 1977. "Citizenship Test for Secondary Schools." In National Task Force on Citizenship Education. *Education for Responsible Citizenship*. New York: McGraw-Hill Book Co., pp. 213-221.

Gamson, William A. 1968 *Power and Discontent*. Homewood, IL.: The Dorsey Press.

Gans, Curtis B. 1978. "The Empty Ballot Box: Reflections on Nonvoters in America." *Public Opinion*, 1 (September/October): 54-57.

Gilmour, Robert S., and Lamb, Robert B. 1975. *Political Alienation in Contemporary America*. New York: St. Martin's Press.

## References

Glenn, Norval D. 1972. "Archival Data on Political Attitudes: Opportunities and Pitfalls." In Dan D. Nimmo and Charles M. Bonjean, eds. *Political Attitudes and Public Opinion*. New York: David McKay Co., Inc., pp. 137-146.

Glenn, Norval D. 1977. *Cohort Analysis*. Sage University Paper series on Quantitative Applications in the Social Sciences, series no. 07-005. Beverly Hills, CA.: Sage Publications.

Glenn, Norval D., and Grimes, Michael. 1968. "Aging, Voting, and Political Interest." *American Sociological Review*, 33 (August): 563-575.

Greenstein, Fred I. 1965. *Children and Politics*. New Haven, CT.: Yale University Press.

Greenstein, Fred I., and Polsby, Nelson W., eds. 1975. *Handbook of Political Science*. 8 volumes. Reading, MA.: Addison-Wesley.

Grund, Francis J. 1959. *Aristocracy in America*. New York: Harper Torchbooks.

Gutek, Barbara A. 1978. "On the Accuracy of Retrospective Attitudinal Data." *Public Opinion Quarterly*, 42 (Fall): 390-401.

Guterbock, Thomas M., and London, Bruce. 1983. "Race, Political Orientation, and Participation: An Empirical Test of Four Competing Theories." *American Sociological Review*, 48 (August): 439-453.

Hadley, Arthur T. 1978. *The Empty Polling Booth*. Englewood Cliffs, NJ.: Prentice-Hall, Inc.

Hart, Vivien. 1978. *Distrust and Democracy: Political Distrust in Britain and America*. Cambridge: Cambridge University Press.

Hawkins, Brett W., Marando, Vincent L., and Taylor, George A. 1971. "Efficacy, Mistrust, and Political Participation: Findings from Additional Data and Indicators." *Journal of Politics*, 33 (November): 1130-1136.

Hess, Robert D., and Torney, Judith V. 1967. *The Development of Political Attitudes in Children*. Chicago: Aldine Publishing Co.

Hill, David B., and Luttbeg, Norman R. 1983. *Trends in American Electoral Behavior*. Second ed. Itasca, IL.: F. E. Peacock Publishers.

Hill, Kim Quaile, and Hurley, Patricia A. 1984. "Nonvoters in Voters' Clothing: The Impact of Voting Behavior Misreporting on Voting Behavior Research." *Social Science Quarterly*, 65 (March): 199-206.

Hinckley, Barbara. 1981. *Congressional Elections*. Washington, DC.: Congressional Quarterly Press.

Hofstadter, Richard. 1965. *The Paranoid Style in American Politics*. New York: Alfred A. Knopf.

Hofstadter, Richard. 1970. *The Idea of a Party System*. Berkeley, CA.: University of California Press.

Huntington, Samuel. 1981. *American Politics: The Promise of Disharmony*. Cambridge, MA.: Harvard University Press.

Hutchins, Robert Maynard. 1954. *Great Books of the Western World*. Quoted in John Bartlett, *Familiar Quotations*. Ed. Emily Morison Beck. 15th ed. Boston: Little, Brown & Co., 1980, pp. 845-846.

Hyman, Herbert H. 1955. *Survey Design and Analysis*. New York: The Free Press.

Hyman, Herbert H., Wright, Charles R., and Reed, John Sheldon. 1975. *The Enduring Effects of Education*. Chicago: University of Chicago Press.

Inter-University Consortium for Political Research. 1974. *The SRC 1960 American National Election Study.* Ann Arbor, MI.: Inter-University Consortium for Political Research.
Jacobson, Gary C. 1983. *The Politics of Congressional Elections.* Boston: Little, Brown & Co.
Janowitz, Morris. 1983. *The Reconstruction of Patriotism: Education for Civic Consciousness.* Chicago: University of Chicago Press.
Jefferson, Thomas. 1977. *The Portable Thomas Jefferson.* Ed. Merrill D. Peterson. Harmondsworth: Penguin Books, Ltd.
Jennings, M. Kent. 1979. "Another Look at the Life Cycle and Political Participation." *American Journal of Political Science,* 23 (November): 755-771.
Jennings, M. Kent. 1983. "Gender Roles and Inequalities in Political Participation: Results from an Eight-Nation Study." *Western Political Quarterly,* 36 (September): 364-385.
Jennings, M. Kent, and Niemi, Richard G. 1974. *The Political Character of Adolescence: The Influence of Families and Schools.* Princeton, NJ.: Princeton University Press.
Jennings, M. Kent, and Niemi, Richard G. 1981. *Generations and Politics: A Panel Study of Young Adults and Their Parents.* Princeton, NJ.: Princeton University Press.
Jensen, Richard J. 1971. *The Winning of the Midwest: Social and Political Conflict, 1888-1896.* Chicago: University of Chicago Press.
Johnson, Haynes. 1980. *In the Absence of Power: Governing America.* New York: The Viking Press.
Kann, Robert A. 1968. "Public Opinion Research: A Contribution to Historical Method." *Political Science Quarterly,* 73 (September): 374-396.
Katosh, John P., and Traugott, Michael W. 1981. "The Consequences of Validated and Self-reported Vote Measures." *Public Opinion Quarterly,* 45 (Winter): 519-535.
Kernell, Sam. 1973. "Comment: A Re-evaluation of Black Voting in Mississippi." *American Political Science Review,* 67 (December): 1307-1318.
Key, V. O., Jr. 1961. *Public Opinion and American Democracy.* New York: Alfred A. Knopf, Inc.
Kirkpatrick, Jeane. 1976. *The New Presidential Elite.* New York: Russell Sage Foundation.
Kirkpatrick, Samuel A., ed. 1974. *Quantitative Analysis of Political Data.* Columbus, OH.: Charles E. Merrill Publishing Co.
Klecka, William R. 1980. *Discriminant Analysis.* Sage University Paper series on Quantitative Applications in the Social Sciences, series no. 07-019. Beverly Hills, CA.: Sage Publications.
Kleppner, Paul. 1970. *The Cross of Culture: A Social Analysis of Midwestern Politics, 1850-1900.* New York: The Free Press.
Kleppner, Paul. 1979. *The Third Electoral System, 1853-1892.* Chapel Hill, NC.: University of North Carolina Press.
Kleppner, Paul. 1982a. "Were Women to Blame? Female Suffrage and Voter Turnout." *Journal of Interdisciplinary History,* 12 (Spring): 621-643.

## References

Kleppner, Paul. 1982b. *Who Voted? The Dynamics of Electoral Turnout, 1870-1980.* New York: Frederick A. Praeger.

Kleppner, Paul, and Baker, Stephen C. 1980. "The Impact of Voter Registration Requirements on Electoral Turnout, 1900-16." *Journal of Political and Military Sociology*, 8 (Fall): 205-226.

Knupfer, Genevieve. 1947. "Portrait of the Underdog." *Public Opinion Quarterly*, 11 (Spring): 103-114.

Kornhauser, William. 1959. *The Politics of Mass Society.* New York: The Free Press.

Kramer, Daniel C. 1972. *Participatory Democracy: Developing Ideals of the Political Left.* Cambridge, MA.: Schenkman Publishing Co.

Labovitz, Sanford. 1967. "Some Observations on Measurement and Statistics." *Social Forces*, 46 (December): 151-160.

Labovitz, Sanford. 1970. "The Assignment of Numbers to Rank Order Categories." *American Sociological Review*, 35 (August): 515-525.

Ladd, Everett Carll. 1985. "On Mandates, Realignments, and the 1984 Presidential Election." *Political Science Quarterly*, 100 (Spring): 1-25.

Lamb, Karl A. 1982. *The Guardians: Leadership Values and the American Tradition.* New York: W. W. Norton & Co.

Lane, Robert E. 1962. *Political Ideology: Why the American Common Man Believes What He Does.* New York: The Free Press.

Lane, Robert E. 1965. *Political Life: Why and How People Get Involved in Politics.* Revised ed. New York: The Free Press.

Lane, Robert E. 1973. *Political Man.* New York: The Free Press.

Langton, Kenneth P. 1969. *Political Socialization.* New York: Oxford University Press.

Langton, Kenneth P., and Jennings, M. Kent. 1968. "Political Socialization and the High School Civics Curriculum in the United States." *American Political Science Review*, 62 (September): 852-867.

Lasch, Christopher. 1979. *The Culture of Narcissism: American Life in an Age of Diminishing Expectations.* New York: Warner Books.

Lasswell, Harold D. 1960. *Psychopathology and Politics.* Revised ed. New York: The Viking Press.

Lasswell, Harold D. 1962. *Power and Personality.* New York: The Viking Press.

Lazarsfeld, Paul M., Berelson, Bernard, and Gaudet, Hazel. 1968. *The People's Choice.* Third ed. New York: Columbia University Press.

Lemann, Nicholas, 1985. "Implications: What Americans Wanted." In Michael Nelson, ed. *The Elections of 1984.* Washington, DC.: Congressional Quarterly Press, pp. 259-275.

Lewis-Beck, Michael S. 1980. *Applied Regression: An Introduction.* Sage University Paper series on Quantitative Applications in the Social Sciences, series no. 07-022. Beverly Hills, CA.: Sage Publications.

Liebert, Robert. 1971. *Radical and Militant Youth.* New York: Frederick A. Praeger.

Lippmann, Walter. 1925. *The Phantom Public.* New York: Harcourt, Brace & Co.

Lippmann, Walter. 1927. *Men of Destiny.* New York: The Macmillan Co.

Lipset, Seymour Martin. 1972. *Rebellion in the University.* Boston: Little, Brown & Co.

Lipset, Seymour Martin. 1981. *Political Man: The Social Bases of Politics.* Enlarged ed. Baltimore, MD.: The Johns Hopkins University Press.

Lipset, Seymour Martin, and Raab, Earl. 1977. *The Politics of Unreason.* Second ed. Chicago: University of Chicago Press.

Lipset, Seymour Martin, and Schneider, William J. 1983a. *The Confidence Gap: Business, Labor, and Government in the Public Mind.* New York: The Free Press.

Lipset, Seymour Martin, and Schneider, William J. 1983b. "Confidence in Confidence Measures." *Public Opinion,* 6 (August/September): 42-44.

Luskin, Robert C. 1978. "Estimating and Interpreting Correlations between Disturbances and Residual Path Coefficients in Nonrecursive (and Recursive) Causal Models." *American Journal of Political Science,* 22 (May): 444-474.

Lynd, Robert S., and Lynd, Helen Merrell. 1929. *Middletown: A Study in Modern American Culture.* New York: Harcourt, Brace, and World, Inc.

McClosky, Herbert. 1968. "Political Participation." In David Sills, ed. *International Encyclopedia of the Social Sciences.* New York: Macmillan Co., Vol. 12: pp. 252-265.

McCormick, Richard P. 1973. *The Second American Party System: Party Formation in the Jacksonian Era.* New York: W. W. Norton & Co.

McPherson, J. Miller, Welch, Susan, and Clark, Cal. 1977. "The Stability and Reliability of Political Efficacy: Using Path Analysis to Test Alternative Models." *American Political Science Review,* 71 (June): 509-521.

Margolis, Michael. 1983. "Democracy: American Style." In Graeme Duncan, ed. *Democratic Theory and Practice.* Cambridge. Cambridge University Press, pp. 115-132.

Matthews, Donald R., and Prothro, James W. 1966. *Negroes and the New Southern Politics.* New York: Harcourt, Brace, & World.

Merriam, Charles E., and Gosnell, Harold F. 1924. *Non-Voting: Causes and Methods of Control.* Chicago: University of Chicago Press.

Milbrath, Lester W. 1965. *Political Participation: How and Why Do People Get Involved in Politics.* Chicago: Rand McNally Co.

Milbrath, Lester W., and Goel, M. L. 1977. *Political Participation: How and Why Do People Get Involved in Politics.* Second ed. Chicago: Rand McNally Co.

Mill, John Stuart. 1952.,*Considerations on Representative Government.* Ed. Currin V. Shields. Indianapolis, ID.: Bobbs-Merrill Co.

Miller, Arthur H. 1974a. "Political Issues and Trust in Government." *American Political Science Review,* 64 (September): 951-972.

Miller, Arthur H. 1974b. "Rejoinder to 'Comment' by Jack Citrin." *American Political Science Review,* 64 (September): 989-1001.

Miller, Arthur H. 1979. "The Institutional Focus of Political Distrust." A paper prepared for delivery at the Annual Meeting of the American Political Science Association, Washington, DC., (September).

Miller, Arthur H. 1983. "Is Confidence Rebounding?" *Public Opinion,* 6 (June/July): 16-20.

Miller, James. 1985. *Rousseau: Dreamer of Democracy.* New Haven, CT.: Yale University Press.

## References

Miller, Warren E. 1979. "Crisis of Confidence, II: Misreading the Public Pulse." *Public Opinion*, 2 (October/November): 9-15, 60.

Miller, Warren E. 1980. "Disinterest, Disaffection, and Participation in Presidential Politics." *Political Behavior*, 2(1): 7-32.

Miller, Warren E., Miller, Arthur H., and Schneider, Edward J. 1980. *American National Election Studies Sourcebook, 1952-1978*. Cambridge, MA.: Harvard University Press.

Morris, Charles. 1984. *A Time of Passion: America 1960-1980*. New York: Harper & Row.

Munro, William B. 1928. "Is the Slacker Vote a Menace?" *National Municipal Review*, 17 (February): 80-86.

National Task Force on Citizenship Education. 1977. *Education for Responsible Citizenship*. New York: McGraw-Hill Book Co.

Nelson, Dale C. 1979. "Ethnicity and Socioeconomic Status as Sources of Participation: The Case for Ethnic Political Culture." *American Political Science Review*, 73 (December): 1024-1038.

Neumann, Franz. 1957. *The Democratic and Authoritarian State*. New York: The Free Press.

Nexon, David. 1971. "Asymmetry in the Political System: Occasional Activists in the Republican and Democratic Parties, 1956-1964." *American Political Science Review*, 65 (September): 716-730.

Nichols, Roy Franklin. 1967. *The Disruption of American Democracy*. New York: The Free Press.

Nie, Norman H., with Andersen, Kristi. 1974. "Mass Belief Systems Revisited: Political Change and Attitude Structure." *Journal of Politics*, 36 (August): 540-591.

Nie, Norman H., Verba, Sidney, and Petrocik, John R. 1979. *The Changing American Voter*. Enlarged ed. Cambridge, MA.: Harvard University Press.

Nunn, Clyde Z., Crockett, Harry J., Jr., and Williams, J. Allen, Jr. 1978. *Tolerance for Nonconformity*. San Francisco: Jossey-Bass.

Nunnally, Jun. 1967. *Psychometric Theory*. New York: McGraw-Hill Book Co.

Oldendick, Robert, and Bennett, Stephen E. 1978. "The Wallace Factor: Constancy and Cooptation." *American Politics Quarterly*, 6 (October): 469-484.

Olsen, Marvin E. 1970. "Social and Political Participation of Blacks." *American Sociological Review*, 35 (August): 682-697.

Olsen, Marvin E. 1982. *Participatory Pluralism: Political Participation and Influence in the United States and Sweden*. Chicago: Nelson Hall.

Orum, Anthony M. 1966. "A Reappraisal of the Social and Political Participation of Negroes." *American Journal of Sociology*, 72 (July): 32-46.

Orum, Anthony M., Cohen, Roberta, Grasmuck, Sherri, and Orum, Amy. 1974. "Sex, Socialization, and Politics." *American Sociological Review*, 39 (April): 197-209.

Parenti, Michael. 1977. *Democracy for the Few*. Third ed. New York: St. Martin's Press.

Parry, Geraint, ed. 1972. *Participation in Politics*. Manchester: Manchester University Press.

Parsons, Talcott. 1959. " 'Voting' and the Equilibrium of the American Political System." In Eugene Burdick and Arthur J. Brodbeck, eds. *American Voting Behavior.* New York: The Free Press, pp. 80-120.

Pateman, Carole. 1970. *Participation and Democratic Theory.* Cambridge: Cambridge University Press.

Pedhazur, Elazar J. 1982. *Multiple Regression in Behavioral Research.* Second ed. New York: Holt, Rinehart & Winston.

Pennock, J. Roland. 1979. *Democratic Political Theory.* Princeton, NJ.: Princeton University Press.

Pennock, J. Roland, and Chapman, John W., eds. 1975. *Participation in Politics: Nomos XVI.* New York: Lieber-Atherton.

Perry, Paul. 1973. "A Comparison of the Preferences of Likely Voters and Likely Nonvoters." *Public Opinion Quarterly,* 37 (Spring): 99-109.

Pomper, Gerald M. 1985. "The Presidential Election." In Marlene Michels Pomper, ed. *The Election of 1984: Reports and Interpretations.* Chatham, NJ.: Chatham House, Publishers, pp. 60-90.

Pomper, Gerald M., with Lederman, Susan S. 1980. *Elections in America: Control and Influence in Democratic Politics.* Second ed. New York: Longman, Inc.

Poole, Keith T., and Zeigler, L. Harmon. 1985. *Women, Public Opinion, and Politics.* New York: Longman, Inc.

Potter, David. 1976. *The Impending Crisis: 1848-1861.* New York: Harper & Row, Publishers.

Pranger, Robert, 1968. *The Eclipse of Citizenship.* New York: Holt, Rinehart & Winston.

*Public Opinion.* 1983. "Opinion Roundup." *Public Opinion,* 5 (December/January): 21-40.

Rapoport, Ronald B. 1981. "The Sex Gap in Political Persuading: Where the 'Structuring Principle' Works." *American Journal of Political Science,* 25 (February): 32-48.

Rapoport, Ronald B. 1982. "Sex Differences in Attitude Expression: A Generational Explanation." *Public Opinion Quarterly,* 46 (Spring): 86-96.

Rapoport, Ronald B. 1985. "Like Mother, Like Daughter: Intergenerational Transmission of DK Response Rates." *Public Opinion Quarterly,* 49 (Summer): 198-208.

Reiter, Howard. 1979. "Why Is Turnout Down?" *Public Opinion Quarterly,* 43 (Fall): 297-311.

Remini, Robert V. 1963. *The Election of Andrew Jackson.* Philadelphia: J. B. Lippincott Co.

Riesman, David, and Glazer, Nathan B. 1950. "Criteria for Political Apathy." In Alvin W. Gouldner, ed. *Studies in Leadership.* New York: Harper & Brothers, pp. 505-559.

Riesman, David, with Glazer, Nathan, and Denney, Reuel. 1961. *The Lonely Crowd.* New Haven, CT.: Yale University Press.

Robinson, John P., Rusk, Jerrold G., and Head, Kendra B. 1968. *Measures of Political Attitudes.* Ann Arbor, MI.: Institute for Social Research, University of Michigan.

## References

Roelofs, H. Mark. 1957. *The Tension of Citizenship.* New York: Rinehart & Co.

Rollenhagen, Rick E. 1984. "Explaining Variation in Concern about the Outcome of Presidential Elections, 1960-1980." *Political Behavior,* 6(2): 147-157.

Roosevelt, Theodore. 1958. *The Free Citizen.* Ed. Hermann Hagedorn. New York: The Theordore Roosevelt Association.

Rose, Richard. 1980. "Preface." In Richard Rose, ed. *Electoral Participation: A Comparative Analysis.* Beverly Hills, CA.: Sage Publications, pp. 1-3.

Rosenau, James N. 1974. *Citizenship Between Elections.* New York: The Free Press.

Rosenberg, Morris. 1954-1955. "Some Determinants of Political Apathy." *Public Opinion Quarterly,* 18 (Winter): 349-366.

Rosenberg, Morris. 1961. "Self-Esteem and Concern With Public Affairs." *Public Opinion Quarterly,* 26 (Summer): 201-211.

Rosenberg, Morris. 1968. *The Logic of Survey Analysis.* New York: Basic Books.

Rosenstone, Steven J. 1982. "Economic Adversity and Voter Turnout." *American Journal of Political Science,* 26 (February): 25-46.

Rousseau, Jean-Jacques. 1968. *The Social Contract.* Trans. Maurice Cranston. Harmondsworth: Penguin Books, Ltd.

Rusk, Jerrold G. 1970. "The Effect of the Australian Ballot Reform on Split-Ticket Voting: 1876-1908." *American Political Science Review,* 64 (December): 1220-1238.

Rusk, Jerrold G. 1971. "Communication." *American Political Science Review,* 65 (December): 1152-1157.

Rusk, Jerrold G. 1974. "Comment: The American Electoral Universe: Speculation and Evidence." *American Political Science Review,* 68 (September): 1028-1049.

Salamon, Lester M., and Van Evera, Stephen. 1973. "Fear, Apathy, and Discrimination: A Test of Three Explanations of Political Participation." *American Political Science Review,* 67 (December): 1288-1306.

Sapiro, Virginia. 1983. *The Political Integration of Women: Roles, Socialization, and Politics.* Urbana, IL.: University of Illinois Press.

Schattschneider, E. E. 1960. *The Semisovereign People.* New York: Holt, Rinehart & Winston.

Schuman, Howard, and Presser, Stanley. 1981. *Questions and Answers in Attitude Surveys.* New York: Academic Press.

Schumpeter, Joseph A. 1975. *Capitalism, Socialism and Democracy.* New York: Harper Colphon Books.

Sears, David O. 1975. "Political Socialization." In Fred I. Greenstein and Nelson W. Polsby, eds. *Handbook of Political Science.* 8 volumes. Reading, MA.: Addison-Wesley, Vol. 2: pp. 93-153.

Shaffer, Stephen D. 1980. "The Policy Biases of Political Activists." *American Politics Quarterly,* 8 (January): 15-33.

Shaffer, Stephen D. 1981. "A Multivariate Explanation of Decreasing Turnout in Presidential Elections, 1960-1976." *American Journal of Political Science,* 25 (February): 68-95.

Shaffer, Stephen D. 1982. "Policy Differences Between Voters and Non-voters in American Elections." *Western Political Quarterly,* 35 (December): 496-510.

Shaver, James P. 1981. "Citizenship Values and Morality in the Social Studies." In Howard D. Mehlinger and O. L. Davis, Jr. eds. *The Social Studies: Eightieth Yearbook of the National Society for the Study of Education.* Chicago: University of Chicago Press, pp. 105-125.

Shingles, Richard D. 1981. "Black Consciousness and Political Participation: The Missing Link." *American Political Science Review,* 75 (March): 76-91.

Shklar, Judith N. 1985. *Men and Citizens: A Study of Rousseau's Social Theory.* Cambridge: Cambridge University Press.

Shortridge, Ray M. 1980. "Voter Turnout in the Midwest, 1840-1872." *Social Science Quarterly,* 60 (March): 617-629.

Shortridge, Ray M. 1981a. "Nineteenth Century Turnout: A Rejoinder." *Social Science Quarterly,* 61 (September): 450-452.

Shortridge, Ray M. 1981b. "Estimating Voter Participation." In Jerome M. Clubb, William H. Flanigan, and Nancy H. Zingale, eds. *Analyzing Electoral History.* Beverly Hills, CA.: Sage Publications, pp. 137-152.

Sigel, Roberta S., ed. 1970. *Learning About Politics: A Reader in Political Socialization.* New York: Random House, Inc.

Sigel, Roberta S., and Hoskin, Marilyn B. 1981. *The Political Involvement of Adolescents.* New Brunswick, NJ.: Rutgers University Press.

Sigelman, Lee. 1982. "The Nonvoting Voter in Voter Research." *American Journal of Political Science,* 26 (February): 47-56.

Skolnick, Jerome H. 1969. *The Politics of Protest.* New York: Ballantine Books.

Smith, Tom W. 1980. "America's Most Important Problem—A Trend Analysis, 1946-1976." *Public Opinion Quarterly,* 44 (Summer): 164-180.

Sniderman, Paul M. 1981. *A Question of Loyalty.* Berkeley, CA.: University of California Press.

Somit, Albert, and Tanenhaus, Joseph. 1967. *The Development of American Political Science.* Boston: Allyn & Bacon, Inc.

Stokes, Donald E., and Miller, Warren E. 1966. "Party Government and the Saliency of Congress." In Angus Campbell, Philip E. Converse, Warren E. Miller, and Donald E. Stokes. *Elections and the Political Order.* New York: John Wiley & Sons, pp. 194-211.

Sullivan, John L., Piereson, James, and Marcus, George E. 1978. "Ideological Constraint in the Mass Public: A Methodological Critique and Some New Findings." *American Journal of Political Science,* 22 (May): 233-249.

Sullivan, John L., Piereson, James, and Marcus, George E. 1982. *Political Tolerance and American Democracy.* Chicago: University of Chicago Press.

Sullivan, John L., Piereson, James, Marcus, George E., and Feldman, Stanley. 1979. "The More Things Change, the More They Stay the Same: The Stability of Mass Belief Systems." *American Journal of Political Science,* 23 (February): 176-186.

Sundquist, James L. 1980. "The Crisis of Competence in Our National Government." *Political Science Quarterly,* 95 (Summer): 183-208.

Thompson, Dennis F. 1970. *The Democratic Citizen.* Cambridge: Cambridge University Press.

Thucydides. 1972. *The Peloponnesian War.* Trans. Rex Warner. Intro. M. I. Finley. Harmondsworth: Penguin Books, Ltd.

Tocqueville, Alexis de. 1966. *Democracy in America*. Trans. George Lawrence. Ed. J. P. Mayer. Garden City, NY: Doubleday Anchor Books.

Traugott, Michael, and Katosh, John. 1979. "Response Validity in Surveys of Voting Behavior." *Public Opinion Quarterly*, 43 (Fall): 359-377.

United States Bureau of the Census. 1984. "Current Population Reports," Series P-20, No. 390. *Education Attainment in the United States: March 1981 and 1980*. Washington, DC.: U.S. Government Printing Office.

Verba, Sidney, and Nie, Norman H. 1972. *Participation in America: Political Democracy and Social Equality*. New York: Harper & Row.

Verba, Sidney, Nie, Norman H., and Kim, Jae-On. 1971. *The Modes of Democratic Participation: A Cross-National Study*. Beverly Hills, CA.: Sage Publications.

Walker, Jack L. 1966. "A Critique of the Elitist Theory of Democracy." *American Political Science Review*, 60 (June): 285-295.

Wattenberg, Martin P. 1984. *The Decline of American Political Parties: 1952-1980*. Cambridge, MA.: Harvard University Press.

Welch, Susan. 1977. "Women as Political Animals? A Test of Some Explanations for Male-Female Political Participation Differences." *American Journal of Political Science*, 21 (November): 712-730.

Wilson, Francis G. 1930. "The Pragmatic Electorate." *American Political Science Review*, 24 (February): 16-37.

Wilson, Francis G. 1936. "The Inactive Electorate and Social Revolution." *The Southwestern Social Science Quarterly*, 16 (March): 73-84.

Wolfe, Tom. 1977. *Mauve Gloves & Madmen, Clutter & Vine*. New York: Bantam Books.

Wolfinger, Raymond E., and Rosenstone, Steven J. 1980. *Who Votes?* New Haven, CT.: Yale University Press.

Woodward, Julian, and Roper, Elmo. 1950. "Political Activity of American Citizens." *American Political Science Review*, 44 (December): 872-885.

Wright, Gerald, C., Jr. 1976. "Linear Models for Evaluating Conditional Relationships." *American Journal of Political Science*, 20 (May): 349-373.

Wright, James D. 1976. *The Dissent of the Governed: Alienation and Democracy in America*. New York: Academic Press.

Young, James Sterling. 1966. *The Washington Community: 1800-1828*. New York: Columbia University Press.

Zeller, Richard A., and Carmines, Edward G. 1980. *Measurement in the Social Sciences*. Cambridge: Cambridge University Press.

# INDEX

Abramowitz, Alan, 1, 2, 62
Abramson, Paul, ix, 27, 54, 66, 71, 85, 86 (ftn.), 111, 114, 119, 156, 168, 169
Adamany, David, 43
Adams, John, 15
Age (and Political Interest), 70, 72, 76, 93, 96-112, 113-115, 116-118, 121, 122, 164-167
Aldrich, John, 66, 116
Alienation, Political, 26, 127, 158-160, 170-171
Almond, Gabriel, 4, 7, 9, 29, 36, 38, 41, 43, 47, 61-62, 68, 69, 72, 78, 84, 159, 163, 168, 173
American Political Culture, 14, 20, 27, 38
Andersen, Kristi, 104
*Apatheis*, 3
Apathy (*See* Psychological Involvement in Public Affairs)
Aristotle, 6
Athens, 11
Attentive Public, The, 9

Baker, Stephen, 21
Balch, George, 27, 86, 116, 153
Baxter, Sandra, 75
Beck, Paul, 88, 89-90, 105, 165
Bennett, Linda, 75, 141, 147, 151
Bennett, Stephen, 75, 141, 147, 151
Benson, Lee, 13
Berelson, Bernard, 4, 12, 24-25, 28-29, 36, 51, 68, 78, 165, 169
Birth Cohorts (and Political Interest), 100-102, 104-105
Bishop, George, 44, 45, 50, 65
Blalock, Hubert, 120, 174
Brody, Richard, 40, 173
Bryce, James, 12, 13, 20, 28, 33, 51, 134, 176

Bunker, Archie, 151
Burke, Edmond, 12
Burnham, Walter Dean, 18, 21

Caddell, Patrick, 156
Campaign Activism, 2, 55, 56, 129, 145-147
Campbell, Angus, 34, 39-40, 54, 58, 68, 83, 86, 87, 90, 141
Candidate Preference (and Political Interest), 79, 84, 93, 121, 122
Carmines, Edward, 52
Carter, Jimmy, 5
Census, U.S. Bureau of the, 103
Center for Political Studies' New Panel Study, 89
Chambers, William, 17
Citizenship, Norms of, 33, 166
"Citizenship" Thinkers, 6
Citrin, Jack, 85, 158, 170
"Civic Cognition," The, 37, 41, 62
Civic Duty, 6, 12, 13, 14, 15, 33-34, 40, 79, 83, 87, 93, 121, 122, 167
*Civic Culture, The*, 4, 47, 62
Civics Education Courses, Impact of on Political Interest, 69
Civil War (Excess Political Interest as Cause of), 18
Cohort Analysis, 96-97
Competence, Political, 25, 78 (*See also* Efficacy, Political)
Concern about the Election's Outcome, 39-40, 41
Connelly, Gordon, 33
Converse, Philip, 18, 19, 21, 39-40, 54, 76, 90, 128, 165
Coolidge, Calvin, 23, 89
"Core Voters," The, 58, 141
Craig, Stephen, 83

*195*

Crockett, Harry, 172
Cronbach's *Alpha*, 52
Cynicism, Political, 34 (*See also* Trust in Government)

Dahl, Robert, 38, 151
Davis, Phillip, 17
Democracy, 2, 34-36, 152, 160, 161, 169-170
Democratic Theory: empirical, 7, 29, 139, 167; critics of, 29, 167; normative, 12, 141, 169-170
Denney, Reuel, 32, 38
DeNardo, James, 36
Devine, Donald, 9
Dewey, John, 34
Dinkin, Robert, 14-15, 33
"Disengagement Phenomenon" (among the Elderly), 70, 76, 164
*Disruption of American Democracy, The*, 18
Duncan, Graeme, 169

Economic Conditions (and Political Interest), 23, 77-78, 173
Education, 68-69, 72, 77, 78, 87, 90, 93, 103, 106, 109, 111, 113-118, 121, 122, 128-129, 164, 165
Efficacy, Political (Sense of), 27, 40, 78, 79, 84, 87-88, 115-118, 121, 122, 153-156
Elderly, The, 70, 76, 98-99, 164
Elites, Political, 13, 14, 16, 21, 28, 29, 36, 88, 153, 169

"Fatalism of the Multitude," The, 20
Field, H. H., 33
Finifter, Ada, 85, 158, 167
Finley, M. I., 11
Forrest, W. G., 11
Futility, Political (Sense of), 27 (*See also* Efficacy, Political)

Gallup, George, 135
Gallup Organization, 66
Gamson, William, 153, 154
Gans, Curtis, 1, 3 (ftn.),
Gaudet, Hazel, 4, 24-25
Gender (and Political Interest), 69-70, 72, 75, 93, 103-112, 121, 164-165, 174
"Generational Effects," 101-102
Gilmour, Robert, 26, 33, 152, 177
Glazer, Nathan, 25, 32, 38
Glenn, Norval, 8, 96, 97 (ftn.), 101

Goel, M. L., 38, 68, 69, 70, 71, 131, 140, 141, 143
Gosnell, Harold, 21-22, 72, 106
Government, National: impact on Citizen, 16, 39 (n.2), 79, 168, 173-174; interest in, 15-16, 45-50, 78
Governmental Attentiveness, Perceptions of, 83, 86-87, 121, 122, 167
Greenstein, Fred, 167
Grimes, Michael, 97, 99 (ftn.), 101
Gurin, Gerald, 78, 86, 87
Gutek, Barbara, 43
Guterbock, Thomas, 70

Hadley, Arthur, 26, 35, 152
*Handbook of Political Science*, 167
Hinckley, Barbara, 66, 138
Hill, David, ix, 171
Hofstadter, Richard, 17
Hoskin, Marilyn, 167
Huntington, Samuel, 88
Hutchins, Robert Maynard, 169, 170
Hyman, Herbert, 94, 135

Ignorance, Political, 14, 168-169
Income (and Political Interest), 77-78
Index of Psychological Involvement in Politics, 39
Information, Political, 55, 56, 58, 129, 135-139
"Inside Dopester," The, 38
Interest, Political: Before 1900, 13-21; 1920s, 21-23; 1930s, 23-24; 1940s, 28; During Eisenhower Era, 61-62, 100; 1960-1984, 62-67, 88-90, 102, 161; in campaigns, 24-25, 31-32, 39, 42-45, 51, 52; in Democratic Theory, 12-13, 28-29; in public affairs generally, 15-16, 45-50, 51-52 (*See also* Psychological Involvement in Public Affairs)
Interest, self-, 6, 12, 13

Jackson, Andrew, 16, 17
Jacobson, Gary, 136
Janowitz, Morris, 7
Jefferson, Thomas, 13
Jennings, M. Kent, 4, 69, 89-90, 105, 112, 166, 174
Jensen, Richard, 19-20
Johnson, Haynes, 32
Johnson, Lyndon, 5

Kann, Robert, 13

# Index

Kennedy, John F., 5, 67, 102, 159, 163
Kennedy, Robert, 102
Kernell, Samuel, 32
Key, V. O., Jr., 9, 86, 87, 115, 153, 166
Kim, Jae-On, 39, 140
Kleppner, Paul, 18, 19, 21, 24
Kornhauser, William, 35

Ladd, Everett Carll, 165
Lamb, Robert, 26, 33, 152, 177
Lane, Robert, 38, 51, 55, 68, 69, 125, 134, 145, 158, 176
Langton, Kenneth, 69
Lansing, Marjorie, 75
Lasch, Christopher, 102
Lazarsfeld, Paul, 4, 24-25, 29, 39, 51, 165
Letter-writing, 2, 147-148
Lincoln, Abraham, 27
Lippmann, Walter, 6-7, 23, 34, 77, 89
Lipset, Seymour Martin, ix, x, 35, 68, 79, 85 (ftn.), 171, 172, 173
London, Bruce, 70
Lukes, Steven, 169
Luttbeg, Norman, ix, 171
Lynd, Helen, 21, 22-23
Lynd, Robert, 21, 22-23

McCarthy, Eugene, 102
McCormick, Richard, 17
McPhee, William, 29, 39, 51, 78, 165
Marital Status (and Political Interest), 112
Mass Media, Utilization of, 55, 56, 129, 131-135
Matthews, Donald, 71
Men (and Political Interest), 105-112 (*See also* Gender)
Merriam, Charles, 21-22, 69, 72, 106
*Middletown*, 21, 22-23
Milbrath, Lester, 38, 68, 69, 70, 71, 131, 140, 141, 143
Mill, John Stuart, 6, 169
Miller, Arthur, 85, 158, 170, 171, 172
Miller, Warren, 2, 39-40, 54, 62, 78, 86, 87, 136, 158
*Modern Democracies*, 12
Morris, Charles, 5
Munro, William, 23, 164

National Opinion Research Center's 1982 General Social Survey, 175-176
*Negroes and the New Southern Politics*, 71
Nichols, Roy, 18
Nie, Norman, 39, 51-52, 62, 68, 77, 83, 140

Niemi, Richard, 4, 54, 105, 166, 174
Nineteenth Amendment, 106
Nixon, Richard, 5
*Non-Voting*, 21-22, 24
Nunn, Clyde, 172

Occupation (and Political Interest), 109 (n.12)
Oldendick, Robert, 44, 45, 50, 65, 112 (ftn.), 177

Parental Status (and Political Interest), 112
Parenti, Michael, 32
Parochial, The, 8, 38, 168, 173
*Participation in America*, 140
Participation, Political, 2, 20, 32, 112, 127, 129, 140-160
Participatory Democracy, 7
Partisanship, Strength of, 41, 78, 83-84, 90-91, 93, 113-115, 121, 122, 165-166
Partition Design, 94
Pateman, Carole, 12
Pedhazur, Elzar, 120
*People's Choice, The*, 24
Pericles, 11, 17
Period Effect, 87-90
"Peripheral Voters," 58, 90, 141
Perry, Paul, 36
Personal Efficacy, 172-173
Petrocik, John, 62, 85
"Political Involvement" (SRC Measures of), 39-40
"Political Apathy," Index of, 41-58, 65
Political Protest, 2, 71, 148-150
*Political Science: The State of the Discipline*, 167
Political Socialization, 167
Polsby, Nelson, 167
Pomper, Gerald, 165
Poole, Keith, 104
Presser, Stanley, 8, 42
Prothro, James, 71
Psychological Involvement in Public Affairs: As Entertainment, 17, 18, 20; Causes, 7-8, 22, 23, 25, 27-28, 29, 68-71, 78-79, 93-118, 121-122, 163-164; Changes in (between 1960-1984), 72-88; Conceptualization of, 3, 24, 25, 29, 31-39, 169; Consequences of, 6-8, 22-23, 25, 34-37, 38, 56-58, 125-126, 131-139, 140-151, 160, 161, 168-172; In Democratic Theory, 12-13, 141, 167-168; In Congressional vs. Presidential Election Years, 64-65, 76-

*197*

77, 90, 143; Measurement of, 4, 8-9, 24, 26, 29, 39-58, 174-176; Typical American's (from 1960-1984), 67, 176; Typologies of, 25, 26
Psychopathology (and Political Apathy), 25, 32-33, 34
*Public Opinion,* 66

Race (and Political Interest), 70-71, 72, 75-76
Rapoport, Ronald, 106, 111, 165
Reagan, Ronald, 5, 67, 75, 159
Reed, John Sheldon, 135
Regression Analysis, 94-95, 119-121
Remini, Robert, 17
Revolution, American (Political Interest during), 14-15
Riesman, David, 25, 32, 38
Roelofs, H. Mark, 33
Rohde, David, 66
Rollenhagen, Rick, 41
Roper, Elmo, 145
Roosevelt, Theodore, 23, 34, 79
Rose, Richard, 150
Rosenberg, Morris, 27-28, 94, 172
Rosenstone, Steven, 36, 112, 173
Rousseau, John Jacques, 12, 169
Rusk, Jerrold, 19, 21

Salamon, Lester, 32
Sapiro, Virginia, 69, 112
Schattschneider, E. E., 35
Schneider, William, 85 (ftn.), 171, 172
Schuman, Howard, 8, 42
Schumpeter, Joseph, 169
Sears, David, 167
Senate, U.S. (Republican control of), 138
Shaffer, Stephen, 36
Shaver, James, 7
Shelley, Mack, 43
Shortridge, Ray, 18
Sigel, Roberta, 167
"Silent Generation," The, 100
Sniderman, Paul, 158, 177
*Social Contract, The,* 12
Socio-economic Status (SES), 68, 72, 75, 87
Stokes, Donald, 39-40, 54, 136
Sullivan, John L., 42, 172
Surveys, (secondary analysis of), 8, 42

Thompson, Dennis, 29
Thucydides, 11
Tocqueville, Alexis de, 16-17
Tolerance, Political (and Political Interest), 172
Trust in Government, 79, 84-86, 88, 153, 156-158, 170
Tuchfarber, Alfred, 44, 45, 50, 65
Turnout (in national elections), 1, 2-3, 17, 18, 21, 23, 26, 35-36, 40, 41, 56, 58, 65, 87, 90, 112, 116, 129, 141-145, 153-160

Van Evera, Stephen, 32
Verba, Sidney, 2, 4, 8, 29, 36, 37, 38, 39, 41, 43, 47, 51-52, 61-62, 68, 69, 72, 77, 78, 84, 85, 127, 140, 159, 168, 173
"Vietnam Generation," The, 105

Walker, Jack, 29
Wallace, George (supporters of), 177
*Washington Community, The,* 15
Wattenberg, Martin, 165
Welch, Susan, 104
Williams, J. Allen, 172
Wilson, Francis, 23, 170
Wilson, Woodrow, 23
Wolfe, Tom, 102
Wolfinger, Raymond, 36, 112
Women (and Political Interest), 72, 75, 103-112 (*See also* Gender); and Age, 109-111; Childhood Socialization of, 106, 111; Educational Attainment of, 103, 109; Employment Status of, 103-104, 106, 109, 111; Housewife, 106; Marital Status of, 111; Motherhood, 111
Woodward, Julian, 147
Wright, Charles, 135

Young, James, 15-16
Young, The, 70, 89-90, 96, 102-103, 111-115, 116-118, 165-167
"Yuppies," The, 102-103

Zeigler, L. Harmon, 104
Zeller, Richard, 52, 54